Friends like Henry

of related interest

Introducing a School Therapy Dog
A Practical Guide
Cherryl Drabble
ISBN 978 1 78592 477 4
eISBN 978 1 78450 861 6

Coming Home to Autism
A Room-by-Room Approach to Supporting Your Child at Home after ASD Diagnosis
Tara Leniston and Rhian Grounds
ISBN 978 1 78592 436 1
eISBN 978 1 78450 808 1

Fifteen Things They Forgot to Tell You About Autism
The Stuff That Transformed My Life as an Autism Parent
Debby Elley
ISBN 978 1 78592 438 5
eISBN 978 1 78450 810 4

Autism in My Family
A Journal for Siblings of Children with ASD
Sandra Tucker
ISBN 978 1 78592 707 2
eISBN 978 1 78450 264 5

Animal-assisted Interventions for Individuals with Autism
Merope Pavlides
ISBN 978 1 84310 867 2
ISBN 978 1 84985 466 5 (Large Print)
eISBN 978 1 84642 795 4

Friends
like Henry

Everything your family needs to know
about finding, training and learning
from an autism companion dog

Nuala Gardner

Jessica Kingsley *Publishers*
London and Philadelphia

First published in 2019
by Jessica Kingsley Publishers
73 Collier Street
London N1 9BE, UK
and
400 Market Street, Suite 400
Philadelphia, PA 19106, USA

www.jkp.com

Library of Congress Cataloging in Publication Data
A CIP catalog record for this book is available from the Library of Congress

British Library Cataloguing in Publication Data
A CIP catalogue record for this book is available from the British Library

ISBN 978 1 78592 678 5
eISBN 978 1 78592 848 2

Printed and bound in Great Britain

Dedication

*This manual is dedicated to the incalculable number of pet,
assistance and working dogs who have served humanity
well, given companionship and unconditional love,
and helped so many people to overcome adversity.*

*I also want to acknowledge the innumerable dogs that, due
to lack of knowledge or respect in their human homes, have
suffered physical and emotional neglect – a neglect that in
some cases has had tragic, fatal consequences for the dog.*

*May this manual help in some way to prevent that injustice.
Dogs are man's best friend for a reason – and deserve no less!*

Contents

Foreword by Jim Taylor 9

Acknowledgements 15

About the Author 17

Adapting This Programme for Other Disabilities 19

Entering the World of Autism 22

Introduction 23

Is a Dog the Right Intervention for Your Child and Family? 35

Why This Programme? 39

Overview of the Programme 55

Success Story 1: Makenzie Gets Heather 63

Success Story 2: Andy and Bailey 66

Points to Remember When Helping a Child with ASD or
Learning Difficulties 70

Points to Remember When Helping an Adult with ASD or
Learning Difficulties 83

**STAGE 1: PLANNING AND TRANSITION
FOR THE CHILD AND DOG** **87**

What Age and Breed of Dog is Right for the Child's Disability? 91

Transitions 98

The Transitional Kit 102

Resources for the Child 124

STAGE 2: INTRODUCING THE DOG TO YOUR HOME . . .   **125**

Planning for the Arrival of the Dog.   131

Avoiding Stress in Dogs.   136

**STAGE 3: USING THE DOG AS AN EDUCATIONAL
FACILITATOR TOWARDS THE BEST POSSIBLE
INDEPENDENCE FOR THE CHILD** **147**

Caring for Your Dog   154

Meaningful Dog Commands.   204

The Principles of Dog Training with Alberto Alvarez-Campos   219

How to Use the Dog as an Educational Facilitator   238

**STAGE 4: LETTING GO! TRANSITION FOR THE CHILD
TO PREPARE FOR THE DEMISE OF THE DOG** **273**

Care of the Senior Dog   277

Letting Go!   286

Afterword.   302

Useful Resources   305

Endnotes   307

Index   310

Foreword

JIM TAYLOR

Finding approaches or methods that will have an immediate impact and can achieve long-lasting gains can be a challenge when parents and professionals are faced with the diagnosis of Autism Spectrum Disorder (ASD). A good team of professionals working alongside a family, along with a broad-based education, will have the most positive impact on the development of young people. However, at times, added value is needed and may be sought through resources such as music therapy, physical therapies, a focus on individual enthusiasms, and others. The introduction of dogs or pets into the lives of young people with ASD and their families is an approach that has gained increasing credibility in the last number of years. As with all approaches or interventions, this is not just an easy fix, and families embarking on this route need to explore further how best to implement this approach to ensure greater and more meaningful success.

Following media stories regarding the success of introducing therapy dogs, many families have taken such a step, and the canine addition to the family has undoubtedly added to the quality of life of the whole family. The public profile of guide dogs, hearing dogs, etc. is such that we understand and acknowledge the intensity of the training that both the animal and the owner experience. What has been less clear, up until now, is the extent of the preparation and training involved when placing/receiving a dog into a family of a child with autism. This manual is therefore especially relevant as it demonstrates the author's own unique experience and the range of experiences she has had with, initially, a pilot group of eight families across the UK and beyond.

Nuala's personal experience in developing partnerships with dogs, families and individuals is well documented and has provided inspiration and guidance for many families. Her own experience, as described in her first book, *A Friend Like Henry*, and the subsequent film version, was the first in the country to gain major exposure and publicity. 'Therapy dogs' have since been introduced to some schools, with detailed evaluations highlighting the benefits to those involved in the programme.

My role here is not to evaluate the outcomes of such initiatives but to explore how Nuala, through the pilot programme involving eight families and her specialised approach, addresses the very specific learning styles and strengths found in autism. I will also examine the consideration Nuala gives to some of the barriers to learning – for example, how the differences in interaction and the development of meaningful relationships may be addressed positively through the introduction of a specially trained dog into family life.

As with all approaches in autism, it is essential to identify and clarify what it is that makes a significant difference and what makes such approaches especially suitable for young people with ASD. Experience shows us, though, that it can be difficult to identify what it is about any approach that makes it unique to autism. This manual illustrates just how Nuala's approach directly addresses the autism. For example, it outlines those elements of the young person's autism that are supported through the programme; it highlights the advantages that can be gained through the introduction of the dog into the young person's life; and, crucially, it emphasises the importance of planning, preparation and correctly matching dog to child/family in order to maximise the chances of sustainable success.

The concept of introducing a dog into a family is an attractive one and, as such, there is a risk that some families might rush into this without the adequate planning and preparation that Nuala outlines in her manual. She also advises that school-based programmes involving a therapy dog should be underpinned by a policy, procedures and, certainly, by a set of agreed aims and targets. Nuala's work demonstrates how this type of planning can also be reflected in family life and how, if the experience and guidelines can be followed closely, positive outcomes can be almost guaranteed. Often, generic responses and a 'one size fits all' approach lead to forgetting the most critical factor: that each young person is unique. In fact, the family, the experience and training of the dog, the interaction style of each individual, and the home environment are all critical factors.

Nuala's success within the pilot project has been based on directly addressing these factors. As she writes, each child, each family and each dog is unique.

So what, then, are the important factors in ensuring success, in ensuring that each partnership adds significant value to lives? And how does this fit in with current thinking about autism?

First of all, it is important to stress that one of the guiding principles here is that the partnership/relationship with the dog provides opportunities for the young person to learn about many things and to acquire new skills, some of which may be challenging. For instance, skills such as learning about relationships, learning about making a contribution to a companion and family group and so on may need to be introduced and taught to the learner with autism. The case for using dogs within autism is less about compensating for the challenges and more about empowering and enabling the young person in ways which this manual illustrates.

As with all the best therapies/methodologies, the way forward should be decided upon after careful assessment. The cases and examples that follow in this manual keenly demonstrate the level of detailed information that needs to be amassed about the child, his or her life experiences and the family situation.

Before matching the dog and the child, Nuala's programme takes into account the child's social understanding, the communication level and the environment that the child is living and working in. This degree of detail, especially through the transition phase, is critical. There may only be one chance to get this right, and the detail in the following pages shows the distance that must be covered. Nuala describes how important it has been to introduce her own dog, who has on many occasions played a heroic part in making immediate connections with young people! In many of her case studies, by the time a dog has been selected and has been introduced, the possibility of failure has been drastically reduced. Many of the stories from the pilot project demonstrate that the timing of the introduction of the dog into the family, the language used and the understanding of the impact of the environment are all critical.

It is impressive at this stage in the process that a strong team is created; in the case studies, the team involved Nuala, the family and, of course, the young person. Together, the team decides what the focus of the programme needs to be, as well as agreeing the precise purpose behind the introduction of the dog into the team. What is often missing from programmes for young people with autism, especially outside schools, is a clear and agreed plan for learning outcomes. It is important to stress again that this programme is not about compensating for the autism but directly addressing strengths and learning styles, developing and nurturing skills and strategies, and building on confidence and self-esteem. The transition programme is directly and effectively teaching and facilitating the development of companionship, interaction skills and strong, meaningful relationships.

Nuala's examples illustrate the degree of detail and personalisation inherent in her approach; the importance of this is well described. I have read many examples of how dogs and other animals are used in many different ways, but Nuala's insistence on attention to the detail of individuals and families is critical to successful outcomes. Each and every example is different. She advocates not simply one generic approach, but the flexibility to tailor each intervention to the particular child and family.

This detailed gathering of evidence around successful interventions and insights is, of course, important, but the programme goes on to demonstrate how this becomes a shared approach. It demonstrates:

- how a team, including the young person, the family, professional advisors and the dog, work together to share aims, to ensure consistency of understanding and approaches

- how each part of the team interacts with the others.

All parties are involved in the decision making, planning and evaluating. The dog becomes not just a companion but a pivotal factor in pulling together the whole team including, where relevant, the school. In a few instances, the dog may become the subject of a full class project in school, thus involving the young person's peers. The learning opportunities are considerable and include the promotion of self-esteem and confidence for all who are involved in the project. This can be a critical part of the whole process. As previously stated, whilst there may be a common understanding of the purpose of working dogs in a variety of other situations, the purpose of a dog in the life of the person with autism may not always be obvious to the wider community. The success of the programme will therefore be greatly enhanced by increasing the understanding and involvement of the whole community.

The most impressive aspect of this programme is that the young person is firmly at the centre of it, with the power and the control to direct and influence the process. The young person's choices and preferences direct every aspect of the process, including: the type of companion needed; the type of personality the dog needs to have; the most effective communication partner the dog can be; the sensory impact the dog can have; and how some of these factors can be addressed and supported. Nuala's pilot project demonstrated well just how the individual is at the absolute core of the process and the future planning.

For many young people with autism and their families, being a part of a community is a real challenge. The isolation felt and thrust upon families can have a profound impact on their well-being. Nuala's approach meets that head-on and, in many cases, the partnership with the dog provides so many opportunities within the community for the family but, most critically, for the young person. These are the very real and long-lasting outcomes of the approach: the confidence and the self-esteem young people experience along with the dog as part of the community.

In summary, I can highly commend Nuala's programme as one that directly addresses the challenges faced by people with autism and their families. The entire process is detailed and highly personalised and, when followed carefully by a team working together, will be highly effective. When we are looking for a programme to add value and to secure significant gains, then this type of positive, directed intervention can provide these added benefits. I look forward to watching it grow and benefit many more families.

Jim Taylor
www.jimtaylorknowsautism.com

Acknowledgements

I would like to give my sincerest thanks to Alberto Alvarez-Campos, National Programs Manager for Assistance Dogs Australia, for his long-standing collaboration and for contributing the excellent material in this manual on dog training and obedience. Thanks also for the support and work of Alberto's wife, Jane Kefford. Without their belief in my work, this educational facilitator dog programme would not be where it is today and neither would I – gracious!

I would also like to thank my son Dale and my daughter Amy for their support and love and their insightful input that has made this unique programme possible.

This manual would not exist if it weren't for the two Henrys, our wonderful Goldies that made it all happen; this is truly their legacy. Thomas, my own and Dale's Goldie, now fills the void the two Henrys left behind and has also played his part.

As always, my respect and gratitude go to Jim Taylor, for his unlimited advice on my work and for his tireless support of me and my children over the past 25 years. I couldn't have managed as a mum without it – and my children wouldn't be where they are today without Jim's presence in their lives.

I would like to thank every child and parent who worked with me for research purposes and allowed me to share the resulting findings throughout this manual so that others could access and benefit from this knowledge. I would like to acknowledge my appreciation of

Kim and Sinclair Macleod at Indie Authors World for giving me the courage to get this manual published. I couldn't have undergone this process without the professionalism and wonderful support of my editor, Julia Lister.

Finally, I would like to thank my partner Michael, for his learning, continued encouragement and support of my work – despite it being as different a world he could ever have expected to meet.

About the Author

Nuala Gardner is the mother of Dale, now aged 29, who had severe autism but now has high-functioning autism, and of Amy, aged 17, who also has high-functioning autism. For 25 years, while bringing up her children, Nuala worked as a registered general nurse. In July 2007, her international bestseller *A Friend Like Henry* was published, followed in November 2013 by the sequel, *All Because of Henry*. Telling the remarkable, thought-provoking story of her children's autism, both books have given hope to hundreds of thousands of others affected by autism all over the world. Nuala's children owe a lot to the gift that the family's Golden Retrievers gave both of them, helping them to be the independent young people they are today.

Nuala gave up her nursing career in 2011 to concentrate on her work using trained dogs to help reach children with autism and others with a diverse range of disabilities. This change in career direction allowed Nuala to continue researching the positive effect that animals, specifically dogs, can have on children, particularly those with autism.

In the course of her research, Nuala discovered that the right dog – properly trained and cared for – could benefit all children, adults and families irrespective of their abilities.

Writing on autism, Nuala says:

Autism Spectrum Disorder (ASD) has a complex, frustrating and totally devastating impact on children's and families' lives.

Within those affected is the greatest desire to connect and express themselves and their love in their own, unique way. Autism may lock a person in a world we do not fully understand. An early diagnosis and a good education should be a person with autism's right – not a privilege. A condition-specific approach to the education of a child with autism – and ongoing support of an adult with autism – is the key to helping them safely emerge from their autistic world. This alone will allow them to cope and be able to live and enjoy a good quality of life in our world. The power of animals, especially dogs, is that, in the right hands, they can have a life-enhancing and life-changing effect for those with autism and other disabilities. May this manual be the catalyst to create more canine successes and many new wonderful friendships between mankind and dogs.

Adapting This Programme for Other Disabilities

I developed this programme to be accessible for a child with Autism Spectrum Disorder (ASD). Autism is a lifelong condition that isolates the child or adult from the world as we know it, affecting their ability to communicate. Verbal communication can be totally absent or very limited. Deciphering facial expressions and understanding non-verbal communication is confusing and complex to interpret. This has an impact on the person's ability to form relationships and understand everyday activities. Many people with autism have problems with sensory issues that affect their ability to cope in different environments; those that are noisy, too bright, visually over-stimulating or pungent, for example, can overwhelm them. Autism is described as a spectrum condition because people can be affected to different degrees, some severely and others in a subtle way.

Adapting the programme for different disabilities

Due to the nature of autism and the way it affects a child's ability to learn, the resources and strategies used throughout this programme have been devised to be meaningful, consistent, seamless and adjustable to the intellectual capacity of the child. As a result, the information and resources in this manual enable parents to adapt this programme to the individual needs of children with other disabilities that affect their ability to learn, develop and reach their full potential.

In addition, while this programme is tailored for a child with difficulties, the simplicity of the approach will enable anyone to adapt it to suit any child or adult. This programme will help any family or individual wanting to introduce a dog into their lives, for all the benefits they bring.

This manual documents all the knowledge I have acquired from raising Dale and using his dog as an educational facilitator. It is unique because I have incorporated all I have learned through collaborating with the working dog world, so that this programme can be universal and accessible for the majority of disabled children and adults.

I understand parents know their children best and know how their disability affects them; you can adapt this programme based on the needs of your child.

Similarly, the knowledge and strategies described in this manual will enable adults with autism, or with other disabilities, to successfully source the right dog to enhance their quality of life.

While this manual is designed to be accessible to all, in order to make the information here as succinct as possible, I primarily talk about the child with autism. Please note that, throughout this manual, when I use the term 'child', this encompasses all children with autism or a disability and the adult where applicable.

Using the principles of this programme with other pets

You can adapt the principles of this programme to use any pet a child might connect to. The programme can be used, in its widest sense, as an aid to using a whole range of different pets as educational facilitators for disabled children. Using cats, rabbits (and their furry counterparts) or horses can all help the child progress. Horses were the key to reaching my daughter Amy and the teaching opportunities were endless.

Think out of the box about what pets could be used; how about a simple wormery or a small reptile or mouse? Think how even a humble little goldfish needs a 'master' to meet its daily needs. As water is a magnet for many children with autism, a goldfish – with its need for a healthy water environment – has the potential to be a goldmine of education for the child!

A goldfish will also allow you to take your child through all the stages of this programme at your own pace. Given the lifespan of a goldfish, the child will experience the fish's demise; when you have exhausted the learning possibilities for your child with countless incognito 'replaced' fish, you can use the fish's demise to teach the child the concept of letting go, as described in Stage 4 of this manual. Better a child learns bereavement via this process than from the acute stress of a family member's demise.

If the child has responded well to the concept of looking after a goldfish, you can then consider 'upgrading' to a pet like a hamster or similar which will increase the child's learning all over again.

All of these creatures can be living educational tools; they have physical needs, including the need to be cared for and loved – just like us. Adjusting the strategies described in this manual will allow success for the child and their pet.

Entering the World of Autism

The psychiatrist Lorna Wing, one of the co-founders of the National Autistic Society in 1962, revolutionised the way autism was thought about around the world. She developed the concept of an autism spectrum and, as a mother of a daughter with autism, championed the rights of families. She proposed that every child should be treated as an individual and that parents and professionals should work closely together. She wrote:

> Those of us who live and/or work with children and adults with autistic disorders have to try and enter their world, since they cannot find their way into ours. We need to learn to comprehend and empathise with autistic experiences in order to find ways to help each individual cope with a system of social rules that is alien to them.
>
> The reward for the effort involved is a deeper understanding of human social interaction and an appreciation of the wonder of child development. The key to autism is the key to the nature of human life.[1]

Introduction

The birth of a child and the birth of this programme

On the 13th June 1988, in the west of Scotland, I was elated while tinged with anxiety as I held my first newborn child, Dale, in my arms. My apprehension for my son grew; as his mother and a trained midwife, I realised he was unlike any other baby I had ever known.

My fears were soon realised. Dale was not a typical baby, but different, showing signs of delayed development. As days passed, he appeared increasingly withdrawn. By the age of three, Dale had been diagnosed with severe classical autism – at the time, a rarely recognised global developmental disorder.

Months later, Dale became increasingly isolated and I found him more and more challenging to manage at home, especially when I tried to take him out. Every day, trying to care for Dale's basic needs was near impossible. He had no language and didn't know who I was, let alone understand emotions. Caring for Dale's physical needs – washing him, dressing him and trying to get him to eat – was a daily battle. Dale was stuck in a bubble, with no connections between his world and mine. As his mother, I was lost and desperate to try anything that could reach him. Then a chance in a million gave me some hope!

When he was five, I witnessed Dale's first emergence from his autistic bubble, when he became 'alive' – interacting and verbalising some words – while playing with a family member's two Scottie dogs. From that day in February 1993, I was on a mission, to find the right puppy for my son's autism, one that might help him in some way, in any way!

I grew up with mixed-breed mongrel dogs. My dad taught me how to core train them, albeit at a basic level. But, with Dale's challenging autism, and the extreme environment living with Dale created, I needed to source a dog with an exceptional temperament to cope with Dale's individual autism and associated unusual behaviours. The puppy would have to be the most loving, obedient, trustworthy and best canine companion for Dale.

Because of my nursing knowledge, and all that I had learned in the first five years of raising a non-verbal child with severe autism, I understood that thoroughly preparing Dale to help him understand this major event – the arrival of a dog in his life – was imperative to success.

From the outset of introducing the puppy, which Dale named Henry, I was determined to use the dog as an educational facilitator to address the triad of impairments of Dale's autism – all at the same time. This objective is *essential* for any partnership between a disabled child and a facilitator dog. However, with all my educational goals for Dale, for me there was *one* factor alone that was the most important of all when planning the transition to the arrival of the puppy: *the dog's welfare!* As a child, I learned how sensitive dogs are; they need proper and caring handling. With the enormity of what I was hoping to achieve for Dale, I was determined that the transitional work I implemented would ensure the puppy would not be stressed or mistreated in any way despite Dale's autism.

In 1993, helping to support a child with a communication or learning disability by using social stories and similar transitional resources was a rarely used or understood educational practice. Today, these are common and effective educational tools. I was fortunate because I learned so much about basic and major transitional planning from Dale's wonderful teacher, Maureen Anderson, at the Highlanders Academy pre-school language unit in Greenock. Maureen taught me how to use visual resources – pictures with real-life content – to make social stories to help Dale learn about and cope with transitions he would meet in life, like the arrival of his baby sister, getting new shoes and moving on to his new school.

Undoubtedly, Henry coming to live in our home was a major transition for Dale! Little did I know at the time that the resources I developed in 1994 would be the foundation of this manual.

Dale is now a fine young man of 29 and has qualified with an HNC in Early Education and Childcare, having obtained seven GCSEs in mainstream school. He plays bass guitar and regular gigs in a successful Glasgow rock band called Century Thirteen. He was a volunteer worker for Barnardo's Scotland for eight years and, to this day, is an ambassador of hope for raising awareness of autism.

At present, Dale works as an administration assistant for a Social Enterprise company called REACH for Autism in Greenock in Inverclyde. REACH is a hub for children, adults and families affected by autism to help them access social groups with the right support. REACH provides educational therapies like arts and crafts, music, etc. Dale is a popular member of staff, liked by parents and children, and the adult service users hold him in high regard.

An integral part of Dale's success is the result of the communication system, intervention and support Henry provided for 12 wonderful years. Henry not only became Dale's educational facilitator; more importantly, he was Dale's first successful friend.

The story of this incredible partnership is told in my first book, the international and *New York Times* bestseller, *A Friend Like Henry* (AFLH). When writing AFLH, I knew that what I experienced with Dale and his amazing dog wasn't a one-off. While Dale's story of how his dog had totally transformed his life was unique, it was far from unusual. There have been many accounts of the therapeutic benefit and impact dogs have had on children and adults alike, allowing them to triumph over adversity. For decades, the assistance and working dog world has embraced this initiative with much success and has given a better quality of life to many affected by disabilities.

It is only in the past two decades that the assistance dog world has adopted a model derived from Canada Service Dogs, to help children on the autistic spectrum and others with disabilities. Ensuring the best chance for a successful partnership between a child and dog is possible – with the right educational approach to each child's individual autism or disability. This is a real factor; there is no denying that Dale and his sister Amy's stunning progress to date is testament to this. Neither Dale's dog nor Amy's love of horses would have had the incredible impact and positive results on their progress if, in the first place, the approach to their individual autism had not been right.

Following the release of the award-winning TV drama *After Thomas*, and my memoir AFLH, I was inundated with requests from parents who wanted to explore the possibility that a dog 'like Henry' could help their children. Twenty-three years ago, I did my research and brought home our puppy, aged 10 weeks. It wasn't lost on me that Henry came with no instructions for use or guidance manual on how to use a dog to help a child like Dale, with his challenging autism! I know from the many parents who contacted me that, without access to the kind of support this programme offers, numerous puppies have been returned to their breeders, with much regret and upset to the child and parents.

Undeniably, with the little dog experience I had, I was fortunate to find such a reputable and supportive dog breeder in Valerie Keill. It is never lost on me that it could have turned out horribly different. I will cover this subject later in more detail but, with this manual, I hope to offer the best chance of success for the child and dog partnership; luck has no bearing in this very specialised field.

The autism/disability facilitator dog programme – research and development

I developed this programme to help those on the autistic spectrum, and others with disabilities or medical conditions, to replicate what I did with Henry and Dale. Inclusion for all means so much to me.

When creating this programme, I was determined it should be possible to tailor it to enhance the life of other children with disabilities, not forgetting adults too! While inclusion for the child is paramount, inclusion is a human right for all: 'The idea that children have special needs has given way to the conviction that children have rights, the same full spectrum of rights as adults: civil and political, cultural and economic'.[2] I will cover how dogs assist inclusion for those with disabilities later.

I am aware of so many heartfelt stories of partnerships with companions and working dogs that have had life-enhancing impacts on individuals. Many of them are anecdotal of the power of the dog, as another mother wrote:

> We found having a dog and training the dog in road safety etc helped reinforce better behaviour for our quite severely autistic son when he was a child… Our non-pedigree dog lived to the good old age of 21 and gave our son a great gift: the breakthrough of communication, friendship and devotion. (Maureen Erdwin[3])

There is an abundance of published accounts and countless stories on social media, together with scientific evidence, to support the positive life-changing affect dogs have had on individuals with disabilities, including those with autism. Scientific findings have shown that the dog has a calming effect on the child, helps reduce or prevent sensory and communication meltdowns, and much more. Children's confidence and self-esteem improves and, if involved with the care of the pet, they transfer these new learning skills to their own independence. The companionship and emotional support given by domestic and working dogs to children and adults with emotional and physical disabilities is as vast and immeasurable as the conditions themselves.

From all the research I have looked at, one point has struck me – the age a child gets a pet is crucial. When I was desperate to help Dale, I knew he had to be a suitable age and at an appropriate developmental stage to be able to interact with and be involved with the dog. As luck would have it, Dale was five when we introduced Henry and, thankfully, this is the age research suggests is the best for optimal success. I believe the combination of introducing the dog at around this age (no younger than four) with good transitional care is paramount to the child's progress.

Marine Grandgeorge and colleagues,[4] researching on dogs and children with autism, found pet ownership improved two areas of social functioning: showing comfort to others and improved sharing behaviours. Children interacted more with the pet, for example petting and stroking them. Time spent with the pet, caring for and playing with them, was more often reported for children who got their pet at age five and over.

There is support for my theory about using Henry as an educational facilitator: a study of 12 children with Autism Spectrum Disorder (ASD) by Rederfer and Goodman confirmed that the dog served as a conduit for interactions with the therapist. Just as I did with Dale, 'the therapist carefully coordinated interactions between the child and dog and took an active teaching role in terms of how to communicate, play with the dog, as well as to sustain activities and broaden the children's range of responses.'[5]

Again, the benefit of canine intervention reported for emotional disabilities like Post Traumatic Stress Disorder (PTSD), depression and many physical disabilities is incalculable.

The first key to success is obtaining the right age, breed and type of dog suitable for the individual's needs and the family's lifestyle and dynamics. This is a detailed manual on how to create a meaningful and successful relationship between a child with a disability and a dog. It's been written following eight years of personal research with eight families whose children have severe autism, and in collaboration with Alberto Alvarez-Campos, National Programs Manager for Assistance Dogs Australia.

With our combined experience and knowledge, we've brought autism, disability and the working dog worlds together to create this unique facilitator dog educational programme. This programme has been successful with families I have worked with in Scotland. It has been implemented by Alberto via a charity he set up in Zamora, Spain, called PAAT, and was the foundation for a successful autism assistance dog pilot programme in December 2013, when Alberto worked for Guide Dogs Queensland (GDQ).

The GDQ pilot involved a range of families, adults and children. Two families each had two children with severe autism; both children shared the dog (undoubtedly ground-breaking work). Two other families with one child with autism were also on the programme. What was significant about this work is that none of the children were physically tethered to the dog, a key point that I will cover later. One adult client on the pilot suffers from lifelong severe and debilitating PTSD. The programme and training of the dog was tailored to this client's individual needs. The dog has had a profound life-changing effect on the client's quality of life.

All five dogs on the GDQ pilot were former guide dogs that didn't make the grade to become guide dogs; Alberto and his team modified these dogs' training to enable them to become assistance dogs for these very different clients. Each dog was assessed and trained to be suitably partnered with each child and to fit the dynamics of the whole family's lifestyle.

The emergence of this work, together with Dale's plight as an adult with autism in today's society, has been told in *All Because of Henry,* published in October 2013, with numerous five star reviews on Amazon!

In September 2011, I left my career as a community staff nurse to devote myself full-time to developing a programme for canine intervention for those with disabilities. My decision was inspired and motivated by the response from parents who had read my books – especially those seeking guidance on how to replicate what I'd done with Dale and Henry in order to help their own children.

My experience as a community staff nurse – with patients with a diverse range of disabilities – gave me real insight into managing and living with other emotional and physical conditions, providing me with so much of the knowledge and practical experience that I use in the work I do now!

Alberto continues to enhance the autism assistance dog programme, working now as National Programs Manager for Assistance Dogs Australia (ADA). ADA trains dogs for many disabilities including autism and PTSD.

In March 2013, I was honoured to present my story and facilitator dog programme at the first International Conference on Animal Intervention in Lleida, Spain. At this conference, I learned that the range of animals – horses, various breeds of dogs and even chickens – being used for human therapy was as varied as the conditions and disabilities themselves. The possibilities for using animal intervention, particularly dogs, were virtually endless.

It was heartening to witness children with autism and other disabilities overcome long-term problems (like sensory issues with food) or improve their intellectual capacity due to the specific teaching from specially trained dogs and their handlers. It struck me that the animal trainer and family therapist in Lleida, Mylos Rodriguez, was using dogs as conduits for children to learn independence skills. Mylos also used her dogs to work with groups of elderly clients suffering with dementia. To witness the elderly clients work as a team with their peers, and have lucid and intellectual episodes emerging because of the dogs' work with them, was wonderful and professionally humbling.

In October 2015, I spent a wonderful and successful week in the beautiful town of Elgoibar in the Basque region of Spain. I was invited to share my work and collaborate with Eneko Kortabarria, the manager of a charity called Anateusk. Eneko uses his own dog, Lynne, a sprightly 10-year-old collie, and sources suitable dogs to train, using their new skills in their widest sense. As a qualified physiotherapist, Eneko has used his professional background to give specialised physiotherapy and occupational, social and communication therapy to children and adults with various disabilities.

Like Mylos, a lot of Eneko's community work involves reaching people with dementia in residential homes. I have learned so much from Eneko and the amazing work of Anateusk. I felt so privileged to share a platform at San Sebastian University with Eneko, the university director and a local child psychiatrist who specialised in autism. After seeing a Spanish subtitled version of *After Thomas*, the audience of future doctors, psychologists and psychiatrists appropriately grilled us. I'm pleased to say we left them enlightened and reassured that canine intervention was a specialised and powerful therapy in its own right!

I was pleased that the first question from the audience was related to the welfare of the dog. Later you will learn how I cover this vital aspect of the programme, via a cuddly dog transition kit I have researched and devised. Before I said my goodbyes to Anateusk, I gave Eneko one of these transitional kits, to use in his work with the children with various disabilities Anateusk helps.

Finally, after eight years of helping parents in the UK and internationally to replicate what I'd done with Dale and Henry, my frustration about the supply of assistance dogs not meeting the demand for them, particularly in Scotland, is at last slowly being addressed. I am now collaborating with Glynn Morris, Chief Executive of Friendly Access, a charity in Scotland that works to ensure inclusion for those with autism and disability wanting to access public places like theatres, etc. Glynn and I are working with a Chocolate Labrador dog breeder called Lynda Hall. Lynda kindly donated a puppy to a family who have a daughter with Asperger syndrome. The new owner and family are thriving as a result of Lynda's tireless support of them. The impact of the dog has been immense, and my involvement in sharing my dog programme with the family has made a real difference.

My collaboration with Glynn and Lynda is timely given the findings of research published in July 2016.[6] This research showed that families with autistic children who owned a pet dog experienced significantly reduced stress in their lives – so much so that the family as a whole functioned better. Carried out at the University of Lincoln, UK, and funded by the US-based Human-Animal Bond Research Institute (HABRI), the research also found a marked decrease in the number of 'dysfunctional interactions between parent and child among the families that owned a dog'. Professor Daniel Mills (Professor of Veterinary Behavioural Medicine at the School of Life Sciences, University of Lincoln) headed the research.

Significantly, this work addresses the question: 'Are assistance dogs the best intervention to improve the quality of life for the child with autism and the immediate family?' Professor Mills has said:

> While there is growing evidence that animal-assisted therapy can aid in the treatment of children with autism spectrum disorders, this study is one of the first to examine how pet dog ownership can also improve the lives of those more widely affected by autism. Researchers have previously focused on the positive effects that assistance dogs can have on the child's well-being and have passed over the impact they might also have on close relatives, but our results show that owning a pet dog (rather than a specifically trained assistance dog) can considerably improve the function of the whole family unit. We found a significant, positive relationship between parenting stress of the child's main caregiver and their attachment to the family dog. This highlights the importance of the bond between the carer and their dog in the benefits they gain.

I couldn't agree more with Professor Mills' findings and comments and that's why I felt compelled to develop this programme and write this manual. Undoubtedly, many families will find the right breed and temperament of dog and enjoy the benefits Professor Mills' study describes. However, there are still too many families facing upset and regret because it all went horribly wrong. My programme offers an increased chance of success for the child and the whole family. As Professor Mills highlights, there is increased bonding between the carer and their dog. Using the dog as an educational facilitator for the child (where the child thinks he or she is the dog's carer) will therefore increase that all-important bond between the child and the dog. With this now understood – and Dale is proof that close bonding and caring for the dog will lead to increased independence – the publication of this manual and work is coming at a favourable time. It is also now widely accepted that pet ownership and caring for a dog is good for everyone in the family's well-being.

I hope to continue to carry on my work with autism and working dog organisations, and continue to speak at conferences and public events. Throughout all this, I will endeavour to give my own time to any parent who seeks my help or advice. My role as an autism parent will never change. I wouldn't have survived without the many parents in the past who gave me their time!

For those who seek my services or want to explore canine intervention, I will give my all – to give them the best chance of success! That is what this manual is all about.

Now, anyone seeking knowledge about how a dog can help a child with a disability can access all I have learned. I have written this manual, painfully aware of what Henry has done for me, but especially of what he did for Dale. As Dale reminds us all:

> Henry brought me through all of my childhood and because of that I was able to help him at the end, when he needed me to help him. It was the hardest thing I have ever had to do, but due to him I am not scared any more of the thought and responsibility of being an adult. I have decided that for the rest of my life I am never going to let my amazing dog down, so that he will be as proud of me as I will always be of him.

Dale with Henry Two on Gourock shorefront

Note: We had two dogs called Henry – known as Henry One and Henry Two. In this book, when I mention Henry in relation to Dale growing up as a child, I simply refer to him as Henry. This always refers to Henry One, which is the main dog that was the facilitator for Dale growing up.

Additional reading for the parents of those with ASD

I recommend that, before implementing this programme, parents of children with ASD read *A Friend Like Henry*,[7] as it is the foundation of this programme. Parents of adults with autism will find the sequel, *All Because of Henry*,[8] insightful reading as it shows how dogs have helped adults and explains how to navigate the many problems and barriers adulthood brings.

Is a Dog the Right Intervention for Your Child and Family?

While there is no denying the benefits the right dog can have for a child and family, it is crucial to establish that the decision is the right one and that the family is ready to own a dog. In the Introduction, I explained that it is important to think about the age of the child when considering getting a dog. It's also important, in the case of a child with autism or a learning disability, that you consider the impact of that child's disability. Can the child understand (albeit at a basic level) that, in a way, a dog is like them and has feelings and needs? The answer will determine what transitional resources are required and how the dog's training can be tailored to improve the child's quality of life.

Practical points to consider

Allergies

Remember anaphylaxis can occur immediately, weeks, months or even years after regular exposure to an antigen. If a child or person has a medically proven allergy, then no dog – despite its breeding – can reduce the risk! Those with allergies and asthma need to seek medical advice but, to reduce the risk, it is wiser not to get a dog. Dogs that have been bred to reduce moulting (or even moulting-free dog breeds) can still produce spores in the air that can produce the same antigens as those from moulting dogs.

Think about dog phobia
Dog phobia is a massive issue that warrants intensive work and education to help the child learn to cope with meeting dogs. A child with a dog phobia will need to be taught about dog behaviours and build up contact with a dog slowly and carefully.

Parents' work patterns
Parents need to consider their work patterns, because *a dog should not be left on its own for any longer than four hours at the most.* If the dog is left too often for too long, the emotional welfare of the dog is compromised and the dog's good temperament will deteriorate. Lonely dogs may adopt antisocial behaviours due to boredom and anxiety. In addition, it is cruel and neglectful not to allow the dog to relieve itself regularly for toilet purposes.

Other pets
Another important point to consider before a dog arrives is whether you have any other pets. Cats, in particular, can cause conflict and unwanted negative behaviours in the dog.

Think about your home
What size is your home and what size will the dog be? Where will the dog sleep? The dog will adopt a few favourite areas in your home to sleep in or retreat to. Do you have a private garden or access to a good-sized garden for play and toilet purposes for the dog?

Costs
Think about the monthly and lifetime costs of food, veterinary fees and health insurance, third-party indemnity insurance, kennel care and costs for holidays. These will cost a minimum of around

£25 a week. Are you willing to commit to all this until the dog's demise? (The average lifespan of a dog is about 12 years.)

Exercise

For the psychological and physical well-being of the dog, it must be walked and interacted with by playing games at the very least once a day.

Can you make time…

…to train and generally take care of the dog for its entire lifetime?

Neutering

I will cover the pros and cons of neutering later. I am of the same mind as those in the working dog world, where all working dogs are neutered around the age of six months. The dog needing to be neutered will be a pivotal part of your plan in Stage 2.

Legal responsibilities of dog ownership

In the UK, the Control of Dogs Order 1992 states that all dogs outdoors and in public have to wear a collar with an identity tag that has the owner's name and address on it. Putting on your personal phone numbers is optional.

Since May 2016, it has been a compulsory legal requirement to microchip your dog by the time it is eight weeks old; failure to comply with this could lead to a fine of up to £500. If local authorities find a non-chipped dog, owners have 21 days to adhere to the law. Primarily, this law was designed to reunite lost or stolen dogs with their owners; it also aims to reduce the massive problems of strays roaming the streets and to ease the burden for dog charities. For the owner, it is a one-off fee; some charities will do this for free. The chip itself is the size of a grain of rice and is inserted under the dog's loose skin on the back of its neck. The chip has a unique 15-digit code that is stored on a national database.

The right veterinary care

The veterinary practice you choose for your dog needs to be suitable for your child too. Look for a practice that embraces the idea of – and gives time to – a child accompanying the dog to the vet. This will mean spending time contacting and meeting vets to explain the aims you have for the child and dog. Dale was involved with visits to the vet with his puppy from the outset; this opened up a whole new social world for him. It also contributed in the long term to helping Dale cope with going to see his own doctor, dentist, etc.

Note: The above points are not exhaustive, and I will cover these and many more issues later, including the legal aspects of poop-scooping, responsible dog-friendly ownership, the Countryside Code and much more!

Identify the behaviours a dog will need to cope with, and plan ahead!

If you feel a dog is the right intervention for your child and family, then this is the time to make a plan.

In the case of a child with autism or a learning disability, your plan needs to identify any behaviours and traits relating to the child's disability that the dog needs to be prepared for in advance. Both the new puppy (from birth) and the more mature dog need intensive socialising and desensitising to the specific disability behaviours of the child, well before the child meets the dog! For example, aspects of a disability such as stimming behaviour must be recognised, as well as poor coordination (relevant to handling the pup or dog), screaming, hand flapping, over-excitement, etc. With key aspects of the child's disability in mind, you then need to decide what age and breed of dog is needed and where you would source the dog. I will expand on this crucial element later, as this is particularly important for the child with autism.

Why This Programme?

I developed this programme to make it accessible for anyone who wants to get a dog for their family. Given the complexity of autism, the meaningful dog commands I've developed for people with ASD will also work very well for all people and be more effective for everyone involved with the dog. As you read on, you'll find lots of common-sense advice on how to look after your dog's welfare as well as discussions covering all the issues surrounding owning a dog.

Sharing experiences from the disability and working dog worlds

Since the publication of *A Friend Like Henry*, I've been contacted by parents, professionals and working dog organisations, both within the UK and internationally, wanting advice on how to use dogs to improve the lives of those with a disability. Parents wanted to source the right puppy or mature dog for their child; others wanted to know which programme or assistance dog charity would best suit their child's needs. Some wanted guidance because they had two children affected and nothing was available for families with two children with disabilities. Some professionals from the working dog world wanted my help to further develop their autism assistance dog programmes. Dog trainers and breeders also wanted my advice on how they could enhance the role of the dog for the client or improve their practice.

I was like these parents before I found Henry. I was desperate to reach Dale and would have paid literally any price to find a suitable dog for Dale. But I knew I had to do my homework, to get it right; the consequences for Dale and the dog's future well-being were not lost on me.

However, 23 years ago, I was fortunate because Dale accessed the right education for his autism and his teachers' practice was exceptional. I learned so much from them and, as time passed, they taught me how to work with Dale's individual autism to achieve the best chance of success in allowing him to progress and reach his full potential.

I also had the advantage as a child of being brought up with mongrel dogs. In those days, owning a pedigree was rare and very much a luxury. I was fortunate to gain my dad's knowledge of how to treat a dog and to core train it to be obedient and socially well behaved.

I have many aspirations in writing this manual; the most important is to share my personal experience and many years of accumulated dog knowledge with others, especially the parents of children and adults who have a disability. My ultimate goals include:

- preventing financial exploitation of parents

- preventing unnecessary harm to the child due to dog bites

- reducing the number of puppies being returned to breeders.

Most important of all, I want to prevent the risk of dog stress, bearing in mind the working role the dog has and its wonderful gift of independence to the child. For me, *dog welfare is at the forefront of this programme!*

Having been involved in disability and the working dog world for the past nine years, one issue alone has become apparent. Within the autism and other disability assistance dog worlds, the demand for these dogs will always supersede the supply. While there are now numerous breeders, organisations and charities endeavouring to help families, sadly there have also been those who have misled and exploited vulnerable families.

There is also the problem that too many puppies are being bred in the wrong environments, such as horrific puppy farms or rural settings that have no plans or facilities for socialising puppies to adapt them to a domestic household. I will cover this important subject in detail later, as sourcing the right dog or puppy is absolutely critical to success.

Aside from sourcing a dog that is suitable for a child's individual disability, addressing the transitional care required for the child and dog is essential. Good autism and disability practice should be universal, no matter what the intervention is. The key components on how to teach a child with a disability should be the same throughout all organisations. The reality, though, is that it is not! That is why it is vital to research what is available and which dog programme will suit the child's individual needs. Choices about the age and breed of the dog and where to ethically source the right dog for the child are critical for success.

In fact, *careful planning beforehand for any family seeking a dog is the best way to create success*; this programme will give you the guidance needed to plan ahead.

Another vital purpose this manual should serve is to allow some parents to decide that a dog is not the right intervention for their child or family circumstances. That outcome alone will save much time emotionally as well as saving parents financial cost, reassuring them that they made the right decision for their child and a dog's future welfare.

I have witnessed lots of success in some programmes; sadly, I have seen the other side as well. Breeders with the right intentions, but little to no knowledge of autism, can compromise the best outcome and cause more upset to families. While I have endeavoured to provide as much knowledge as possible on this massive subject, this manual by no means fully covers this very specialised field. It will, though, give the reader the knowledge, tools and best practice needed to help achieve the best chance of success.

Assistance dogs, inclusion and independence

An autism assistance dog differs from a therapy or companion dog. If you Google 'assistance dogs for disability or autism', you will be overwhelmed by the result; the working dog world has come a long way in training dogs for numerous conditions and medical problems. Think of the many condition-specific working dogs being trained these days, with their varied tasks. There are too many – all doing amazing work – to mention them all, but here is a sample.

- Medical detection dogs can alert those with diabetes when blood sugars are falling dangerously low, well before the client feels early symptoms of hypoglycaemia. The same is true for epilepsy or seizure alert dogs, who can detect a change in their client's breath that signals an imminent convulsion, giving the client the chance to get to a safe place. Again due to breath smell changes, dogs alert clients with Addison's disease when cortisol levels are dangerously out of control. The dogs are specifically trained to nudge or lick the face or hand of the client when they are in danger due to their condition. These dogs are literally life-savers, as the client can avert the crisis by taking glucose for their hypoglycaemia or the desired medical intervention their condition warrants. The benefits in terms of the quality of life these dogs give to their clients, let alone the costs they save the NHS, are incalculable!

- Cancer-sniffing dogs can sniff out deep tissue, early cancer cells occurring well before physical symptoms appear. There are also dogs that help our soldiers from the armed forces who are suffering from Post Traumatic Stress Disorder (PTSD). The list of different types of working dog is virtually endless!

While there is historic and overwhelming proof of how dogs have and still do help mankind, particularly children and adults with various disabilities, a new study, 'Canines and childhood cancer', carried out by the American Humane Association™, is showing the incredible power of the dog.[9] The research is taking place within five hospitals from around the USA. So far, the results have proved that dog-assisted therapy is an effective intervention for children with cancer, giving the children and their families a happier and better quality of life while the children are in hospital fighting the condition. The dogs have been shown to alleviate the boredom and associated depression children have while they are going through long and painful treatments. The study has also shown that the dogs help distract the child from their pain and nausea. The cancer therapy dogs have decreased children's stress levels and combated loneliness while improving the child's social skills and physical exercise levels. One young boy with leukaemia on the study said it all: 'I didn't feel like I was in hospital, I just felt like I was at home playing with a dog.'

Getting back to autism and dogs for disability, the different types of dog available in the working dog world are as numerous and varied as the conditions themselves. Examples include: Service Dogs, Autism Assistance Dogs, Support Dogs, Therapy Dogs, Enabling Dogs, Companion or Buddy Dogs, Emotional Support Dogs and many more. These labels can create the impression that the client is dependent on the dog, *whereas the dog's main role is to increase inclusion and independence for the client.* The dog is purpose-trained to assist the client to do physical and psychological tasks a human counterpart would have done. In my opinion, all dogs that are in a working role are social and educational facilitators, enabling the child or adult with a disability to have as full inclusion as anyone without a disability.

Inclusion is based on nine principles (adapted from Tassoni[10]):

- a person's worth is independent of their abilities and achievements

- every human being is able to feel and think

- every human being has the right to communicate and be heard

- all human beings need each other

- real education can only happen in the context of real relationships

- all people need support and friendship from their peers

- progress for all learners is achieved by building on what people can do, rather than on what they can't

- diversity brings strength to all living systems

- collaboration is more important than competition.

While the dog is trained to perform specific tasks for a client, many other positive outcomes happen spontaneously and inadvertently – things that the dog wasn't trained for! There's an example of the guide dog a dad with sight-loss had: the dog alerted him during the night that his son, sleeping in another room, was having a life-threatening asthma attack.

The tasks of the Autism Assistance Dog (AAD)

The trained AAD's task is to help keep a child calm and confident when they are out and about and in public places, like shops and cafes.

It is well recognised in the field that dogs have an incredible calming effect on a child with autism, particularly when the child is distressed or angry. The dog can distract the child and help the child reach resolution quicker. The AAD is trained to assist with road safety via the use of a special harness the dog wears and that the child is attached to via a long lead. This practice prevents bolting behaviours in the child with autism or a disabled child who may wander off. Attachment to the dog keeps the child safe at busy roads and stops them running off into danger. The security the dog gives the child helps them cope within busy, noisy, sensory-inducing public places like shopping malls and helps facilitate inclusion and increased independence for the child.

Public access trained dogs

For the majority of people living with disabilities, not having access to full inclusion is a great barrier. That is why many working dogs are trained to such a high standard – dogs trained to the level where they have full public access rights can facilitate social inclusion for the client.

As well as keeping the child safe and increasing inclusion, a public access trained dog brings many other proven benefits for a child with autism. The dog promotes social belonging for the child, as some assistance dog programmes encourage the public to interact with the child via the dog. They display notices on the lead or jacket that say 'Please feel free to pat me'. This initiative has increased the confidence and self-esteem of many children with autism by improving their social interaction and communication skills. This is also true for children with physical disabilities – the child's confidence and physical independence soar due to having the dog in public places.

The advantages of public access dogs are well recognised, especially for those with physical disabilities which are lifelong and may deteriorate, increasing the need for more support from the dog or human counterpart. However, I feel that, particularly for a child with autism, there needs to be caution about how public access is managed. The aim, in the case of autism and related learning disabilities, is that *the dog should facilitate overall improvement and increased independence for the child.*

A child with autism learns literally – and it is harder to un-teach a learned behaviour (one that may not be appropriate later, like being physically attached to the dog), once the child is an adult.

In my opinion, tethering the child to the dog should be done as a last resort. As my own experiences, those of PAAT in Zamora, Spain, and of the pilot programme from Guide Dogs Queensland show, it is good transitional education that prevents the child from bolting or wandering. I found with Dale and Amy, and the majority of children Alberto Alvarez-Campos and I have worked with, that most children didn't require tethering. It was apparent they wanted to stay or be near the dog, just as Dale and Amy did!

There is one crucial issue to think about regarding a public access dog. *What do you do if the dog is suddenly ill or subsequently dies?* I feel, for children with autism, that it is vital to build educational goals for the child into a public access dog's objectives so that, when the time is right for the child, the dog doesn't need to be with him or her. If the public access dog is improving social inclusion for the child, then the child should progress towards coping in some places in public without the need for the dog to be with them. There may be the rare case where this cannot be done but, for the majority who will always have human support as well as the dog, public access without the dog in the long term has to be more realistic for an independent adult life.

We cannot forget that the majority of children with autism and disabilities learn social and independence skills from their schooling and with human support to access public places. In my opinion, whether the child has a dog with or without public access rights, that dog should enhance the child's educational process towards the best independence possible in adulthood.

The dog's welfare – an essential key to success

Another crucial issue to think about when choosing a dog programme for a child is: which programme is best for the dog's welfare? Later in this manual, I will cover what makes a happy, content, loving companion dog and family pet. If you want to reduce or eradicate the risk to the child from nipping or, at worst, dog bites, then nurturing the dog's temperament is vital. To ensure this, the dog's well-being has to be at the forefront as well as the child's.

A study by Burrows, Adams and Millman[11] highlighted many of the concerns I had when I first learned that the working dog world was providing dogs for children with autism and disabilities. When I met charities from the working dog world in the UK and internationally, I was worried about the lack of understanding of autism, particularly about the importance of transitional care for the child before and after the dog arrives. Many organisations leave this area for the parents to cover, and problems that should have been avoided (like the child overwhelming the dog, dog aggression and changes in the dog's behaviour) have to be dealt with when they occur, rather than being prevented in the first place. Sadly, the majority of problems that arise (and serious issues like the dog retaliating due to stress) could be avoided with the right transitional intervention from the outset – weeks and even months before the dog is placed in the home.

The study looked at factors that affected the working role of assistance dogs and had a negative impact on dog welfare. Issues that could contribute to an assistance dog's stress included:

- the dog not being given sufficient time to rest from working

- limited opportunities for the dog to relieve itself

- the dog wearing its jacket for too long

- a lack of consistent daily routines

- insufficient time given for the dog to free run, go on child-free walks or other recreational activities.

For me, the most important issue of all was highlighted in this research: the authors found that assistance dogs that worked and slept with children were exposed to 'unintentional mistreatment by children with ASD'. Dogs that slept with the child were tired due to being up with the child during the night and didn't work as well the following day because of it.

Due to the lack of recognised dog welfare-specific transition plans, assistance dogs were exposed to added stress until the dog itself learned that the different probing and handling by the child was normal. Within the first three months, the dogs desensitised themselves in order to cope; in this way, the dog was able to avoid mistreatment and not display any aggression towards the child. One factor from the study that struck me was that, if a dog didn't receive any affection from the child during the first three months, then the parents tried to improve matters by prompting the child to groom, feed or play with the dog, etc. Every dog bonded and engaged with the child it was paired with in a different way, based on the child's autism, development and personality. Parents accepted that the first year of placement was a settling-in period for the child and dog to find their way with hopes that the dog's future years would increase the benefits for the child.

The key benefits of transition planning – for both child and dog!

The 2008 study (Burrows, Adams and Millman) and my own research both point to the need for adequate transitional care for the child months before the dog arrives; transitional care for the dog is equally vital. With all this in mind, I devised the *cuddly dog transitional kit*, to address the issues of dog welfare and much more before the dog arrives.

None of the problems highlighted by the research surprised me; without an adequate, consistent and recognised transition plan aimed at the welfare of the dog, the problems reported in the study were to me inevitable!

That is why, in 1993, I went to extremes to teach Dale via a cuddly dog and all the equipment a real dog needs – to help him support his puppy's physical, emotional and social well-being. As a child, I wanted Dale to learn by looking after 'his' dog. He could then transfer the same skills to looking after himself – which he did! Transitional interventions are far more difficult, almost impossible, to implement after the dog arrives. Good transitional practice should always take place weeks or months before the major event.

Nowadays, the benefits of good transition for children with sight loss are recognised by Guide Dogs UK. During the guide dog training process, many dogs, at different stages of the training, fail to make the grade for a guide dog. Some dogs fail at around the 14-month age and more mature dogs fail for various reasons. Some don't like wearing the metal-framed harness or are too playful or boisterous; others are easily distracted; some may have developed health problems that a person with sight loss couldn't manage. Some of the dogs that fail the training have become 'buddy dogs' for children with sight loss, but they have a different role from a guide dog's. Buddy dogs provide companionship and emotional support for the child, with all the advantages of owning a dog coming with it. The children learn to become more confident with dogs, thereby preparing themselves for successful partnerships with guide dogs in the future.

Your decision – a pre-trained assistance dog or a dog you train yourself?

Having explained all of the above, here are the reasons why, for the majority of parents, the only way to acquire a dog to help their child with a disability will be to *do it themselves!*

I totally understand why parents or disabled clients would want the luxury of an assistance dog. In essence, they are the perfect calibre of trained dog and amazing role models for those with disabilities, given they are on a par with a fully trained public access guide dog. They are a luxury because the cost of breeding and training them, and then maintaining them with the client, is far from cheap! Some charities will provide a dog – either training the family's own pet or providing a trained dog – from around £5000 to £10,000. The reality is that providing a fully trained public access assistance dog costs the charity around £12,000 for training and then around another £20,000 for the working life of the dog. This is because the organisation providing the dog keeps ownership of that dog and therefore pays all the costs of maintaining the dog up to its retirement at around 10 years old.

Today, despite these costs, many autism assistance dog charities have waiting lists that are as long as two years or more; many lists are now closed! New organisations are emerging offering similar trained dogs. They will source puppies and mature dogs or train a family's dog, for a fee, usually of around £5000. But, even at this price, many of these dogs won't have public access rights. Here's why...

Legal ownership of all public access dogs in the UK, for their entire working lives, remains with the charity or organisation that supplied and trained the dog. (When the dog has to be retired at around aged 10, some organisations allow the family to keep the dog up to its demise. Alternatively, depending on the nature of the client's disability, the dog may have to be retired to a new home.)

What is crucial to know is this: all organisations who supply public access dogs in the UK have to be accredited by or members of Assistance Dogs International (ADI) or members of the International Guide Dog Federation. In the UK, the organisations that are members of ADI have merged to become Assistance Dogs UK (ADUK). At the time of writing, members of ADUK include: Guide Dogs UK, Hearing Dogs for Deaf People, Dogs for Good (formally known as Dogs for the Disabled), Canine Partners, Support Dogs, Dog A.I.D., and Medical Detection Dogs. It's worth checking online to find out which organisations are current members.

Core training, behaviour and obedience of the dog are of ADUK standard, for the safety of the disabled child and the public. Dog trainers must be ADUK-accredited to train dogs to public access standard. Therefore, only dogs from the above-named organisations have public access rights that are the same as the clients', under the Equality Act of 2010 (where public premises have to make reasonable adjustments for the client and their dog). All assistance dog owners carry an ID card (an identification book), showing the dog's certification for public access and certifying that the dog is no threat to health and safety or hygiene issues (because the dog is groomed daily and has regular health checks by a vet).

ADUK and ADI have a register of all public access dog charities and organisations that have successfully met intensive criteria, a good standard of training and practice, to supply public access dogs for those with disabilities.

All public access dogs are tested working with the 'designated dog handler' (i.e. a parent or disabled adult) in public by an independent, qualified assessor from ADUK, Assistance Dogs Europe (ADE) or ADI. The dog and recognised handler have to meet strict assessment criteria and pass an assistance dog public access certification test. The purpose of the test is to ensure all public access dogs are trustworthy temperament-wise, obedient, well behaved and unobtrusive in public places. The recognised dog handler has to display full control of the dog and demonstrate that the dog partnership with the child or client themselves is not a danger to the public. The test is strict but tailored to the client's individual need to have the dog in public with them. The slightest indication that the dog is not under good control, with any signs of growling, biting, etc., or relieving itself, will lead to the dog being immediately disqualified. The crux of the test is that the dog must demonstrate it is safe to be in public places and that the handler has full control of the dog at all times!

The test is carried out in a real public setting, like a noisy and busy shopping mall, with lots of people and natural distractions going on. Shopping malls allow the assessor to test the dog and handler in coffee shops and supermarkets and in how they safely access lifts and, most dangerous of all, escalators! In the working lifetime of the public access dog, the organisation will keep regular contact with the family and monitor the dog's progress to ensure its training and public access skills are maintained up to the dog's retirement.

The criteria to be met and the auditing process involved in a working dog charity or organisation becoming a member of these bodies are intensive, with strict guidelines, and can take months or even years to achieve. The lesson here is: *beware of organisations that are not members of at least one of these three bodies, especially if you want a public access dog!*

Many of the above-listed organisations are members of all three bodies, including ADE, because they run regular conferences to promote the sharing and learning of new practices. ADI runs international conferences every two years. I was fortunate to attend the 2007 conference held in Frankfurt, where I met Alberto Alvarez-Campos and Jane Kefford (a meeting which started my new journey in this field).

A vital part of a public access dog's assessment is ensuring that the dog can perform three main tasks that will alleviate problems or assist the client in a public place. In the case of a child with autism or a similar disability, these could be:

- The dog is there to calm the child to facilitate access to public places and to provide good companionship and emotional support for the child.

- If a child with autism won't move on, or is facing a negative or sensory issue in public, the dog will prompt the child by diverting them or moving them on. The dog could also help reduce the child's anxiety in busy, noisy public places. If the child is upset, the dog can support the child by lying beside them, with its head on the child's body, to enable them to reach resolution quicker, especially if a challenging tantrum occurs due to the child not being able to communicate their distress.

- The dog is trained to keep the child safe at kerbs and ensure road safety and to prevent the child from bolting or wandering off. As discussed earlier, many children are tethered to the dog!

All public access working dogs in public places must wear their charity's jacket which clearly shows the organisation's name and logo.

In the nine years of researching and working with people from the dog world, I have learned many wonderful stories that convey how life-enhancing a public access assistance dog can be for a child or adult with a disability.

Of all of them to date, there is one story told in February 2016 that really struck a chord with me.[12] It occurred on the other side of the world. Assistance Dogs New Zealand trained Mahe, a black Labrador, for James Issac, aged nine, who has non-verbal autism. Mahe was trained to keep James safe and calm when he was out in public and, since the day they were partnered, they have been inseparable.

Naturally, due to sensory issues, James doesn't like being touched, and unfamiliar situations like medical appointments are also difficult, so having to get an MRI scan to investigate the cause of his seizures was a massive challenge to overcome! James would need to be sedated for the scan, a traumatic procedure itself. This was frightening enough for James to cope with, but he also had to deal with the sensory chaos of having to be in hospital. However, James did cope, due to one special support mechanism being put in place. From the outset of James being in hospital, Mahe stayed by James's side throughout, lying beside him on the hospital bed and theatre trolley. Mahe nuzzled James to keep him calm while he was sedated; James's mother noticed that the dog seemed worried for James. I understood this, as I had seen Henry looking worried for Dale when he was upset. Like Mahe, Henry never left Dale's side – and I didn't train Henry to have this skill!

In 1993, I vividly remember seeing Dale always give the correct eye contact with Henry, but struggling with mine or others'. It didn't surprise me to read these words from Mahe's trainer, Wendy Issacs:

There is such magic that happens with a child with autism and the dogs, they just calm the kids down. The kids will maintain eye contact with the dogs, but often not with their own parents and siblings.

The vital message for parents

It is vital that parents empower themselves with as much knowledge as possible on how dogs can assist those with disabilities so that they are confident that the type of dog and the programme they choose for their child is the right one.

For those who want guidance on how to train a socially well-behaved, obedient dog, the Kennel Club[13] has a three-tier award scheme (bronze, silver and gold) that will guide the owner in training the dog to an adequate or high standard. However, this will not be sufficient to enable the dog to access public places.

I have no doubt that choosing the right dog for the child with autism is critical to success. It is vital that the dog's training is specific to the child's disability. How the dog is used as a facilitator for the child's future is paramount. Incredible results can and have been achieved with this approach, some with dogs like Henry without public access and others with public access assistance dogs. This manual is about replicating what Maureen Erdwin (see earlier) and I did with our family dogs to help our severely disabled sons. We didn't have this manual, but now here it is – the best chance of success – with or without a public access dog!

Overview of the Programme

This is a unique four-stage educational programme on how to ensure the best chance of success for a child with their dog. The objective is to achieve the best level of independence possible for the child or adult. It is important that the educational approach described in this manual is tailored to each child's individual needs, autism or disability. In the case of children with autism, the approach should be tailored to address the triad of impairments of their autism simultaneously.

This model allows the inclusion of siblings, the immediate and extended family, and the child's schooling, with dog ethics at the forefront. In the nine years I have been involved with parents and professionals in this field, I have encountered many issues and scenarios. I understand parents' apprehension in their search for a therapy that will help their child, especially given all that a dog can bring to the entire family. However, most important from the outset is making the right decision – is a dog suitable and the right intervention for the child and family in the first place? This alone is an area that needs in-depth thought and research. Many parents who have contacted me have changed their minds when they understood all that was involved in sourcing and owning a dog, let alone having to personally train it and look after it for the rest of the dog's life.

To make the decision process easier and to try to avoid puppies being returned to breeders for re-homing, I have compiled a 'dog checklist' that helps parents make the right decision before they proceed. This checklist is described in detail in the chapter 'Is a

Dog the Right Intervention for Your Child and Family?' If you've not already done so, *please read this chapter before you embark on this programme.* This checklist has saved parents financial loss and, more importantly, prevented upset for the child and family.

The aim of the programme is to use a dog as an educational facilitator and motivator for a child, by creating a strong bond between the child and dog, and with a holistic ethos throughout.

Throughout, the programme is devised to:

- promote improved communication skills, both verbal and non-verbal

- increase the child's imagination and thought processes

- improve social understanding and belonging, allowing better social inclusion and quality of life for the child and the family.

The programme's educational approach is compatible with the strategies and curriculum used by a school working with a child with autism. This enhances the work being done with the child and their dog, giving a seamless educational approach throughout.

I believe that, to ensure the best chance of success, the safest and best choice is an ethically sourced puppy or mature dog that has been professionally bred in relation to the Kennel Club registration standard. The dog must also have been assessed as having a trustworthy good temperament and nature. It is essential that the puppy, from its birth until it is re-homed, is given adequate socialisation and domestication; the same need exists for the mature dog. I discuss this in detail later in the manual. It is imperative for the child's and the dog's welfare that the dog is desensitised to, and familiar with, the child's individual autism, behaviours or specific disability traits.

To assist bonding with the dog, I have modified dog training core commands that will be meaningful to the non-verbal child with autism and assist the child with a learning disability. These are described in the chapter 'Meaningful Dog Commands'.

Note: While this model is tailored for a child with autism, the basic language and meaningful dog commands and the ethos of the entire programme will allow it to be used by anyone who wants to get a dog. This manual will give the reader the best chance of success by providing the knowledge to ensure the dog has the best care.

To ensure I had the right educational approach with this dog model, I piloted the transitional resources with eight autistic children to ensure they were beneficial for the transition period before the dog arrived. I needed to find out if this essential element of the programme would help the child to connect and bond with the dog before the real dog arrived!

I learned that modifying standard dog training commands to create meaningful instructions that children could learn allowed them to understand core dog commands and the associated actions. These new commands provide a platform of meaningful, key language for the non-verbal child to learn as well as empowering the verbal child. The child can then use this language to communicate with others – precisely because the language is comprehensible and consistent.

This made sense to me because you train a dog using the same strategies and approaches you would use to work with and teach a child with autism. In essence, the dog learns with the same approaches and manner as a child with autism!

Throughout this programme, all those involved with the child must have a consistent approach to using the dog as an educational facilitator. In this way, repeatedly throughout every day, the child sees and hears – in a literal way, via the dog complying – that communication works!

The adjusted dog commands and transitional resources allow the child to be involved with the dog's needs from the outset of the programme, using the cuddly dog transitional kit and other resources I have developed. The eventual aim is that the child will be able to transfer these skills in order to take care of themselves, and be more socially included, leading towards a more independent life.

The outcomes of any autism or disability intervention, immediate and long term, should facilitate improved communication and social skills leading to the best possible independence for each child as they approach adulthood. Interventions should be planned, implemented and evaluated with realistic objectives for the long term! This is vital for any child but particularly the child with autism because they learn in a literal way. We don't want to introduce the child to a behaviour or technique that is not appropriate for an adult. This is why tethering the child to the dog is, for me, a last resort, and should be a temporary strategy.

This whole programme has been developed to allow the child to understand and cope with all of life's transitions, each of which I have covered in the four stages of the programme.

To help me devise this programme, I had the best resource of all – my son Dale! Dale (now aged 29 and a professional himself) allowed me to unzip and probe what used to be a severely autistic mind. Via Dale, I could decode autistic puzzles and find the answers to the countless questions I had. In Dale, I had the ultimate and unique expert to help me try to solve the biggest mystery and most vital question of all: *Why do dogs or animals manage to reach many affected by autism, when their human counterparts have been unable to reach them?*

The four stages of the programme
Stage 1: Planning and transition for the child and dog
One of the successful resources from the pilot programme that I use within this stage (as long as it is age- and stage-appropriate) is the cuddly dog transition kit. This kit helps the child:

- cope with the transition to having a dog

- care for the dog by learning skills using the cuddly dog

- transfer these skills to the real dog when it arrives.

During this stage, the transition kit is essential and can be used extensively with the child. You'll find detailed guidance on the use of the kit – to help the child learn through play and in a fun way about all that is concerned with the dog – in 'The Transitional Kit: What You Need and How to Use It', later in this manual.

The kit has helped all the children in the pilot projects, to various degrees, to:

- connect, understand and communicate better with their dogs

- bond with their dogs and understand the dogs' needs many weeks before their real dogs arrived.

This alone has been reassuring given the findings of the 2008 assistance dog study,[14] which showed that these same skills could take months (even up to a year) to develop. In my own research, early intervention and adequate transition strategies have been proven to lead towards real success.

With any intervention to help a disabled child, it is always worth remembering that the earlier the education begins, the better the results. This is especially true for a child with autism. The transition kit also helps children with autism engage in imaginative play as well as enabling siblings to be involved as perfect role models to teach the autistic child.

It was important to me to ensure siblings were included throughout the programme; any disability in a family affects siblings and the whole family. Again, the holistic approach of this programme can address many aspects of a child's disability simultaneously.

A NOTE ABOUT DOG PHOBIA

This programme could be adapted to help a child or adult with dog phobia, but it is not described here in the detail this intervention warrants. Nevertheless, there is much information and many strategies in this manual that can help with this delicate issue.

Stage 2: Introducing the dog to your home

As well as preparing your child for the arrival of the dog, this stage involves helping your child understand that the dog has daily needs – just like they do!

During this stage, with the seed well planted in the child's mind about a dog's needs, it is time for parents to source the right dog for their child. This stage allows parents to prepare the child and the home for the arrival of the dog.

This stage is similar to Stage 1 but teaches the child, via social pictures and stories about their real dog, to make sense of what they have learned in the previous stage. This is a vital stage of transition with many practical strategies for the child and the family home to be implemented – all of which need to be done weeks before the dog arrives.

During this stage, there is much to do. To source the dog – and get it right – will take months in the first place. When this has been achieved, there is much to organise within the home. Advance planning of a workable structure and routine for the dog and child at this stage is imperative for success! This stage also encourages as much involvement of the child and siblings as possible so they feel a sense of ownership of the dog prior to its arrival. Good planning and preparation beforehand will assist bonding between child and dog and make the transition through the stages seamless.

Stage 3: Using the dog as an educational facilitator towards the best possible independence for the child

This is the stage where all the planning should pay off, from achieving stress-free settling in of the dog to establishing a workable routine for the child and the whole family. This stage is the crux of the programme and continues throughout all the transitions and life stages of the child until the dog reaches old age.

The dog is used as an educational facilitator throughout this stage, during all transitions – at the child's school, on birthdays, for seasonal events like Christmas, etc. Just as with Dale and his dog through the years of their life together, there are endless learning opportunities for the child to learn to care for all his or her dog's needs – as if the dog were a human counterpart.

Using the dog extensively and holistically throughout this stage is designed to help the child learn to look after themselves, lead a more independent life and have a better quality of life towards adulthood. At his or her specific intellectual level, the child is included in the training of the dog and learns how to appropriately and safely engage and interact with the dog.

A vital aspect of this stage involves the child and parents learning dog behaviour, albeit at a basic level. Everyone in the family must have enough knowledge of how to prevent and identify dog stress. This is paramount for dog welfare and essential to preventing the risk of nipping or bites to the child.

If you have read *A Friend Like Henry*, you will understand how using the dog as a facilitator for a child, as described in this stage, is a very powerful educational tool as they grow up. With a successful partnership established, the dog can be incorporated into the child's schooling. New social worlds like dog reading schemes and dog agility and walking/social clubs can be opened up for the child.

Another important component of this stage involves parents gauging the right time to introduce and teach the child about the transition of the dog getting older, leading towards its demise. With good transition practice, this major event is introduced within this stage. I cover this important and delicate subject in detail.

Stage 4: Letting go! Transition for the child to prepare for the demise of the dog

As important as it is for the child to learn from the outset all that a dog is and needs, it is also imperative they learn about the ageing process of the dog towards its inevitable demise.

Of all the lessons Dale learned from Henry, this issue was the most life-changing for him. Due to good transition practice, Dale learned total empathy for his old dog and how to take care of him.

It empowered Dale to plan ahead for Henry's expected demise and how he would manage the entire process. No matter what impact a child's autism or level of learning disability has, giving the child a concept of death is vital to their emotional well-being and development. In discussing this stage, I share recent research as well as personal knowledge about this subject.

This stage of the programme uses transitional strategies, social stories and other resources to help the child to learn the concept of dogs – and people – getting old. Regardless of culture or religion, I feel it is helpful to give the child a concept of Heaven or similar, so the child can connect with the idea that the dog or person is no longer in this life and that they or their remains have gone somewhere else that the child understands or recognises.

Whatever voyage the child and family go through with this programme, by the end, they will know what is best to do about moving on! If the programme has achieved its objectives, the family may choose not to seek another dog. Or it may be that the child as an adult could manage a dog themselves. Or a companion dog or pet may be best.

And finally...

No matter what, I hope this programme will be the catalyst that allows the child and family to enjoy similar success as Dale and others who have been on the same road! I sincerely hope this manual is a significant contribution to their special and successful journey.

Success Story I:
Makenzie Gets Heather

I n her own words, Makenzie Garrett, aged 14, describes the arrival and training of her dog Heather.

I started asking my parents for a dog in 2014. Mum started looking into getting an Autism Therapy Dog for me. This was when we found out how long the waiting list for getting a Therapy Dog was. It can take *years* to actually get a Therapy Dog. The waiting list is so long, that any child who goes on the list to receive one will be an adult before they will ever get to the top of the list.

You can buy an Autism Therapy Dog but they cost a lot of money and my family could never afford one.

Then one day a friend of my mum's sent her a story about the NAS giving away a chocolate Labrador to an autistic child. Mum immediately sent off an email about me. Out of the hundreds of emails that they received, they picked me! When I found out that I was chosen to get Heather, I was excited and scared at the same time. As the time grew closer to get her, the more scared I got. I was still getting over my fear of dogs, but what if I was terrified of her? What if we didn't bond? What if she didn't listen to me and I couldn't train her? What if this didn't work out and we had to give her back!

I decided that I wanted a female Lab as they are a little smaller than the males. I wanted a Scottish name for my dog as we live in the Highlands of Scotland, so I named her Heather.

When Heather was eight weeks old, we finally got to meet her. I was so nervous that I had my dad hold onto her at the beginning because I was scared I would drop her. She was so beautiful and sweet! Instead of taking her home at eight or nine weeks old, the breeder and our family decided that Heather would stay with the breeder till she was five months old to do some more training with her.

We agreed to meet up with the breeder a few times before we got her to build up a bond. This really helped me as I got to feel what it was like to walk a dog and I could feel a bond starting.

Mum phoned around the local area to find a dog trainer that could help me train Heather for my autism. There was no one in all of Scotland at the time that could help us. My mum and dad had watched the movie *After Thomas* and found out the author Nuala Gardner lived here in Scotland. Mum then found Nuala's website and sent her an email about Heather. Nuala emailed her back and they talked on the phone.

Nuala told mum she was writing a training manual and that she would send us a draft of the dog commands for all of us to learn before we got Heather. I'm glad my mum got in contact with Nuala before we got Heather. My whole family learned the commands so we would all be teaching Heather the same thing.

After talking to Nuala, we learned why it was so important to start transitioning ourselves now to get ready for Heather's arrival. Nuala told us to get a Panda Harness. She also asked us if we were planning on using a doggy crate. We were, so Nuala taught us about crate training. We knew that puppies liked to chew, and Nuala told us to buy a Kong chew toy. We bought a purple one.

When the day finally arrived to collect Heather I was so nervous! All my old fears were back. I was going to get my dog today! I was very overwhelmed and had to calm myself down because I was getting worked up about it. I was going to be Heather's 'Mum' and that was a lot of responsibility. Could I do it? My family helped calm me down and kept reassuring me that it would all work out and that I was just scared. Once I was with Heather everything would be fine. To make it worse, I had a film crew filming me because this was such an honour to be getting Heather. I was the first person to be getting a puppy from the National Autistic Society and it was such an important occasion. So now I really didn't want to cry on camera and be all embarrassed. Thank goodness it all went smoothly with Heather and I bonded right away. I was finally taking my dog home.

Heather is so smart that it didn't take her long to learn the basic commands. When it was time for Heather's feeds, Nuala taught me to have Heather sit and wait while I got her food ready. She had to continue to wait while I placed her food bowl down. When I blew the whistle twice, that was her command to come and eat her meal. She learned this very quickly. This was Heather learning recall. Mum and dad phoned Nuala a few times because of some problems we were having with Heather. She wouldn't let us know when she had to pee and ripped to shreds her nice fleece bed. Nuala took the time to give us advice we needed to stop this. (Although to this day she still rips any soft toy to shreds.)

Nuala also taught me about low and high rewards. When Heather did a basic command correctly, she got a doggy biscuit. When she went to the toilet outside, she got a high reward like a piece of cooked chicken.

My favourite thing to teach Heather was to give a paw. She's figured out that if she does this, she gets a reward. I continue to train and practise with Heather every day and I hope to be able to take her into stores with me very soon. She is now a member of this family and I am her proud Mum.

Makenzie with her dog Heather

Success Story 2:
Andy and Bailey

Autism dad Duncan MacGillivray describes what led to the arrival of Bailey the Labrador in their home and the effect the dog has had on the whole family.

An autism dad

I am an autism dad. I have three children – two boys and a girl. My middle child, Andy, is 10 years old and has non-verbal classic autism and a globalised developmental delay (viewed from a neurotypical perspective). I am also a social worker. In my 'spare time' I run a small charity – Inspired by Autism.[15] I provide advice, support, advocacy and representation for autistic people and their families.

I run a local drop-in/support group, Dunoon Autism Support Group, and promote local peer support. I lobby for autism rights and services at local and national level and chair my local health care forum. I also provide autism awareness talks, presentations and lectures.

My central goal is to go beyond autism awareness to autism acceptance to make our world a better place for my precious boy and everyone living with autism.

Andy and Bailey's story

My wife, Jenny, had been suggesting a dog in our home would have lots of benefits, not only for Andy but for the whole family. We investigated the possibility of a specially trained autism support dog but found this to be almost impossible to obtain here in Scotland. To be honest, I had concerns about the whole idea. What if it didn't work out? What about the mess and extra work? I am happy to admit that much of the time I was coming from the perspective of a stressed-out and tired parent/carer. Each stage in supporting Andy had been a real challenge and we had just emerged from an ultimately successful but exhausting toilet-training period.

Andy's carer is Nuala Gardner, who had introduced Andy to her retriever Thomas and under her supervision Andy has made progress. From being initially very unsure he was now comfortable around this large dog and he and Nuala had started walking with Thomas. With great patience, Andy was making progress and the social and physical benefits to him were starting to emerge.

Despite my pessimism, my wife began making plans and researching about which dog might be best for our family. Together with Nuala and with Thomas, the transition work began. A large cuddly toy dog arrived in our home with a bed, food and water bowls and a lead. Andy's carer's dog became a regular visitor and accompanied them on outings and walks.

Andy with cuddle dog

Jenny's research had pointed to a Labrador and she had located a couple of possibilities. Again, I moaned about more toilet training that a puppy would require and remained unsure generally.

A reputable breeder emerged and Jen was particularly keen due to the fact that the household was one with several young children in it. This she hoped would help the pups be used to having noisy and unpredictable young children around. Jenny discussed this with the mum in the breeder family and she was very receptive to this. She prompted her kids to stim around the puppy, explaining the purpose to her own kids.

Nuala continued the transition work, modelling life with a dog using the toy dog and of course including Thomas. Social stories with lots of pictures were used with Andy. A safe space for the dog to have his sleep was emphasised with Andy, using do-not-disturb pictorial signs. Jen and Nuala visited the breeder, met the pups with their mother, and had more discussions on how to desensitise the chosen pup. Nuala commented that the breeder had created the perfect environment for the pups – the whelping box was ethically perfect, in a secluded and calm place, but adjacent to all the noise and goings-on from the kitchen, allowing appropriate socialisation of the pups to enable them to cope in a domestic setting. We paid a deposit and it all became very real, especially for me. I made a last ditch and concerted effort to express the doubts I harboured. Jen stood firm.

With Nuala's guidance, Jen selected our dog as one that appeared particularly relaxed about being handled. Oh and he was the cutest! (They were all cute.) The mum at the breeders agreed to keep our pup a week or so longer than the normal weaning period to fit in with our plans around a short break. This would then allow us a long and uninterrupted settling-in period at home.

We visited the breeder's home with Andy and the other kids, but Andy refused to get out of the car. This is not uncommon with Andy who struggles greatly with new places and situations. We decided not to force the issue in any way to avoid any negative feelings related to our new arrival. Nuala, Jen and Andy went to visit the breeder's home again, but Andy wouldn't budge from the car. So, the breeder took the pup out to the car to let Andy see it; he took a calm and fleeting look at the pup.

We all redoubled our efforts in the final lead-up period, talking about the new pup and using the cuddly toy dog to model the events that were to unfold. We settled on a name – Bailey – as Andy, though non-verbal, could produce a B sound. We also liked the name!

The day finally came and Bailey arrived. We did our best to contain the excitement and all behave as normally as possible. Bailey won our hearts immediately. He was gentle but playful. We attempted to let Andy and Bailey interact on their own terms – slowly, cautiously checking each other out. It was a slow burner but all positive, and that was fine by us. Bailey was and still is a very quiet dog, who very rarely barks, and this certainly helped. Andy's habit of carrying finger food around with him also helped their early bonding! They began sharing space and experiences; more and more Andy appeared to really enjoy this engagement that did not involve uncomfortable social intrusion like eye contact and overwhelming questions or demands. Bailey took the spotlight from Andy and that was very agreeable to him. Another major characteristic of their engagement was humour. Andy found Bailey very amusing and still does to this day. He is open to interactions with Bailey at all times, even when waking up, as Bailey sometimes helps Nuala to get Andy to rise in the morning and get dressed. Andy and Bailey hang out together during the day. They cuddle up in the evenings. They go in the car together. They are quite simply best friends.

Oh and guess what? Bailey has changed my life. I walk him most days and miss him when away at work. He sleeps on our bed and he makes our whole family complete.

Andy with his dog Bailey

Points to Remember When Helping a Child with ASD or Learning Difficulties

G iven the progress of both my children, I'm mindful never to take anything for granted with them. I always adhere to the adjustments they need in order to fully express themselves and engage with me and others. I have had the privilege to meet and work with many children with different levels of autism, and I find I need to remind myself regularly of basic ASD adjustments. Over the years, Alberto Alvarez-Campos and I have found that, in order to implement this programme successfully, we need to ensure *everyone involved adheres to the same adjustments* for the child.

Without good working practice, specific to the child's needs, any intervention programme will be compromised and progress and the chances of success for the child will be adversely affected. With that in mind, it is appropriate to remind ourselves that we must never become complacent about good practice when working with a child with autism.

As well as providing an overview of the key points we need to remember, *this chapter introduces some specific examples of ways in which working with a dog can help the child overcome the many communication hurdles they face.*

Note that the guidelines in this chapter are also suitable for a child with a learning disability or similar communication or sensory processing problem.

> Communication is one person having the ability to send a message to another, either verbally or non-verbally, to allow interaction between the two and to elicit an appropriate response, thereby allowing two-way communication. Children with ASD have difficulty understanding spoken language and interpreting non-verbal communication. Therefore, meaningful communication between the two will inevitably break down. This negatively impacts the child's ability to interact and respond appropriately.

Imagine being in a world in which everyone speaks a language you don't understand! You will then have a fleeting insight into what life is like for the child with autism. However, unlike the child with ASD, you will still be able to interpret visual cues like facial expressions, tone of voice and body language.

To assist the child, the person engaging with them should be mindful that, for many children, *communication does not need to involve the use of speech.* Other methods – picture systems like Picture Exchange Communication Systems (PECS) or photographs, visual timetables, etc. – can help the non-verbal child express their needs. Using these resources is the first step towards the child learning basic verbal language.

Often, parents of ASD children feel confused about how to communicate and interact with their children, because the children do not give them any positive cues on how to react with them. The child does not understand the pragmatics of two-way communication in the first place. Parents find that, despite all their efforts to elicit the most basic response from their child, their efforts seem futile. To the parents, the child appears to be deaf.

The child may not even respond to hearing his or her name and may be aloof or indifferent to any attempts at communication with them. However, *the child's daily activities and play opportunities give parents and practitioners the opportunity to bathe the child in basic, consistent language.* This must be done at the level of language and comprehension at which the child is functioning.

Imagine bringing a facilitator dog into the many daily activities of a child's life as a living educational tool – one that makes these learning opportunities more motivating, meaningful and, most importantly, more fun for the child!

To understand what level of communication a child is at, you need to observe the child in the first instance and understand his or her individual communication strengths and needs. For example, in the case of a non-verbal child not using any sound or speech, rather than trying to engage with them with direct speech, try using gestures only.

All children with ASD do communicate in their own individual and unique way: via tantrums, crying, taking an adult's hand to objects or things they want, or simply looking at the object they want or reaching for it.

Some children develop echolalia speech – repeating in the same tone words they have previously heard. This could be in or out of context (the latter is called delayed echolalia). For instance, a child may repeat the phrase 'Would you like a biscuit?' exactly as it was heard previously, when they mean 'I want a biscuit'.

Some children may just point at the object or thing they want. Understanding the purpose of the child's attempts to communicate with you allows the child to find more ways and reasons to communicate. You achieve a level of two-way communication by breaking it down to the child's own level of comprehension and into its most basic of components.

There are two main types of communication:

- *Pre-intentional communication.* The child says or does things spontaneously, without intention to affect those around him or her and without expecting any response. This type of communication is used by a child when he or she has extreme anxiety. Children will do this to calm themselves, to focus themselves or as a reaction to an upsetting or fun experience. (The 'Who's on first base?' scene in the film *Rain Man*[16] is a good example of this.) Stimming behaviours like hand flapping are used in a similar way, as calming strategies.

- *Intentional communication.* This is when a child says or does something with the purpose of sending a message to another person. This is easier for the child to develop once they understand that their actions and what they say have an effect on others and they begin to learn how basic communication works.

The facilitator dog has a very powerful role to play in helping the child to learn intentional communication. For example, the child will hear the command 'Rover, sit' and then see the dog comply. Unlike humans, who would tire of such repetition, a dog doesn't judge and will always reply to its core-training commands. This area alone illustrates the power of the dog to help children with communication problems learn the meaning of good communication skills.

The four stages of communication

There are four different stages of communication, as defined by the Hanen Programs®.[17] Each stage of communication that the child can reach depends on three things:

- the child's level of understanding (comprehension)

- the child's ability to interact with another person

- how and why they communicate.

Stage 1: The 'own agenda' stage

Many children first diagnosed with ASD are at this stage. The child appears to be uninterested in people around them and will tend to have solitary play. Their communication will be dominantly pre-intentional.

Stage 2: The requester stage

At this stage, the child begins to learn that their actions have an effect on people. They are likely to communicate to the adult their wants and needs, what they enjoy, etc., by pulling the adult towards objects, areas or games. Some take the adult by the hand to do this as well.

Stage 3: The early communication stage

The child's interactions begin to increase in length and become more intentional. Echolalia (repeating phrases they have heard before from another person or source, such as a TV advert) may be used to communicate their needs. Gradually, the child will begin to point to things they want to show the adult. Notably, at the same time, their gaze will improve to be more appropriate.

This stage is a sign that the child is beginning to engage in a two-way interaction.

Stage 4: The partner stage

When the child reaches this stage, he or she has become a more effective communicator. The child uses basic language and can carry out simple two-way conversations. He or she will be more confident and capable of basic communication in familiar places, such as the home, but less confident and perhaps struggling in socially challenging, unfamiliar environments. Examples of the latter include changes to existing environments – such as when a dog suddenly appears in the home – as well as new physical environments such as a new nursery or school.

Ways that adults can affect the communication of a child with ASD – and how the dog can help

Take on the role of a helper and teacher

Say the child's name to get their attention, so they know you are talking to them. This is exactly the same approach as when you are training a dog. You need to get the child's/dog's attention so they know you are talking directly to them.

When your child is not communicating their needs, it is so tempting to barge in and help them by constantly doing things for them. By interrupting too much or too early, though, you reduce the child's ability to learn themselves. *Give the child time to process language and work things out.* Bear in mind the six-second rule: allow six seconds for the child to process your request before you repeat that request.

Try to get them to join in and engage with others

While there are times when solitary play is important, to give the child space and time out, our objective is to teach the child to engage and interact with others – not simply to let them be! This is what I call 'breaking in' to whatever the child is doing, but it should be done in a delicate way on the child's own terms!

Even if it's playing with or taking toys in and out of the box, *it is the language and interaction between the child and adult that is important* – not the function of the play. Here's an example. The child is lining up his or her toys. Gently break in and use minimal language throughout: 'Dale, where does Teddy go?' 'Dale, which toy next?'

The child stays in control of the play. If the child displays a little upset at the intrusion, give them space and time to recover and then try again. Anger or an upset response is an interaction itself; the adult reacting in a positive way teaches the child that their communication works! This is better than no interaction at all.

While this type of play may seem laborious and repetitive while you are involved in the most basic of play, the child is learning that two-way interaction with another person can be fun and meaningful.

Slow down the pace to give the child a chance to communicate

This has to be the most vital rule if the child is going to be able to learn from any experience of interaction. The parent has to allow lots of extra time for the child to engage with, understand and enjoy an experience – whether it's eating breakfast or getting dressed. It could take a half hour or more to get Dale dressed because the act of dressing was done at a slow pace, an item at a time in the same sequence. The whole process allowed Dale to be bathed in familiar associated language. Put a sock on the child's right foot and encourage him or her to pull it up. Use the same language and sequencing for all daily activities of living. Use the same process when working with the child via the dog.

When playing with the child, take on the role of partner, not leader – be led by the child

As the child's comprehension improves and their communication and interaction skills increase, they need less direction. Remember not to overload them. It is vital to follow the child's lead and respond to what the child does. Always try to get down to the child's eye level so they will have some chance of eye contact with you.

Praise the child for trying to communicate with you

This will encourage the child to communicate with you again, as they learn they have been successful. For example: 'Dale, good patting the dog.' 'Dale, good sitting.'

A positive tone of voice and regular praise is crucial in encouraging the child and, again, this is also true when you are training a happy obedient dog!

Give the child with ASD a reason to communicate!

If the adult provides the child with what they want, then the child will not need to communicate their needs. Try to prompt the child to tell you what they want. For example, say: 'Dale, you want a...' [then pause]. Child says 'biscuit'.

Encourage requests from the child

Place a favourite food or toy where the child can see it but not reach it. This will encourage him or her to ask for the object, with prompting from the adult. You could do the same with the dog's toys or lead, etc.

Give things gradually to the child

If the child wants a biscuit, give them small pieces at a time so they have to ask or gesture for more. Getting the child to feed the dog with dry food pellets one at a time will create the same learning opportunity.

Let the child decide when to end an activity

Encourage words such as 'finished' or 'all done' to let the child know when things are coming to an end. This again can be used when giving the dog treats as the dog has to learn the same lesson!

Say less; say it slowly!

Use meaningful key words that are specific to the situation. Repeat them to the child and stress them using many visual cues as well, such as pointing or gestures. Examples include:

- using a drinking action for a drink

- nodding or shaking your head to indicate yes or no

- using visual aids or pictures.

When the child clearly understands, use the verbal prompt only. *Remember the six-second rule, then repeat.*

Encourage the child to learn the value of direct eye contact
This is very difficult for the child but, again, using the dog as a conduit can be very helpful. We know many children give appropriate eye contact to a dog, so getting down to the dog's eye level will promote eye contact with the human counterpart.

Remember — always one question or one request at a time
Do not use abstract language like irony, sarcasm or metaphorical phrases such as 'I laughed my head off'. Due to the literal learning method of those with ASD, extreme remarks like this can cause upset and confusion. Always say what you mean and mean what you say!

Don't tell the child what they shouldn't be doing...
...instead, tell them what they should be doing!

Understand how a child with ASD learns to communicate
I have adapted the basic dog-training commands to facilitate the learning of meaningful core language for the child. Every day, as he or she repeatedly sees the dog respond to these specific commands, the child develops their understanding of how communication works! These commands are described later in the manual.

Remember the impact that sensory issues have on the child's ability to process information from others and their environment
Being a neurological condition, these problems are not specific to autism. Around one in five children are affected by sensory processing differences. Sensory processing can be heightened or reduced, causing a child to perceive the world differently. In relation to using a dog as an intervention, the dog itself is a sensory minefield (as are the dog's accessories and food, etc.) that will have

an impact on all seven sensory systems: sight, sounds, smells, taste, touch, balance and body awareness.

With sensory issues in mind, I developed the cuddly dog transitional kit to make a real difference to the child overcoming sensory issues. The chapter 'The Transitional Kit: What You Need and How to Use It' gives detailed guidance on using the kit to reduce the impact of sensory problems for the child. It also describes how using the kit increases the child's understanding of the dog and improves bonding between a child and dog.

An autistic person may respond in a way you wouldn't link to a sensory impact. Sensory overload in everyday activities can cause increased stress, anxiety and physical pain such as headaches, earache or eye pain. If not recognised or addressed, the result could be challenging behaviour or extreme distress.

Let's look briefly at each sense and how the dog intervention would be related to it.

SIGHT
Under-sensitive: Objects like the dog's feeding bowl, collar, lead and brushes, etc. could appear darker and lose some of their details. The child's central vision is magnified but peripheral sight is blurred. The child may have problems with perception; games they can play with the dog, such as fetch, will enable them to improve those skills.

Over-sensitive: The child can have distorted sight, causing objects and bright lights to seem erratic. Images may fragment. The child may appear to be stimming over an object when they are really seeking comfort by focusing on the detail rather than the entire object.

SOUND
The under-sensitive child's hearing will be affected in a similar way to his or her sight. A child may hear just in one ear while the other has partial or no function at all. The child might cope with crowded, noisy environments, and bang doors and objects for stimulus.

The over-sensitive child will find noise is intense and sound can be distorted, and that they can hear distant conversations. Not being able to cut out background noise affects their ability to concentrate. Therefore, think about how this will relate to the unusual noises from the dog, such as growling during boisterous play, barking and (with some dogs) howling!

SMELL

Under-sensitive: Many have no sense of smell at all, while others may lick things to explore them to get a sense of meaning of what they are. Many children take a liking to the dried dog food and eat it.

Over-sensitive: Smells can be magnified and overpowering, so think how awful the dog food will smell to the child. Also, dogs – despite regular grooming and bathing – do smell (especially wet dogs). The over-sensitive child will have to learn to cope with the smell of dog breath and dog poo and when the dog burps or has flatulence.

> Smells like dogs, cats, deodorant and aftershave lotion are so strong to me I can't stand it, and perfume drives me nuts.[18]

TASTE

Under-sensitive: The child seeks stimulus from spicy foods, adding too much salt or pepper, and adding vinegar to foods. Some will have what is known as pica where they seek stimuli from chewing on items like stones, dirt, grass or even metal. This may be why many children taste and try to eat the dry dog food.

This is an area where the child could learn from the dog. In the same way that the dog is encouraged to chew safe toys or Kong-type bones rather than people's shoes or the furniture, the child could also be diverted to more positive items to chew to satisfy themselves.

Over-sensitive: Foods can be too strong and overpowering. Even the textures of the food can cause discomfort; in this case, children may prefer to eat smoother foods like mashed potato, yogurt and ice cream.

TOUCH

The under-sensitive child tends to hold onto things, people and the dog tightly, to gain a sensation of applied pressure. The parent of this child needs to be mindful about how the child handling the dog like this could add to the dog's stress and increase the risk of nipping or, worse, a dog bite. This issue is covered in 'The Transitional Kit: What You Need and How to Use It'.

This child will also have a high pain threshold – so unseen nipping from the dog could lead to a harmful bite in the future if not noticed and dealt with.

The over-sensitive child has many issues in relation to touch, which can feel painful or uncomfortable. The child may not like having their hair brushed or washed or wearing clothing on their hands and feet. He or she may only tolerate fabrics like cotton. These problems can be addressed using the cuddly dog transition kit and the real dog as well.

BALANCE OR VESTIBULAR PROBLEMS

The under-sensitive child will try to compensate for this problem by spinning, rocking or swinging. Playing the game of fetch with the dog or walking beside the dog to near-heel position will help the child improve balance and spatial awareness.

For the over-sensitive child, playing with the dog, running with it, playing fetch and walking beside the dog to heel position will help him or her learn to compensate and cope.

PROPRIOCEPTION (BODY AWARENESS)

Being aware of your own body, where it is and how the different parts move, is known as proprioception. This is a sensory area that children with autism find difficult.

Under-sensitive children may be too close to others because judging personal space is hard. Many find it difficult to navigate their environments, seem clumsy and bump into people. Learning to walk beside the dog, near the heel position, while they learn to master good lead control, will help a child slowly improve proprioception issues.

The over-sensitive child will have poor fine motor skills. The child may have difficulty fastening buttons and manipulating small objects, for example. The dog's feeding routine will give plenty of scope for addressing this area, as will grooming the dog.

Sensory issues summary

Being aware of how sensory issues impact your child in relation to the dog is vital. With the right approach, the dog is an ideal facilitator for addressing sensory issues with your child. The dog, with its daily routine, will provide lots of opportunities for the child to be involved and adapt.

> If I get sensory overload then I just shut down; you get what's known as fragmentation…it's weird, like being tuned into 40 TV channels.[19]

Final points to remember

Finally, *use areas of interest to the child*: use his or her obsession to engage or motivate them to learn. Children with ASD will learn better if they are motivated. I used Dale's obsession with Thomas the Tank Engine until it ran out of steam. I also used little dog figures to help Dale learn to count and used dog stories for bedtime reading.

Remember to avoid idioms like 'It's raining cats and dogs' or 'You need to pull your socks up'. The child with ASD will respond to these literally.

In other assistance dog programmes, many found that, when the dog sat at the kerb (as it was trained to do), the child would sit at the kerb too.

To summarise, to give yourself the best chance of success, it is prudent to ensure your approach and educational practice is tailored to the child's disability before introducing a new intervention.[20]

Points to Remember When Helping an Adult with ASD or Learning Difficulties

I t is good practice when working with an adult with ASD or similar processing difficulties to be mindful of adjustments that will help the adult understand us and effectively express themselves.

Remember to build on the adult's strengths and capabilities. Autism Spectrum Disorder affects social and communication skills. The difficulties people with ASD experience can be very subtle – and they will be put under more pressure when doing new activities, including working with a dog! Here are some useful points to remember:

- If you plan to get a puppy or mature dog for an adult with ASD, it is important to empower them and include them in as much of the process as possible. This will help increase the person's confidence and self-esteem and help improve the bonding process between the adult and the dog.

- When training the dog, and especially when meeting the dog's daily needs, involve the adult on their terms and at their pace. Adhering to these basic adjustments will make the learning process much easier for the adult.

- Just as with the child with ASD, it is helpful to address the person by name when speaking to them, so that they know a question or comment is being directed at them personally.

- Looking at the adult when speaking to them will make that person more aware that you are addressing them directly.

- The adult will struggle to concentrate if more than one person is talking to them at once.

- The adult may take a few extra seconds to respond to a question. Leave about six seconds to allow them to reply, while he or she processes the question. Stick to one question or instruction at a time, from one person at a time.

- It helps if language, questions and instructions are given in short, concise sentences.

- Encourage the adult to ask for instructions to be repeated if they are unsure of anything.

- If the person becomes anxious or nervous, they may stutter. In this case, it helps if the person instructing is patient and offers encouragement or reassurance that the person is doing well – this will help him or her recover.

- Find out from the person if they are comfortable discussing their condition, as this may reassure him or her that people are interested in learning about autism and processing problems.

- In terms of language, it is best to be specific! Say what you mean and mean what you say; people with ASD can find vague abstract questions or instructions very confusing.

- Try to ask closed questions and avoid open questions. For instance, saying 'Tell me about yourself' will probably not elicit a good response; instead, say 'Tell me about any interests you have had in the past.'

- Avoid hypothetical/abstract questions, such as 'How do you think you'll cope with owning a dog and people interrupting you to pat it?' A better question would be 'Can you tell us how you coped when people interrupted you?'

- Give the person extra time to follow through instructions and be prepared to prompt him or her in order to confirm they have understood what you expect of them.

- Let the person know if they are talking too much, as they will find it hard to judge how much feedback you need from them and when to start and stop two-way conversations.

- Be aware that the person's eye contact and body language may appear awkward or forced at times due to anxiety or the stress of the newness of working with the dog. This will improve because the dog's daily routine lends itself to lots of repetitive learning for the adult. Quite simply, practice and awareness that the dog won't put pressure on the adult will facilitate improvements for the adult.

Stage 1

PLANNING AND TRANSITION FOR THE CHILD AND DOG

S tage 1 allows you to take note of your objectives and hopes but, more importantly, enables you to plan the transition that helps the child understand what a dog needs. This stage significantly increases the ability of the child to connect and bond with their dog. It is therefore critical to the success of the whole programme.

The main aim at this stage is to get the child involved with all the dog's needs. If you can get the child connecting right away with a cuddly dog, as described in this stage, positive things will come later when the real dog is in the child's life. Planning transition and having these resources at this stage gives parents a baseline from which to monitor progress as the child is led through each stage of the programme.

At the end of this stage, there are outline images of a dog to help educate your child on many levels. These can be used one at a time for the child to colour in; the educational uses of them and their benefits to the child's overall learning are virtually endless. Taking care not to overload the child, you can use the dog pictures in various ways to help teach the child the beginnings of basic dog training. These colouring pictures also give siblings a great opportunity to be involved. Any attempts from the child to colour the picture in should be put up on the kitchen wall. It is helpful even if the parent colours them in – as long as the child is observing, they will be absorbing information.

Introduce the images in this order:

- Introduce the 'Stand' dog picture first, emphasising that the dog is standing.

- Once you feel the child has got as much learning as possible from the picture, move on to the 'Sit' picture and, from there, to the 'Down' image.

An adult can add the dog's collar, with a lead attached, in the child's favourite colour to plant the seed of ownership of the dog in the child's mind.

Using these resources with the child in a fun and relaxed way will help provide the child with a lot of information about the dog before it arrives. The three dog images show the child the dog's basic non-verbal body language which is easier for the child to decipher. Using these pictures with the child in their widest sense – as aids to promoting language, literacy, numeracy and fine motor skills (used in colouring them in) – will help increase the child's motivation to learn via the dog.

As all children learn visually, literally and with repetition, these resources will reinforce learning. We need to start the process right from the beginning – before the dog arrives.

Many of the parents who took part in the pilot study informed me that their children's teachers had been able to fit in some classroom time, using the resources with the child and their peers. There has therefore been an additional social advantage, as the child's peers gained awareness of something exciting happening to one of them.

The cuddly dog transition kit introduced in this stage takes into account the fact that autistic children in particular learn visually and literally; it increases the chances of success by ensuring the child understands the many aspects of a dog. I have provided guidance notes in 'The Transitional Kit: What You Need and How to Use It', so the child can get the optimum learning out of the kit, which will make a real difference to success when the real dog arrives.

It's essential to use all the resources at the child's own pace and as much as possible, so that the child can learn in their own way how a dog is good for them and can be like a friend to them.

After using the resources from the transitional kit, you'll be able to gauge how connected your child could be to a dog. Another worthwhile strategy to try is to find a family or friend with a nice pet dog so that your child can have the opportunity to respond to or have contact with a real dog in their own home.

Think about your immediate educational objectives for using the dog with your child so you can plan realistic goals that can be met. For example, objectives could include:

- using the dog as a diversion when out in public to promote positive behaviours in the child; for instance, you could use the fact that the dog needs to go home to get its dinner to persuade the child to leave the play park when you need to leave

- using the dog to calm down and reassure a child during a tantrum

- teaching the child practical skills in the process of looking after his or her dog, such as washing the dog food bowl after the dog has been fed.

Involve your child's teacher so that the educational objectives you're aiming for via the dog mirror those in the child's schooling.

If your child has bolting tendencies, then this behaviour alone is a good reason to ensure transitional care is done to the fullest at the start of the programme, before the child meets a dog. This will help the child connect better with the dog, increasing the chance that the child will want to stay with their dog. In this way, bolting behaviours can be reduced or stopped altogether.

Stage 1 will show the child and the parent that getting a dog will be a positive and worthwhile intervention not just for the child but for the whole family.

The pilot scheme helped reinforce the fact that detailed and well-implemented transition planning is essential to success. Stage 1 allows seamless progress towards the other stages, which will increase overall benefits for the child.

What Age and Breed of Dog is Right for the Child's Disability?

I t is now time to think about what age and breed of dog is right for your child's needs and your family dynamics. This will help you plan ahead, especially for the transition part of the process for the child and the dog. Good transition is vital for success, and knowing the breed and size of dog you need will enable you to devise a transition kit that's specific to your child's and future dog's needs. I cover the use of the transition kit in detail later in this manual; with the right planning, you will be able to transfer the contents of the kit to the real dog, making the transition process seamless and meaningful for the child.

When choosing a dog for your child's disability there is much to consider, as your child will grow and develop with the dog. When I was looking for the right dog for Dale, he needed a dog that had an exceptional temperament and was good with children. I use the word 'good' lightly as there is much to learn about how children should interact with a dog and how to manage this. I cover how to teach children to interact safely with dogs, and how to prevent dog stress, in detail later on.

It's also important to bear in mind the research findings of Dr Grandgeorge and colleagues that children with autism can improve their social skills if they have a pet to play with after the age of five.[21]

I was fortunate that Dale was this age when we brought Henry home; this has to have been a significant factor in the success of that friendship.

A major factor in choosing a Golden Retriever puppy for Dale was that I wanted the dog's nature and temperament to be right – and I knew Goldens are very sociable and friendly dogs, always seeking attention.

I also knew that Dale was going to grow up to be very tall. The size Henry would become was therefore important, because Dale would feel safer with a bigger dog by his side and the dynamics would work better for dog walks. I wanted Dale to be Henry's master and take care of all the dog's needs; the size Henry would become was therefore also a major factor. Although it made dog grooming a bigger task, playing games with Henry was more fun for Dale.

As another example of the importance of considering the size of the dog, I know of a wheelchair-bound young woman who specifically chose a smaller breed of dog so that the dog could sit on her lap when she was in her wheelchair.

When choosing a dog, it's very important to get all these things right: the size of the dog, how much exercise it will need, its nature and whether it's male or female.

It is impossible to cover all the various breeds and types of dogs here; what is important is getting the right dog for the child's disability. I cannot overstate the importance of researching the type of breed and size of dog; the Kennel Club Assured Breeder Scheme[22] promotes professional breeding so that potential owners can have the best chance to bring home a healthy, well-adjusted puppy and has a wealth of information on how to navigate all aspects of this process. Under this scheme, buyers can be assured that the breeders meet the standard set by the Kennel Club. This covers everything from how the puppies were raised to the legal documentation required to have your puppy registered with the Kennel Club.

When I researched which dog would be best for Dale, I couldn't ignore the working dog world's most commonly used breeds. It made sense to take note of the successful breeds used in the working dog world. Many use Labrador Retrievers, Golden Retrievers and Golden crossbreeds. Dogs are bred for appearance and some for their working ability; there is a vast range to choose from, and it's impossible for me to cover the hundreds of breeds available. Each type of dog is characterised by the work they do and the breed they were designed to be. All breeds have been created by humans, over the years, using selective breeding, to result in a dog that will look a certain way and have a particular character and predisposition to its nature.

No matter what type of breed, each individual dog will have its own character. Therefore, there is no guarantee of the temperament an individual dog will have, despite its pedigree. Many breeds will be prone to hereditary health problems; that is why you have to research thoroughly any particular breed you might think would be suitable for your lifestyle and a child's needs. For the purpose of the child's needs, you should endeavour to choose a breed that is known for its good temperament and that has social skills with children and the general public.

A pedigree dog is the offspring of two dogs of the same breed, whose breeding lineage is recorded with a recognised club, like the Kennel Club. These dogs carry a breed standard, which is the blueprint for their predisposed character, and health needs. A crossbreed is a mixed blood dog, whose parents are two different breeds, or a mixture of other breeds; therefore, what the dog will look like, and the size it will grow to, are hard to determine. This also gives them varied personalities and breed traits. However, depending on the level of crossbreeding, there are benefits: crossbreeds usually have fewer hereditary health problems due to not having close selective breeding.

Gundogs have been bred to retrieve game from hunting shoots; they are soft mouthed so as not to damage the game they retrieve. That is why gundogs are motivated by furry toys and like to replicate their innate breeding by using their toys for the game of retrieval – it's also why they like to carry things in their mouths. These dogs need a lot of exercise and would suit an active family. They are very popular for all these reasons and are well received by the public, as they really enjoy lots of human interaction. Examples in this group include Labradors, Golden Retrievers and Springer Spaniels. Throughout the worldwide autism assistance dog community, these breeds are the most popular due to their temperament, willingness to please, adaptability and kindness to people.

Again, there are low-maintenance breeds to look at, and non-moulting breeds, which have a predisposition not to shed their coats; all have different natures and various caring needs.

As well as choosing the right breed of dog, deciding whether to have a puppy or mature dog is also vital to success. There are advantages and disadvantages to both, and the choice depends on the lifestyle and needs of the family and disabled child.

I chose to have a puppy for Dale because I wanted to delicately mould the puppy to our lifestyle and the extreme environment Dale's autism would create. I wanted the puppy to get used to Dale's autism and have a sense of belonging to Dale. I knew it was a risk despite the impeccable breeding of Henry: all puppies are different, with unique personalities, and they will develop and respond to the environment in which they have been reared.

Puppies are like babies in a sense; they have particular needs and take up a lot of your time and energy. Some of the puppy stages are difficult to cope with, particularly with children. Issues like house-training and the puppy nipping because it is teething can be tricky to manage. Most importantly, puppies shouldn't be left alone for long episodes and must have intensive socialisation to the family, the home and the surrounding environment. If this doesn't occur, then there could be detrimental effects on the puppy's future development.

I will cover socialisation in more detail later, but there is a lot of work needed when rehoming a mature dog as well. The older dog will need a similar socialisation and settling-in period to the puppy, and will need remedial training appropriate to the family's and child's individual needs.

No matter what age and type of dog you choose, the key component to get right is sourcing a dog with a good temperament. No amount of training or work can make up for this characteristic of the dog if it is not present from the outset.

Key points to remember

The main points to remember when choosing a dog for your child are:

- Look for a dog or puppy that is motivated by food, toys or attention.

- Find a sociable dog that is happy to see you and your family and friends.

- Select the right dog that will enhance the life of your child and fit in with the needs of the whole family.

- It's a good idea to seek advice from a prospective vet who could give you personal advice tailored to your child's specific needs and also the dog's.

Planning

Having a plan that defines what you want to achieve with the dog (including reasonable short-term and long-term outcomes) will help you in your search for and communications with the right vet. The plan is also, of course, vital to the whole process of choosing the right dog!

Within this plan, you should note specific disability traits that the dog would be exposed to, so it can be trained to cope with the specific behaviours the child will display. This is vital when choosing a dog for a child with autism. It is crucial to discuss with the dog breeder or trainer the types of individual autistic behaviour the child regularly displays, for example screaming, jumping up and down, hand flapping, stimming or other autistic behaviours. It is vital that the dog experiences these behaviours, in a positive and sensitive way, before it arrives in your home. This will allow an easier settling-in period for both the dog and child. This preparation is also crucial in reducing the risk of dog stress and bites.

The dog's welfare

There is a fine balance to be achieved here, because the dog's welfare has to be paramount, as well as the needs of the child; a balance between both has to be met. However, we must never forget that the dog itself has the right to, and should have, a good quality of life, both emotionally and physically. Just as humans have rights, animals too have five freedom rights:[23]

- Freedom from hunger and thirst. The dog must have easy access to fresh water and an adequate diet to maintain its health and well-being.

- Freedom from pain, injury and disease, via good management of health, prevention or prompt diagnosis, and access to veterinary care.

- Freedom from discomfort. The dog must be provided with a suitable environment, including shelter and a comfortable resting area.

- Freedom from fear and distress, by being provided with appropriate conditions and care that avoid psychological suffering.

- Freedom to express normal behaviour, by being allowed adequate space, facilities and company for socialisation with the animal's own kind.

Sources of further information

For further information, see:

- The PAWS Family Dog service (www.dogsforgood.org/how-we-help/family-dog).

- The Kennel Club (www.thekennelclub.org.uk).

Transitions

Transition can be defined as passing or changing from one place, state or condition to another. The National Autistic Society (NAS) recognises that transitions can consist of anything from quite simple events, such as the classroom getting decorated, to major events such as the child getting a new teacher. There is no denying that a child or adult getting a dog is a major transition! This rings even more true for the child with ASD when you add on the sensory impact the dog will have on the child. The NAS recommends that measures be put in place for major transitions a year before the actual event.

Under the Equality Act of 2010, schools and organisations that employ or work with those affected by ASD have a duty of care whereby they must take into account the needs of people with disabilities and implement effective transition planning for those with ASD. Under this act, schools have to take into account the different learning styles of pupils with ASD and use visual resources, social stories, comic strips or Picture Exchange Communication System (PECS) social stories to relay information to the child about the transition ahead of them.

Many of the autism assistance dog models I have looked at over the past 15 years do not include any transitional mechanisms for the child. Instead, they rely on parents to devise and implement an appropriate transition plan to prepare the child for getting a dog. I understand every parent knows their child's disability best. However, what worries me is this: what is the parents' experience or knowledge of dogs? How can they devise an adequate transition plan when they don't understand this very specialised field? If they have never owned a dog, how can parents tailor a specific plan to meet their child's and a dog's individual needs in a way that will help a child with a disability? I have found that good transition planning is crucial to a successful partnership between the child and dog.

Twenty-four years ago, I devised a transitional plan for Dale. It was basic and, I now know, inadequate in comparison to what I know now on the subject. That is why I have devised this programme. After nine years collaborating with Alberto Alvarez-Campos and those within the working dog world, and combining this knowledge with my experience with autism, I am now confident that the transitional plan in this manual provides the best chance of success for the child and the dog.

In any disability intervention, no matter the tool being used, a good practitioner will have a plan or programme that covers the 'before', 'during' and 'after', to review, update and maintain best practice.

For me, the most crucial aspect of any dog intervention programme – the key to success – is putting mechanisms in place well before the dog arrives. That is why I piloted my own transitions study because I needed to know that my approaches and strategies were workable and allowed the best chance of success.

Guide Dogs UK embraced early transition with their 'buddy dogs' service. So has Alberto Alvarez-Campos, National Programs Manager for Assistance Dogs Australia, learning from all his experience collaborating with me to date. Assistance Dogs Australia have made it a prerequisite that any parent wanting to access the autism assistance dog programme must complete the Parents Autism Workshops and Support (PAWS) programme the organisation runs. This programme was developed in the UK by Dogs for Good and also runs successfully in the Netherlands. The programme covers topics including: the reality of owning a dog, how the dog can help the child, how to source and train the dog and dog welfare issues. They come at a cost and are time consuming, but

I feel these programmes are a welcome option for parents where before they had few or no options.

Another aspect of many of the models I studied from the working dog world was that they did not seem to include any forward planning for the child towards social independence without the dog. What if the assistance dog became ill or, worse, died or could no longer access public places due to a change in its health or public behaviour? I feel that creating social dependence for the child on the dog, rather than using the dog as a social facilitator towards independence, could have implications for the child's overall development and progress towards adulthood. A dog programme that has strategies in place to allow the child to progress, with or without the dog, has to be more conducive to the child's future.

Assistance dogs in various roles do amazing work for their clients. But I feel that, for a child with autism or a similar disability, the use of the dog is very different from other situations in which an assistance dog is used. That's because, with the right education, a child with autism and similar types of disability has the ability to improve.

The roles of assistance dogs for the physically disabled (those with sight-loss, deaf clients, and people who use seizure-alert dogs, for instance) are very specific to the clients' needs. In these cases, continuity is essential. Due to the nature of these disabilities, replacing these dogs after they have retired is right; the needs of these clients will be for life and the roles of the dogs vital. Some clients' needs will change due to the nature of their disabilities, so, for some, dependence on the dog will increase, warranting modification of the assistance dog's role.

However, I have reservations about this same approach – replacing a dog with another dog with an identical role – being used for the child with autism. As the child moves towards adulthood, he or she should, via their schooling and the positive effect of the dog, progress and developmentally change to the point where he or she can move on to a mature, trained companion dog. The adult will have progressed and should be taught to cope with social outings with human help and support and not be solely dependent on the dog. Depending on the impact their autism has on them, this is more beneficial to the adult's long-term needs. Having human support, with or without a dog, should ensure these adults enjoy full social inclusion for the rest of their lives.

It is equally crucial to success for parents to work in unison with their child's school, using the dog as an educational motivator. With realistic and obtainable educational objectives and accessible resources for the child, a dog could increase the progress of a child towards a better and more independent life as an adult. Dale and Henry's story is proof of this, and there are undoubtedly countless untold stories of dogs improving the quality of lives of people with autism and various other disabilities.

The Transitional Kit
What You Need and How to Use It

U sing the transitional kit is your final check to ensure the suitability of this intervention for your child before you introduce a dog to your home.

In early 1994, when I had sourced Dale's puppy, the breeder held on to Henry for a further two weeks, so that Dale had four weeks' transition preparation before I brought the puppy home. I knew this was the most vital stage of transition: teaching Dale that Henry was a living being with needs, not a cuddly toy. Starting with a cuddly dog and all the language and learning derived from that, I involved Dale in the process of getting the things Henry would need. To ensure Dale understood the importance of each item, with Dale by my side in the pet shop, I bought about two items for the pup at a time. All children develop better when they are given choice and can be empowered and involved in an activity. This was especially true of Dale. During the four weeks, as Dale's transitional kit expanded, he learned via the cuddly dog what each item was for and why, as well as how to use them, where to store them, etc.

When the final item was bought off Henry's list, on the day his pup was coming home, Dale knew Henry would need grooming, where the pup would play, toilet, eat and sleep. Such was Dale's understanding of all this that, on the first night Henry had in our home, Dale donated his special train duvet to his dog by putting it in Henry's bed.

I devised the cuddly dog transitional kit with many issues in mind, but ultimately with dog welfare at the forefront. In preparing Dale for Henry coming, I understood the consequences that Burrows and colleagues' research[24] revealed in cases where assistance dogs were exposed to added stress when partnered with children with autism. Prevention of dog stress was my aim in 1994 when I made a transitional plan for Dale so that Henry would not suffer despite Dale's autism.

Using the transitional kit to help your child learn

The purpose of the kit is to help the child learn to connect through imaginative and symbolic play with their cuddly dog. The kit encourages the development of key language, imagination and symbolic play, turn-taking and sharing, and helps address potential sensory issues for the child.

Everything in the kit has been devised to help the child understand the need for a routine with the dog. Teaching the child the dog's needs via the kit will help reinforce the need for the child to have a similar structured routine in his or her life.

The pack is used to teach the child that a dog has needs. The child begins to learn appropriate behaviour and contact with a real dog via the cuddly dog. In time, the learned behaviour will be transferred to the real dog when it arrives. That is why the pack contains all the accessories the real dog needs, so that the child is familiar with how to use these when the real dog arrives.

The aim is to teach the child that the dog – like them – has physical and emotional needs!

While your child may view the transitional kit as a gift, its primary use is as an educational resource so that you can help your child to prepare for, connect and bond better with the real dog. That is why, throughout this programme, I have ensured there is scope for progress for the child – without the need for any dramatic change of the model visually, sensory-wise or in function. It is essential to the success of any intervention that there is a consistent approach throughout; interventions should complement, not compromise, the child's schooling and individual educational goals.

The cuddly dog transition kit has been so successful in pilot studies that some children spoke a few first words while many others showed the green shoots of imaginative play. All the children on this pilot programme had, to a greater or lesser degree, an obsession and/or ritual; a similar vein ran through them all. It is because of this similarity that a condition-specific educational approach is warranted and is essential when working with children on the autistic spectrum.

Before you start: General hints and tips on using the kit

- When creating your child's transitional kit you need to be mindful of the size and breed of dog you are sourcing, so the contents of the pack can be transferred to the real dog when it arrives.

- As their parents know, children with ASD learn literally, visually, then by doing – with lots of opportunity for repetition. So it's best to drip-feed the child with the pack, a little at a time, and build up at the child's pace.

- If your child is more able, and his or her age and stage of development are such that a cuddly dog is not appropriate, then involve the child with the equipment itself, as there is much to learn from it. Giving the child autonomy over their dog will undoubtedly increase bonding with the dog, as well as benefit the child's confidence and self-esteem.

- All members of the family are encouraged to take an active part with the transitional kit, especially the cuddly dog. The child having appropriate regular interaction with the cuddly dog will help reinforce that the dog will be part of the whole family. Siblings can be really helpful in showing the child how to engage and interact with the cuddly dog and how to use all the dog's items in the kit.

What you'll need

- Large cuddly dog (as close to life-sized as possible, to replicate the real dog and take into account the child's literal learning and understanding).

- A metal dog bowl that fits into the raised stand or dog table you will be using with the real dog.

- A whistle (one that's audible to the human ear).

- Wooden-handled, soft-bristle dog grooming brush.

- Real dog collar (in the child's positive colour).

- A keyring picture tag (put a headshot of the child into the tag).

- EzyDog zero shock lead (preferably the same colour as the collar).

- Dog harness (Panda harness or similar, preferably black).

- Kong dog toy.

- Wild Knots teddy.

- Dog towel (preferably in the child's colour or one that the child chooses).

- Real-size dog bed.

- Halti dog head collar, if required for the real dog.

The educational benefits of using these items to help your child learn and develop are discussed in detail below.

Example of a transition kit

Dog cupboard allocation

Allocate a child-accessible kitchen cupboard for all the cuddly dog's things. The cupboard will become the real dog's, as all of the kit except the cuddly is transferred to the real dog. Put a headshot picture of your child on the outside of the dog's cupboard, with a picture of your kit, showing what a dog needs, so all is meaningful for the child. Once you know the colour and breed of your real dog, put its picture on the cupboard too. This will give the child access to the cupboard on their terms, so they may feed their dog treats or groom it.

Use the obsession

In 1990, when Dale was two, I learned how powerful it was to engage and interact with him by using his ultimate and current obsession; back then, it was Mickey Mouse. So, for Christmas, Dale got his first inanimate 'friend' – a cuddly pull-string talking toy, with just five phrases, that became like a second child to me and a sort of brother to Dale.

I used Mickey to teach Dale and address the triad of impairments simultaneously. Using Mickey as a facilitator, I taught Dale communication, imagination and how to successfully socialise, albeit at a basic level.

In both of my first two books, I give many examples of the diverse advantages of using the child's interest or obsession. If I had to give one example of how powerful this educational approach can be, though, here is the best I have come across to date. In Bangkok, an 11-year-old boy with autism was so nervous at his first day at a special needs school that, to get away from the chaos, he climbed onto a third-floor balcony at his school and sat dangling his legs over the edge. Teachers and the boy's mother tried to coax him to safety, but he ignored everyone's efforts. Fire-fighter Somchai Yoosabai was called; the boy cried and refused to let anyone near him. Overhearing his mother commenting 'If only Spider-Man was here', the fire-fighter rushed back to his base and donned a Spider-Man outfit he had. He spoke to the boy, saying, 'Spider-Man is here to help you.' He cautiously asked the boy to walk towards him with a glass of his favourite orange juice in hand, scared the boy might slip. With a beaming smile the boy got to the safety of Somchai's arms.[25]

Why I use the child's favourite colour

To help individual children recognise and make sense of the specific resources in the transitional kit, every resource needs to be adaptable for each individual child. One powerful way of doing this, which I used successfully with Dale and Amy, involves using each child's favourite colour. I invested time finding out whether incorporating the child's favourite colour in the resources would make a difference to a child's level of engagement with and connection to the dog. Throughout the years of bringing up my own children, and because of the many others I have met, I've witnessed how the majority of children adopt a positive interest in or feel a connection with a particular colour. During this time, I also observed that, for sensory reasons, some children find particular colours cause them visual discomfort. The range of colours I have witnessed children 'adopting' are as varied and individual as the children themselves.

The most memorable colour and obsession for me was of course Dale's. It was Thomas blue – adopted the day he found Thomas the Tank Engine when he was two. Blue thereafter was a colour Dale never tired of, and blue things became a big and positive part of his life. Even today, Dale prefers bright primary colours in almost everything and never tires of blue. Amy was two years old when she took ownership of red. When she was six, she told me it was because she loved Winnie-the-Pooh's bright red jumper.

Therefore, it seemed to make sense to try to incorporate each child's favourite colour into the dog programme, via the lead, dog collar, etc.

The need to include siblings

I would encourage your child's siblings to be involved with the cuddly dog kit. Let them choose and have their own coloured lead as a symbol of their own identity and a way of indicating 'my time' with the dog. Siblings could have the opportunity to walk the dog with one parent, while the other could be attending to the disabled child's needs. This initiative allows the child with autism to learn the concept of sharing their dog with siblings, while maintaining they are (in a way) the dog's master! Using the same principle for grooming and feeding the dog will increase sibling inclusion and help create great role models for the disabled child, enabling the child to interact more with their siblings. The child will learn the pleasure of sharing their dog with others and that sharing as a social skill is good for positive social relationships. Devising a dog care rota for the child and siblings will aid inclusion of siblings and teaches the child all the social benefits of sharing.

The cuddly dog

The cuddly yellow Labrador dog I use is two feet long, to replicate the size of a real dog. I source it from IKEA, but it is too floppy to play with. I open up its stomach area and put in more stuffing (especially in the paws), so it can be dressed, have shoes put on it or act as a nice sensory positive pillow for the child.

When she was upset and couldn't sleep, Amy would use our second dog ('Henry Two') as a pillow, to help calm her down. She called this using her 'Golden Pillow'. In doing this, Amy echoed the findings of research conducted in Canada by senior researcher Sonia Lupien, in collaboration with the MIRA Foundation[26] – that many children with ASD would use their dogs in the same way, allowing the dogs to reassure them and to help them settle down. Not surprisingly, the research revealed that the children, as Amy described, liked all the positive sensory aspects of the dog in this situation. When Henry Two lay down to rest, Amy would literally lie on the floor with her head resting on his chest as it rhythmically moved with his breathing. This, with the added stimuli of Henry's soft fur, the dog's relaxed state and the beating of his heart, would really help Amy to settle and sleep. Henry Two never flinched at this; I believe he had a sense of how he helped Amy, and I know this is a common occurrence with many other children with autism.

The cuddly dog makes learning more realistic for the child with autism, who learns in a literal way, and prevents the child being overwhelmed when the real dog arrives. The vital lesson learned from Dale is: always direct everything for teaching the child via the cuddly or real dog first.

If your facilitator dog is to help two ASD or disabled children in the family, then each child, if their ages are appropriate, should own their own cuddly dog that wears a generic black collar (as should the real dog). This will allow sharing of the real dog but, for the child's individual sense of belonging to the dog, the disabled children and siblings should each have their own coloured lead so they can share dog-walking times with their parent.

Encourage the child to name the cuddly dog themselves. This could be a name they like or a dog character the child likes, or a name they can relate to. If that's not possible, simply call it 'cuddly dog'. This will help personalise the cuddly dog, increase the child's sense of ownership and help the child differentiate the cuddly from the real dog. Children who learn literally and those with learning difficulties will be less confused, especially non-verbal children. A severely non-verbal child aged eight, who had a cuddly dog, said 'dog' to his mum when he saw one in a play park he was enjoying.

An essential role the cuddly dog has is to teach the child how to have appropriate interaction with a dog. This is vital for dog welfare and to prevent unwanted nips or dog bites to the child. All children are fascinated by the dog's tail. This is especially true for children with autism – the fact that it is long and moving is very attractive to the child. Using the cuddly dog to reinforce the message to the child that they shouldn't touch or pull at the dog's tail will help teach the child not to do this with the real dog.

For a child with autism, learning contact and petting with a real dog has been proven to be very good for social and emotional stimulation. Hugs and kisses with the dog have aided communication skills that can be transferred to parents and others. By introducing this interaction with the cuddly dog, you give your child the chance to practise and improve their fine motor skills, tactile stimulation, eye contact, social timing, spatial awareness and confidence with their facilitator dog. In the long term, if this positive interaction is learned via the cuddly dog, your child will switch on to the real dog's many emotions and behaviours and gain an understanding of the dog's needs. A vital lesson will be learned; the seeds have been sown for the child to experience empathy via the dog which, in the long term, will help your child relate the same emotion to other people. This is huge, as those with ASD find understanding empathy very difficult.

If the child is interacting well with the dog, then the dog won't become stressed or overwhelmed. I collaborated with Neil Ashworth when he was the dog training manager of the Irish Guide Dogs autism programme in 2008 – he found that children overwhelming their dogs was a common problem. Neil explained that if the child was over-handling the dog or playing too much with it, the dog didn't get much time out. In most cases, the child never hit out at the dog – having the dog in the first place had actually stopped that behaviour. However, it would be better to try to address the issue before a dog is placed permanently in the home.

Sadly, it has to be recognised that this problem can occur despite all efforts. A family with a seven-year-old, severely non-verbal child with autism had much success following the programme and implemented all the dog welfare strategies. The mother even put a taped exclusion zone around the dog's bed, together with child-friendly 'do not disturb' signs. But no matter what preparation was given, the child wouldn't leave the dog alone, pulling at its muzzle and overwhelming the dog. The parents made the right decision to give the facilitator dog back to the former owner for rehoming. It was so upsetting for the family, especially the sibling who clearly loved having the dog, but the risks of the child getting bitten and of extreme stress to the dog were too high. Instead the family opted for a cat. This alleviated the sibling's loss of the dog, and the autistic child was indifferent to the cat.

Encourage the child to take his or her cuddly dog into their bed to sleep with it. This will encourage the child to want to sleep with the real dog, if that is an objective you have. The cuddly dog also makes a great pillow for sitting on the floor with while the child watches television or listens to a story.

Show the child, especially at bedtime, how it's good to kiss their cuddly dog on top of its head with the words 'good night' or 'good morning'. Kissing the top of its head will be tolerated by the real dog; it's also the most hygienic area to kiss the dog. This action shows affection and plants the seeds of appropriate emotions and empathy. Read the cuddly dog a bedtime story with the child. Dale often got involved with simple stories and picture books, developing his language skills, because he thought his dog liked them and Henry was beside him to 'listen' to the stories. Most of the stories were dog-themed.

Addressing sensory issues via the cuddly dog

The tactile sense provides information about the environment and what is within it. The dog itself is a massive object to process, given it is hard in places (like its bones), soft in others (fur), has sharp claws and teeth, hot breath or body heat, and a cold nose or paw pads. In addition, the dog will respond dramatically to touch or contact alone! These areas affect the child as they may find touch uncomfortable. Many don't like their hair being brushed, cut and washed. Using the cuddly dog to show the child how the real dog would like being touched and looked after will help reduce similar sensory problems for the child. I will never forget the day when Henry sat in the bath with Dale and got a good scrub down before Dale did.

Early literacy and numeracy skills

Use the cuddly dog to practise familiar language and the routine that will be used with the real dog. Learning new tasks via the cuddly dog without pressure will, over time, allow your child to gain self-confidence and independence. Use the cuddly dog to familiarise the child with words that relate to a real dog, such as 'sit', 'down' and 'wait'. Teach the child the dog's body parts, then teach the child their body parts. Call the dog's paws 'feet' so it makes sense that the child also has feet. Show your child that the dog has two eyes, four feet, etc., and use all the associated language involved with a real dog.

Try to get the child's teacher and other family members involved using the cuddly dog. In one classroom I visited, the teacher had involved the children to set up a vet's corner and over the weeks the children learned how to take care of their various pets.

The cuddly dog wears a real dog collar with a keyring picture fob attached, showing a headshot picture of the child. Try to source a dog collar with a buckle, so the child can learn to master buckles, just as Dale did. The plastic snap-together collars are tricky for the child to manage and can cause fingers to get caught and injured. In the early days of his dog's arrival, Dale liked taking off Henry's collar every night and putting it back on in the morning. He told me he liked getting Henry 'ready for bed' and that, by putting Henry's collar back on in the morning, he was getting his dog ready for another busy day! This helped him feel he was in control of his dog; he felt he really was Henry's master, because all was done on Dale's terms.

Your child will be slowly processing and retaining the information you give them due to lots of repetition, and learning in a fun, relaxed way, on his or her own terms.

At mealtimes, put the cuddly dog under the dinner table. This is where the real dog will be, whether at home or eating outdoors in dog-friendly cafes and outdoor eating areas. This is what an assistance dog would do, behaving in a socially acceptable way and almost invisible to the public.

Take the cuddly dog with the child in the car, with its lead on, on outings where the real dog would go. Given that your real dog won't have public access rights, you need to practise leaving the cuddly dog in the car, when going shopping for example, so that the child learns to cope with this.

Dale and a child on the pilot programme used to take the dogs' leads with them, like a comfort blanket, when their dog couldn't be with them on outings. Such was the connection to the dog via the child's special lead that one child took his dog lead on holiday abroad with the family and coped very well because of it. This is a great example of how this programme allows for forward planning as the child reaches adulthood, with long-term measures being built into the programme for the child.

If your child isn't showing interest in the kit, continue to include the cuddly dog when interacting with the child, as if it's a new member of your family – in a fun and relaxed way! The first severely non-verbal child (aged nine) on the pilot programme showed no interest in the cuddly dog, but his parents stuck with it, including the cuddly dog in family life on a regular basis. As soon as the child learned he was getting his real dog, he immediately sought out his cuddly dog.

Have as much fun as you can using the cuddly dog to help your child understand how human-like and fun a dog can be. You want the child to get quite obsessed with all dog things: use story books and dog DVDs and dress up the cuddly dog to increase imagination and fun! You could get shoes for the cuddly dog to help desensitise the child that has shoe sensory issues.

Involve the cuddly and the real dog in dressing for hot and cold weather, Halloween and Christmas. Within reason and causing no stress to the real dog, it can be included in some way, perhaps wearing a special scarf that the child likes or a school tie or jumper. Put pyjamas on the cuddly dog, to encourage a bedtime routine for the child.

The cuddly dog has been very successful in the pilot programme, during which most of the children have been able to speak a few words or gain new words. Some of the children displayed the beginnings of imaginative play, while a few started to use a crayon and colour-in for the first time.

Drip-feed the child with the transitional kit, a little at a time, and then build up. Do this at the child's pace, taking into account how a child with autism learns – literally, visually, and then by doing things themselves with lots of opportunities for repetition!

The metal food bowl

Using real dog food with the cuddly dog will prepare the child for sensory issues – dog food is smelly and gritty! Experience how deafening the dry food hitting the metal bowl is to the child. More important is the frightening noise the metal bowl makes on a hard kitchen floor if it is dropped; let your child experience this when the time is right and when your child is prepared for the frightening loud noise. Show your child regularly that the dog needs water in a second bowl. Filling the bowl with water and placing it safely into the dog's food table, without spilling it, is a difficult task for the child to master. Again, give the child practice, allowing him or her to become familiar with all the sensory effects the bowl has – how it feels and how it's shiny, like a mirror, in a way that seems to attract ASD children.

For many reasons, I advocate using a raised feeding table that houses both the food and water bowl. It has been proven that a raised table aids better digestion for the dog and prevents aspiration of water or food down to the dog's lungs. It is far better for the child to navigate as well, and they can see at a glance when the water needs replenishing. More importantly, it provides a safe and comfortable area for the dog to access and prevents people walking into bowls and spilling water over the kitchen floor. Having this as part of the transitional kit before the real dog arrives will really help the child to learn this very difficult skill with the real dog.

There are various types of raised bowl tables available on the market. If you Google 'bone shaped dog feeder', you will find novelty bone-shaped ones that come in primary colours. You can choose your child's favourite colour again to motivate them in this area of feeding the dog. Using a novelty table like this will be more appealing to the child and teaches the child that dogs like to chew on bone-type objects.

I have found that working with the child on the feeding task before the real dog arrives is vital to success. One family on the programme had many breakthroughs with their child along the way. However, when they got their real dog, the raised feeding table had not arrived in time for the child to practise with it. As a consequence, the child used the dog's water bowl for playing with. The child emptied water over the kitchen floor and didn't understand the concept of the dog's feeding table, because the dog had arrived before the table.

Why use an audible dog whistle?

You will need an audible dog whistle for the feeding routine with the dog. (I say audible because some working dogs are used to whistles that are silent to the human ear, but not to the dog, such is the extent of the dog's hearing.) The chapter 'Meaningful Dog Commands', in Stage 3 of this manual, explains how the whistle is used at feeding time to help teach the dog recall outdoors.

The wooden hair brush

Grooming the cuddly dog teaches imaginative play and reinforces to the child the needs of the dog. If you purchase a wooden-handled standard dog brush, the child can use a similar brush on his or her own hair. I have found that, for one severely non-verbal child, the dog brush was less painful and alleviated any negative sensory issues the child had about getting their hair brushed. Another child I worked with didn't tolerate getting his hair touched, let alone brushed, but he would tolerate having his hair brushed with the same standard brush used for the dog. Putting a paw print on the brush head with a permanent black felt-tipped marker gives the child a visual clue that the dog needs its fur brushing regularly – just as the child's hair needs brushing regularly.

Have fun playing with the real dog's hair that's removed and involve the child in the game in any way you can. You might want to have two brushes, so you can give one to a sibling to use and the other to the child the dog is supporting. The sibling can show the child how to use the brush and share the duty of grooming the dog.

Dog collar with picture keyring

Whatever type of dog collar you or your child choose, make sure it has a keyring headshot picture of the child attached, so the child sees that the dog belongs to them. If two children are sharing, use a generic black collar with a picture of both children together attached. Transfer the collar worn by the cuddly to the real dog, so the child or children know that they belong to the real dog.

The EzyDog zero shock lead

The very successful Service Dogs Canada programme developed a shorter lead with a soft, bulky handle for the child to grab. This is attached to the dog's harness and enables the child to walk safely at the dog's side. This type of lead seems to be easier for the child to manage, dexterity-wise, while allowing appropriate adequate space between the child and dog. Bearing in mind the spatial awareness and proprioception problems the child may have, the strategy of using a lead in this manner really makes a difference to dog walking. This initiative gives the child a sense of autonomy and empowerment with the dog; feeling he or she is in control of the dog will undoubtedly improve the child's confidence and self-esteem.

Knowing those affected with autism learn in a literal way, and bearing in mind that other children with disabilities may not like change, I wanted to use this initiative with the half-lead but also enable the technique to progress in a seamless way to help the child adapt as an adult dog-walker. This long-term aim for the child to progress, which is an essential part of the dog programme, would mean him or her being able to manage a real dog lead. When developing the programme, I tried many sizes and types of lead. Following my experience of working with Alberto Alvarez-Campos on the Guide Dogs Queensland pilot scheme, during which Alberto developed a bungee-type lead for children to use, I've settled on the EzyDog lead which works in a similar way.

People using the programme have found that the EzyDog zero shock lead is by far the best of the shock-absorbing generation of leads. It is easily found via Google and can be sourced in many different colours to enable you to personalise it. The lead is attached to the dog's harness in a half-loop for the child to manage.

The concept of the lead is that it has a section that acts like a sprung bungee that absorbs any sudden shocks made by the dog. It is made out of the popular nylon webbing, soft and durable, and is long-lasting. The lead is comfortable for the dog and child, giving good control between the two. The advanced shock-absorbing section in the centre of the lead cushions and eases the pressure for the dog and child. The soft nylon webbing makes the lead easy to hold while maintaining quality and strength. An added feature is it has a reflective trim for night-time safety.

The 48-inch lead, which is what you need, has an extra traffic control handle to grab positioned near the dog's collar, giving better control when at the kerb. The lead is ideal for the child: a D-ring at the handle area allows you to clip the lead into a half-loop for the child to use. When the child is ready, the half-lead can be unhooked to its full length – the transition is seamless and practical. When the child has progressed to using the lead at its full length, the D-ring can be used for adding a poop bag container or similar accessories. The parent can have a black zero shock lead attached to the dog's collar; in this way, the adult is the real dog handler while the dog and child maintain a consistent approach.

Makenzie's experience when she adopted this lead with her adult dog is a good example of the success of this lead. Her mum wrote to me saying, 'Makenzie likes it so much better because she's hanging onto the lead so tight, but Heather cannot feel the tension coming from her, so she is more relaxed walking with her.'

Dog harness

Another important lesson I have learned from the working dog world involves the use of a harness for the dog and child. While developing this programme, I tried many different types of harness. However, as with the dog lead, I have found a brand that is perfect for the dog and child: the Panda dog harness. If you Google 'Panda dog harness', you will find the size you need for your dog. Essentially, this harness is designed to reduce or prevent the dog from pulling. It is so easy for the dog to wear and is easily put on. I recommend the harness should be in black so the child's coloured lead and the dog's collar stand out. This harness is very functional, fashionable and a fun resource for the child. The materials used and the design of the harness allow the dog natural movements; it is extremely comfortable for the dog, allowing great control over it.

A useful addition on the harness is its easy-grab handle at the top which some children might want to use instead of the lead. Alberto told me he used a similar harness for a seven-year-old non-verbal Spanish child who also had neurological coordination problems. To try to promote toilet continence for the child, the child would hold onto the handle of the assistance dog's harness, allowing the child to lean on the dog to walk through to the toilet with it. Within two weeks, the child was toilet-trained because of this strategy with the dog.

Another great feature of the Panda harness is that it has two removable Velcro® tabs at each side of the harness; you can use these to display a Picture Exchange Communication System (PECS) sign or similar initiative for the child to use. The harness has a sturdy central hook for attaching the child's lead; I sew on a second hook so you can add a toy or purse for the child to use.

The rubber Kong

This is a great dog toy for the child to use with the dog, helping to promote new language and improve fine motor skills.

Kongs come in different sizes and colours. The Kong will teach the child that the dog likes to chew things and play with toys. It's a great resource for the child and siblings. They can fill it up with the dog's food, hard or moistened, with treats and cooked meats. It can teach the child new tolerances for different foods, like cooked chicken, ham, etc. You never know, the child's diet could improve because of this initiative.

Get the child to fill the Kong with the dog's food and put it into the freezer, to give to the real dog as a major treat. Frozen Kongs last longer and give the dog more to work for. Kongs also help to prevent boredom and separation problems in the dog. The child filling the Kong will lend itself to addressing many issues simultaneously!

Note: To prevent dog obesity, subtract filled Kong treats from the dog's food allowance.

Wild Knots teddy

A common problem for children affected with autism is that a simple game of fetch is a complex concept to master. It requires many new skills to be learned within all three areas of the triad of impairments – and all at the same time. The child has to:

- engage with the adult and dog, communicating with them verbally and non-verbally

- learn the social timing of the game with the adult and dog: waiting for the dog to sit, throwing the toy and the dog fetching it

- learn good coordination in order to throw the toy and have the motor skills to play with the toy with the dog.

In addition, the child has to process sensory issues (such as the noise of the dog playing the game) and socially time correct interaction with the adult and dog. All this makes the game complex for the child to master.

During the pilot scheme I used a furry, quacking duck toy to play the game of fetch with the children. The dog really liked the duck and it was easier for the child to work with, as well as being a positive sensory toy for the child. Apart from one child who had a dog phobia, all eight severely autistic children on the pilot study played the game of fetch for the first time with Henry and his duck.

While the duck toy has been really successful, I recommend using a Kong Wild Knots teddy instead for the game of fetch. I feel the child will connect better with the dog and the teddy toy because most children like cuddly teddies. The child will understand better that the teddy is a toy and it will be easier to manipulate for the game of fetch.

The Kong Wild Knots teddy is a superb toy for the dog because it is really safe if the dog chews it. It's very soft and the fur is very pleasing for the dog; the teddy has minimal stuffing. The teddy has a very durable knotted rope inside (like a skeleton) that is really appealing to the dog. It is a very popular dog toy and easy to find online.

Playing the game of fetch with the child and dog will lend itself to lots of new language being learnt. You could ask your child to 'fetch' their coat, etc., once they understand the concept.

Dog towel

Again, you can use the child's favourite colour for the dog towel. Decide where you want to hang it up, for the rare occasions the cuddly dog might get caught in the rain. Your child can learn to use the dog towel to dry their dog. An elastic loop attached to the towel makes it easier for the child to hang up the towel on a hook. Again, this may encourage the child to hang up his or her coat.

Real dog bed

Using a real dog bed is a vital part of the kit, because it teaches the child the importance of 'time out' for the real dog. It is essential for dog welfare, and to avoid stressing the dog, that all children in the family understand they must leave the dog alone when it is asleep. The real dog will create a quiet place in the home in which it likes to sleep. Using the cuddly dog with the dog bed will teach the child about the real dog's need to have time out and be left alone. This will prevent dog stress and reduce any risk of dog bites.

Teaching the child proper interaction with the dog will encourage more positive social interaction with others. This allows the child to access other dog social activities like dog agility or dog-walking clubs. The cuddly dog's bed is used symbolically when the cuddly is put to bed for a sleep. To reinforce what a sleeping dog looks like, download a picture of one from Google Images to show your child. This vital lesson will help the child begin to learn the concept of empathy for their dog, and, more importantly, for others!

The dog bed can then be used by the real dog when it arrives. To help your child understand that the dog should be left alone when sleeping, put a sign that he or she is familiar with which means 'no!' by the dog bed. I like the Do2Learn 'Do not enter' sign which is useful to alert everyone to leave the sleeping dog alone.

The Halti, if required

A Halti is placed over the dog's nose and head and is designed to stop the dog from pulling. While the harness can help alleviate this problem, excessive pulling needs a Halti. If your dog requires a Halti, then use it with the cuddly dog first so the child gets used to it and will not be fazed if the real dog wears one.

Songs about dogs to sing for your child

Finally, to help teach your child how to interact with the dog, here are the words to a popular song. Most children like music or singing, so using the cuddly dog as a prop you could sing songs about dogs.

'How much is that doggy in the window?' is a nice slow song that allows a child to pick up the words connecting them with a dog. If you Google the song name the lyrics can easily be found online. For example, the 'waggly' tail is a happy dog! At the beginning, just encourage the child to try and do the 'woof woof' part, to make them aware that sometimes dogs bark. Barking is an anti-social behaviour, but the child should learn that sometimes the dog may bark during excitable play. For this reason, we want the child to learn that positive barking is like the dog 'talking'.

I like the song 'Where, oh where, has my little dog gone?' As it describes how the dog uses its tail to show how it is feeling.

Where, oh where, has my little dog gone?
Where, oh where, has my little dog gone?
Oh where, oh where, can he be?
With his tail cut short and his ears cut long.
Oh where, oh where, can he be?

My little dog always waggles his tail,

Whenever he wants his dinner (instead of grog);
And if the tail were more strong than he,
Why, the tail would waggle the dog.

Resources for the Child

Stage 2

INTRODUCING THE DOG TO YOUR HOME

Stage 2 of the programme is about:

- finding the right dog
- the transition period for the child
- preparing for the dog coming home.

Where and how to source the dog

Undoubtedly, now you have decided on the age and breed of dog for your child, the biggest hurdle is where to source the dog. However, where you source the dog must take into account one vital element – the dog's or puppy's socialisation!

The early human and environmental experiences a puppy or dog has been exposed to will have a significant impact on its behaviour and character for the rest of its life. It is vital to acknowledge this when you are looking at a breeder or other dog sources, because it could make or break success. If you don't get the right dog that has been adequately socialised, then you are inheriting serious problems and potential heartache for the future.

Puppies should stay with their mother until eight weeks old, so that they will be mature enough and will have learned some good dog manners and behaviour. After the first couple of weeks after their birth, puppies should be delicately exposed to and have contact with all kinds of people, including adult men and women, because they smell and interact differently with the pup. The pup must be gently handled with supervised children and even the elderly.

As was the case with Dale's dog Henry, a domestic home environment is by far the best for good socialisation of the pup. A puppy bred in a home environment will, from birth, be exposed to all the sights, sounds and smells of family life that the pup will transition to when rehomed. These points are vital but, when partnering a dog with a child with a disability, the pup or dog must also be exposed to the specific traits of the child's disability – before the dog arrives in your home. When I found our wonderful dog breeder Val, we ensured Dale had regular visits and contact with his pup many times before we took Henry home. Finding a breeder that understands your child's condition is crucial for preparing the dog for its new home.

In the case of a child with a disability, you need to identify your child's specific disability behaviours before you source the dog, so the dog can be desensitised to them before it is taken home. (When I worked with Alberto Alvarez-Campos on the Guide Dogs Queensland pilot programme, staff adopted common autistic behaviours to expose them to mature dogs during their re-training as autism assistance dogs.) If the breeder doesn't understand or support you with this, then the chances are they are the wrong source for your dog.

You can find a reputable breeder via the Kennel Club's Assured Breeder Scheme, but here are essential pointers to remember.

Socialisation of the dog is the most vital aspect, so you need to ensure that the dog's environment and the breeder will provide this. At all costs, you want to avoid the pitfalls of a puppy farm dog (I discuss this later).

The internet and social media have opened up opportunities for sourcing a vast choice of pups and mature dogs but, if you stick to these points, you will have the best chance of success. If you suspect the dog source is of a puppy farm level, then walk away and report your concerns to the relevant animal welfare organisation where you live, such as the RSPCA.[27] The Kennel Club states that around one in four puppies bought have been sourced from puppy farms; such is the extent of the problem.

How to source the dog or pup – the essentials

Always view the mother with the pups

If this can't be done, then do not buy the pup. Ask to see the whelping box, where it is housed, and the mother with the pups. It may sound strange, but do not allow the pup to be delivered to you either, because you don't know what you are getting and why.

If you are getting a big breed dog like a Labrador or Retriever, you should insist that the parents of the pup have been hip-scored. The hip joint of a dog is similar in size and function to a human hip. It has to be healthy and strong for the long-term well-being of the dog. Malformations of this joint can lead to a serious condition called hip dysplasia, which was first recognised in 1937 and can still cause problems for dog owners and breeders to this day. By X-raying the parents' hips, a score can determine the suitability of the dogs for breeding purposes, lessening the risk of hip problems in potential puppies. Generally, the advice given to breeders is that dogs with a hip score of 10 or less are suitable for breeding. Nowadays, it is thought dogs with a score greater than the breed mean shouldn't be bred from. Good examples of this include Labradors and German Shepherds: the breed mean is a score of around 18 or 19. (Non-genetic factors that influence the dog being prone to hip dysplasia include its diet, exercise, weight and injury history.)

Make sure the dog or pup is in good condition and health

- Well-kept pups and dogs should have a healthy weight and clean unmatted fur and be full of vitality. Their eyes and ears should be clean with no staining or notable discharge.

- Remember to take note of the type of environment the pup or dog is being kept in, so you can assess the socialisation of the pup.

- Ask to see a copy of the dog's records, including its vaccination and veterinary health check documents.

Check the behaviour as well as the health of the mature dog

When you are sourcing a mature dog, it should be in a similarly healthy condition to the pup; however, there is more to recognise in terms of the dog's behaviour. You must assess the overall nature and temperament of the dog. Remember its environment and especially how it has been socialised, particularly in relation to contact with children.

The dog should not jump up at you when you meet it, nor bark. Is the dog wary of you as a stranger? Does it back off when approached? How does the dog cope with you handling and petting it? Can it tolerate having its ears, head and neck touched? Can you feed it a treat without it snatching it from your hand? Does the dog allow you to touch its paws and interact with it?

You need to see how the dog handles and walks on the lead; it should walk at a good pace and not pull.

Check how the dog copes with an unusual event like you clapping your hands or the sudden noise of you dropping your keys on a hard floor. See how the owner handles the dog; is it under their full control? Find out if the dog can tolerate cats, doesn't chase them and can cope well with meeting other dogs. Does the dog calm down and settle well after greeting you, or in the company of the owner?

With a mature dog, you need to give the owner information from your plan about your child's disability behaviours and traits, so they can desensitise the dog to the same behaviours before you take the dog home.

Establish a contingency plan

Finally, a good breeder or dog owner will agree a contingency plan with you should the pup or dog not be successful with you in your home. With dog welfare in mind, after an agreed period of trial, you can arrange to return the dog to the breeder or owner for rehoming (albeit with a reduced reimbursement of your fee, because there will be time and costs involved in a rehoming process).

Where to source the dog

As discussed, there are many options open to you in sourcing a puppy or mature dog: breeders, rescue centres or, as some parents do, applying for a failed guide dog from Guide Dogs UK. Wherever you source the dog, the centre will have assessed the dog for its suitability for the type of home it should go to.

Beware of private adverts for puppies or mature dogs, unless you can check out the whole situation as you would with a reputable breeder.

Do not be pressured into taking a dog after a first meeting; there is much about the dog and rehoming it to consider before you make a decision.

Finally, never buy a puppy from a pet shop as it may have come from a puppy farm. Think about the cost of the dog; be wary if it is cheaper. This could be because money has been saved in its breeding environment at the expense of the health and well-being of the mothers and pups.

If you find a breeder that has kennelled dogs and puppies, be aware that this is similar to puppy farm conditions in the lack of adequate socialisation. Do not be tempted to take a dog because you feel you are rescuing it. All you are doing is lining the pockets of the breeder and paving the way for another litter of farmed pups.

The horrors of puppy farming should not be underestimated. The lengths to which callous breeders will go to defraud people seeking puppies of various breeds are despicable and inhumane to the dogs. There have been horrifying cases of people breeding and selling sick pets to unsuspecting families for huge profit. In one case the perpetrators used fake names to set up a 'pedigree registration' company to defraud buyers into believing that they were obtaining healthy puppies reared in a home environment. Thankfully, some of the owners of these puppy farms have been prosecuted, but this form of animal cruelty continues, which is why it is so important to source puppies from the places I have listed.

Planning for the Arrival of the Dog

I t is important to prepare the child and plan for the arrival of the dog in plenty of time, before the dog comes home. There is much to think about. The dog is a pack animal and has a need for resources for its well-being and development. Your child and family will become members of the pack, through the dog's eyes; each one of the family will have a place within the pack. As identified in Rogers Brambell's 'five freedoms',[28] dogs need routine and to have their basic needs met if they are to thrive.

Planning for a safe and suitable home

First, you need to prepare your home so that it's safe and suitable for the puppy or dog. Just as you would child-proof your home to protect and keep a child safe, you need to think about how the dog will explore your home and have a desire to chew anything it can get its paws on.

To dog-proof your home, keep objects at a safe height and keep things you don't want it to get (like shoes) out of the way. Make sure everyone in the family knows how the dog will behave regarding items around the home – especially how they love socks and underwear that could be lying around. As a family, you need to establish the rules that you want to implement with the dog beforehand, so everyone will have a consistent approach and not confuse the dog. Will the dog be allowed upstairs into bedrooms? Will they be permitted to sleep on beds or the sofa?

Beware of house plants as some are toxic to dogs, and ensure household cleaning items are locked away. Remember to ensure that your garden is secure and safe for the dog and think about the best area for the dog to use for toilet purposes.

The dog's toilet

It is preferable to make an enclosed toilet pen in a suitable area of your garden, so you can establish a toilet routine for the dog, and keep the rest of the garden clean for children to play in.

A pen area is less distracting for the dog and it will learn to use the area for all toilet purposes. A pen should be fenced off, and be at least six feet by four, and is better with a gate. This size allows the dog to move around and avoid using other soiled areas in the pen. Most dogs like to relieve themselves on grass or play bark. The bark is more practical for cleaning up purposes and can be replenished when needed. You must be vigilant in cleaning up after the dog when outdoors; as well as providing a positive role model for the child, it is socially more acceptable and a legal requirement that you clean up after your dog. Dog poo takes a year to break down into the ground. It contains lots of bacteria which can make dogs and people ill. In the United Kingdom dogs produce around a thousand tonnes of poop every day, which is the same weight as a thousand cars!

The dog's equipment

Now you know the breed of the dog being partnered with your child, the allocated kitchen cupboard where the cuddly dog's things are kept becomes the real dog's. This cupboard will become the dog and child's special place, helping to reinforce ownership of the dog for the child.

Think about where in the kitchen you will be putting the dog's raised feeding table. Put it in a place where the child can work with it and it is accessible for the dog and not next to a radiator. I cover feeding the dog in more detail later, but deciding beforehand where the dog will eat and drink will help your child get used to what this space is for and will therefore make the learning process easier.

Sleeping arrangements and the 'bolt-hole'

You need to decide where the dog will sleep at night and plan crate training for the puppy. Many parents with children with autism have found their child slept better with the dog in the child's bedroom. It is very much a personal choice whether the dog sleeps on the child's bed, but the dog can sleep on the floor in its own bed beside the child's. Some parents have found that their child slept better with the warmth and pressure from the dog giving the child increased comfort.

Both during the day and the night you will need to give the dog what is called a 'bolt-hole'. This is a place in the home where the dog will sleep and have time out. In this designated area, put up a sign the child is familiar with that means 'no' or 'do not disturb!'

Using puppy crates

If you are taking home a puppy, you will need to plan where you will put the crate. Using a crate is a good prevention resource but it must be used appropriately and for the right reasons. The crate is to be a happy, safe place for the pup and never to be used as a punishment place or a cage.

Selecting the right size is very important for the dog's development. The dog should be able to stand up in the crate and freely move around; therefore, most crates will be quite big and need plenty of space. Don't put it next to a radiator or the television; put it in as secluded and as quiet a place as possible.

The crate is needed because puppies like to explore everything and chew what they can find, especially when you go out and leave them unsupervised. You should put comfortable bedding in the crate with some water and their favourite toys or chews. The crate should be a positive and peaceful place for the dog. When house-training the pup, you need to put a newspaper down for the puppy to use and keep it away from the bedding area.

Planning puppy training

Another issue you need to think about is whether you will take the pup to dog training classes or use a personal dog trainer. The general dog training classes will be different to how you are training the pup, but a personal dog trainer could tailor the dog commands to meet your child's needs.

Keeping your child interested

Remember to keep your child involved when you can and keep their interest in dogs going via story books and online dog games, etc. There are numerous dog gaming sites and software available to keep your child motivated.[29]

Preparing for visits to the vet

Before the dog arrives, it would be prudent to find the veterinary practice you want to use and have a chat with the vet about how you want to include your child during visits. This gives you the opportunity to compile a social story for the child about going to the vet. The child is involved with taking the dog to the vet (what Dale used to call the 'dog doctor'), and this could help alleviate anxiety and fears for the child when visiting their own doctor.

And finally...

The dog coming home is a major transition for both the dog and child. Careful planning beforehand will pave the way for better success in the future.

Avoiding Stress in Dogs

For the dog's long-term health and well-being, and for the safe-guarding of its good temperament, it's essential that you monitor the dog for signs of stress. If unresolved, stress could lead to the dog nipping or, worse, biting. This chapter will explain the main signs you need to look out for.

When I sourced Henry for Dale, I understood that it was essential for the dog's well-being for Dale to learn, as far as possible, how to interact appropriately with the pup, so as not to cause it stress. I achieved this via good transition practice with Dale, but I also studied the topic and learned to recognise when a dog was stressed.

Given Henry was coming to live with Dale's severe and challenging autism, our home would be an extreme environment for the pup to adapt to. I had to make sure I knew the signs of stress and anxiety in the dog, before long-term damage was done and it was too late to modify the trigger of the stress. I did all I could beforehand to reduce the risk of stress to the pup. Undoubtedly, our puppy had immediate stress as it learned to cope with some of Dale's behaviours; this was part of Henry's desensitising process and socialisation in his new environment. I also knew to look out for long-term stress in the pup, as it affects their general health, long-term development and temperament. Long-term stress behaviours could be subtle, like the dog not eating properly or sleeping well, or it adopting negative behaviours, such as being destructive or barking inappropriately.

The common signs of stress to look out for in the dog can come across as normal dog behaviour, but it is important to recognise when these behaviours are out of context and excessive due to the dog being fearful and anxious. As a dog owner using the dog as a facilitator for a child, it is vital you get to know normal dog behaviour and abnormal body language in the dog.

Recognising signs of stress

Here are examples of common signs of stress that could be misinterpreted as normal dog behaviour:

- *Excessive lip and nose licking.* It is normal for a dog to do this when you've just given it a treat or fed it but, when this behaviour is out of context, it may be an indicator of stress.

- *Increased yawning*, which happens repeatedly, is excessive and is not a sleep yawn.

- *Excessive panting.* All dogs pant, but you need to recognise when this is happening at times other than in hot weather conditions and when the dog has not been exercising. Abnormal panting can be associated with marked tension in the dog's mouth area and eyes, with the ears being pinned back and low set.

- *Excessive scratching*, when there is no medical cause for the behaviour. The dog may also over-groom itself or self-mutilate by biting at its coat to pull off sections of its fur.

- *Pinned-back ears.* No matter what type of ears your breed of dog has, if their ears are pinned back against their head, this could be another sign of stress.

- *Avoidance*, which can be displayed in many different ways, like excessive sniffing, lack of attention, or looking or turning away. If the dog is avoiding interacting with people or other dogs, he is feeling uncomfortable. Avoidance behaviour is safer than the dog showing aggressive behaviour; you must acknowledge the dog's choice, and lead them away from the trigger, because the dog doesn't want the interaction to occur.

- *Vigorous shaking.* Another 'normal' dog behaviour that could be misinterpreted is the dog vigorously shaking their body, especially when they are not wet or haven't just woken up. Stress shaking is usually triggered when the dog has experienced something it doesn't like. A good example of when this might occur is after the dog has had an examination from the vet.

- *Low tail carriage.* This depends on the type of tail the breed of dog has, but the tail is a good indicator of how the dog is coping with or feeling about a situation. Most of us know that a tail between the dog's legs is a sign of fear. But the dog's tail can show more subtle changes to let us know the dog is anxious about something. With some dogs, the tail could stop wagging, be stationary and just lying low. This can occur with low pinned-back or low-set ears and tension around the dog's mouth and eyes. Also look out for any change in head carriage as it may be lowered and the dog subdued.

Other dog body language to look out for:

- low body posture
- slight or severe cowering
- weight shifted to the back legs
- excessive coat shedding
- increased whining or other vocalisation
- slow or tense movement
- changes in eating patterns or refusing food

- restlessness or pacing behaviours

- sweating on the paws

- dilated pupils.

Be mindful that the dog is stressed if it continually shows submissive behaviour by snorting a lot and the previously mentioned behaviours. This could lead on to aggressive behaviours like snarling, growling and baring their teeth. If the threat to the dog is great, the dog will escalate its fear to threatening barking or nipping or even a bite, as the dog concludes this is the only way to eradicate the threat.

Look out for changes in the dog's toileting habits. The dog may out of character urinate indoors; this is a behaviour which indicates the dog is in extreme distress, like you could witness on firework night. Be mindful if the dog gets over-excited or starts to have destructive behaviour, or shows signs of aggression towards people or other dogs. A long-term sign could be the dog developing abandonment issues by becoming attached and dependent on their owner or dog handler.

Look out for long-term physical signs that the dog is feeling exposed to stress – signs like the dog having lost weight; increased thirst; loss of appetite; and skin problems or eczema developing. Be aware if the dog has an increase in appetite but doesn't put on weight or has diarrhoea or digestive problems.

There are many stress triggers for the dog and there is increased likelihood of stress caused by children and people who don't know how to greet or handle a dog. How it manifests depends very much on the individual dog. It is helpful to try and identify the trigger of the stress, so you can alleviate the dog's fear.

Just like children with autism and those with sensory processing problems find coping with different environments difficult, the dog has similar issues adapting and coping. Just as you would be mindful of how a child is coping, you have to think about the environmental impact on the dog. This is why early socialisation of the puppy in the first eight to 16 weeks of its life is vital to avoiding stress later.

The dog may not like being in a strange or new environment, especially if it is unpleasant due to too much noise or being too busy with people. Other changes the dog may get stressed over include going to a new home or handler and changes to its routine. Overwhelming the dog can trigger stress, as I highlighted earlier; expecting too much from the dog or over-physical handling from the owner or child can add to the dog's ongoing stress.

Remembering Rogers Brambell's 'five freedoms', which specify how the dog's basic needs must be met, is vital to its development and long-term well-being.

The dog must have adequate exercise for its size and breed, and enough stimulation so it is able to learn and develop. The dog's strong teeth mean that it likes to chew on various types of toys, materials and dog chews. They require a good diet and enough sleep. Most dogs sleep at least 12 to 16 hours a day; puppies will sleep even more. The dog's psychological needs must be met; as they are very active, they must be allowed to run around and explore. A dog needs human companionship, canine interaction and opportunity to thrive, with freedom from pain and discomfort.

Preventing stress

Now that you are familiar with the signs of dog stress, it is vital to prevent the stress before it reaches crisis point. As well as using the transitional kit to show the child how to interact and be with the dog, there are also general points to acknowledge about children and dogs.

The essential rule is to always supervise children when they are interacting with a dog, because most dog bites occur within the home. Never let a child take food from a dog when it is eating. No matter how good the temperament of the dog, never allow a young child to sit astride the dog as this is pinning the dog down and restraining it, and there is a high risk the dog may retaliate.

Your child should never approach a dog they don't know, especially if the dog is tied up. Alberto Alvarez-Campos told me of a sad incident that proves this is a vital rule. Through his work with Assistance Dogs Australia, Alberto was supporting a young severely autistic Aborigine boy with his assistance dog. This partnership was as successful as James and Mahe's partnership discussed earlier, and the bond between the boy and his dog was very strong. One day the boy was out with his mother without their assistance dog. They came across a dog that was tied up with a chain. Before his mother had time to intervene, the boy attempted to pat the dog. The inevitable happened and the dog severely attacked the boy causing him serious injuries. I was stunned to learn that, while the boy was being attended to in the hospital, he was crying and desperate to seek comfort from his assistance dog. Such was the bond and trust between them.

There is much to learn to keep children safe when interacting with dogs. If you are taking your child to meet a potential puppy for the first time, after adequate transition preparation, there are strategies to adhere to that will increase the success of this very important first meeting. Remind the breeder to prepare a calm environment for the meeting – one that is suitable for both the child and the puppy. Make sure your child either sits or kneels on the floor so it is less intimidating for the pup and the child. This will make it safer for any handling and interacting between the two, as puppies have lots of energy and movement, so the child won't inadvertently hurt or, worse still, drop the pup. Once the two have successfully engaged, with the child calmly and gently patting and stroking the pup, and they have interacted well together, give your child a treat that is easy to give to the pup. Throughout the meeting, as best you can, keep the child calm so the puppy remains calm and relaxed.

While it is natural for a child to want to put their face close to the dog's, this should be avoided as the dog may perceive it as a threat unless the dog has instigated it. This is the kind of behaviour that should be dealt with when socialising the dog, so the dog can be desensitised or learn to cope with it when it does happen – but it is best avoided. Again, good socialisation, with supervised contact with children, is vital for the puppy.

Think about the height of a young child in the proximity of the dog and the immature interactive behaviours children present to dogs. Some dogs see eye contact as a threat, so young children, who will walk differently towards the dog, will be at a similar eye contact level to the dog. Unless the puppy has been socialised to cope with young children, the dog could see the child as an unpredictable threat and retaliate with a nip or bite to the child. Most children who suffer dog bites are bitten by their own family dog because these factors were not understood. Children will treat the dog like their peers and mishandle them and overwhelm them if allowed. When playing with a dog, it shouldn't be teased; do not take a bone or toy away from the dog if it is playing with it.

As discussed earlier, measures should be taken, like creating a bolt-hole, and the dog should be allowed to sleep without being touched or disturbed. Do not play rough games with the puppy as this can lead to aggressive behaviour later on. Never let the child force themselves on the dog or puppy; if they want the dog to be included in the game, it should be on the dog's terms.

Make your child aware that puppies and dogs like to chew things. To avoid accidents to the dog, measures have to be taken so the dog doesn't get access to things it can swallow. Children should be able, and at least 10 years old, in order to be legally responsible for a dog outside their homes. It is prudent to teach all children to ask a dog owner's permission before they pat their dog.

If a young child is giving the dog a treat, it is safer to get them to put it on the floor for the dog. The safest way to teach your dog how to receive a treat without snatching is by using the command 'gently'. With the dog in the sit position, show the dog you have the treat in your hand, ensuring he doesn't snatch it from you. If he tries to grab it, then close your hand into a fist. Hold your fist towards the dog and let him sniff your hand with the treat in it. Wait until the dog is relaxed and calm. Let the dog take the treat from your hand saying 'gently'. If he attempts to grab it, close your fist again. The dog will quickly learn that he only gets a treat when he is calm and doesn't try to snatch the treat.

Remember, puppies are like babies and have teething problems. When their teeth are developing, it is normal for them to mouth on objects and people, especially children. Children find this stage difficult to cope with, as they feel the dog is actively biting them and being hostile to them; this can affect the bonding process between the puppy and child.

Puppies will use their mouths to explore people and things within their environment. By doing so, they are replicating their behaviour from when they played and interacted with their litter pups. When a puppy bites another from its litter, the play immediately stops as the hurt puppy yelps with disapproval and will move away from the offending pup. Playful puppies will also bite or nip, snarl and growl and even bark, which is normal behaviour for them. If a puppy, like an older dog, is tired, overhandled or overwhelmed, then anxiety will lead it to nip or bite because the pup cannot cope with the excessive handling.

Again, this is why the safe and secure bed or bolt-hole is essential for transition, as is adequate socialisation, like exposing the puppy to strange noises or the specific disability behaviours of the child, before the pup or dog is taken home.

If the pup continues to mouth or nip when playing with you or the child, then put the pup down, ignore it and stop the play and walk away – just like a litter pup would do. You can divert the pup by giving them a toy or chew toy instead to play with or bite on.

Preventing tragedy

There can be tragic consequences due to lack of early socialisation and irresponsible pet ownership. In September 2016, I was saddened and shocked to hear on the news that a three-year-old child had died after he was attacked by an American Bulldog. The dog was completely out of control and had to be seized by police and put into kennels. The child was rushed to hospital but his injuries were so bad he died.[30]

Some kinds of American Bulldogs have been found to be Pit Bull types. Pit Bull Terriers are on the banned dog list in the UK. In 2013–14, the number of hospital admissions due to dog bites was around 6750.[31] A survey carried out for the Dogs Trust in 2014 reported that 2083 stray dogs were put to sleep due to behavioural problems or aggression, 1042 due to ill health, and 755 under the Dangerous Dogs Act.[32] In 2014, changes to sentencing guidelines raised the maximum jail sentence for a fatal dog attack from two years to 14 years.

The dire consequences of a dog not being adequately socialised can occur to any breed. I have seen this first-hand, when I was involved in the decision to euthanise a beautiful, healthy five-year-old Spaniel because it couldn't cope being out of its owner's home environment. I came across this dog via a friend, who sought my help because the dog was attacking other dogs and strangers that visited its home and when it was taken out for walks. As a pup, the dog came from a farm setting, and was bred in a kennel environment, and could only cope with walks in remote woodland areas. If the dog was out of its home environment, it attacked other dogs, people and even children. The owner sought my help and I did all I could to assess the dog and see if its behaviour could be modified. The dog lived with me for a month, but the reality of the damage done to this dog became very apparent. Such was the lack of early socialisation, the poor dog couldn't even cope when I used the Hoover; it was terrified of it.

I developed a close bond with the dog, and it seemed to trust me, but when I attempted to take it for walks, it was horrendous and tried to attack almost every dog it met and every stranger. One day

I had a close call when it tried to attack an old age pensioner who had an unsteady gait and used a walking stick. Such was the lack of socialisation, the dog perceived the old man as a threat, because it couldn't cope with the old man's different walk and body language.

This is a sad but powerful example of how young children like toddlers are so at risk with dogs. Because of the height of the child, their proximity can be too close to the dog. To a fragile dog, this can be threatening and intimidating.

I did all I could to give this dog the best chance of rehoming, but it was futile. There were times when he bit me and my partner, no matter how gentle our approach. After I got the dog an assessment from my vet, and had sought advice from a rehoming centre, it was a sad but inevitable conclusion that this poor dog needed to be euthanised. It was a heart-breaking decision for the owner and me; the best I could do for the dog, as it trusted me, was to ensure it had a calm and stress-free death. I will never forget the day I took the dog to my vet to carry out this procedure, and it broke my heart. With the dog muzzled as the procedure began, it looked at me with its big beautiful eyes, confused and forlorn. Because the dog was so healthy, it took longer than usual for the drugs to work; the dog was calm throughout, though, as it trusted me. I will never forget that dog and the lessons learned on how vital early socialisation is for the long-term welfare of the dog and the safety of others. That poor beautiful pedigree dog became a sad statistic because people let it down, and I will never forget the painful experience or the lost look in its eyes as it passed away.

This kind of tragedy can be prevented by making sure that the puppy you choose is sourced from a reputable breeder and has been well socialised from the outset, and that you monitor its stress levels and take steps to correct any problems at an early stage.

Stage 3

USING THE DOG AS AN EDUCATIONAL FACILITATOR TOWARDS THE BEST POSSIBLE INDEPENDENCE FOR THE CHILD

T his is the most intensive part of the programme. As you welcome your puppy or older dog home, the partnership between your child and your facilitator dog has begun.

While the dog coming home is a very exciting time for you and your child, this is a momentous event and a potentially stressful time for the dog as it learns to adapt to its new environment. Be particularly careful with the settling in of a puppy, because it has to adapt to living without its mother and littermates for the first time. This is a major transition for the puppy as well as for your child, so there is much to plan and think about.

Remember that, while this programme is tailored for a child with difficulties such as ASD, the simplicity of the approach means it can easily be adapted to suit any child. Stage 3 is no different, in that sense, to the programme as a whole: it will help any family or individual wanting to introduce a dog into their lives for all the benefits that brings.

Settling in your dog

Now that your dog is home, everything from the cuddly dog now belongs to the real dog!

While extended family will want to meet the new member of your family, leave this aspect for a few days to allow the dog to settle and be familiar with its own surroundings and immediate new family. Start with taking your dog into the garden, as it is a calm and stress-free place, and allow the dog to explore it. Try to give the dog time to go to the toilet, as this will enable the toileting training process to begin. If the dog successfully toilets, then praise him and reward with a treat.

When back indoors, limit the dog to exploring the main areas of the house – but not all of it at once. Remember not to overwhelm the dog. Child barrier gates are very useful to allow you to zone your home, especially if you don't want the dog to go upstairs or into bedrooms. This helps keep the pup safe from injury from stairs; its bones are still immature and developing, so they are at high risk of fractures. A child gate will come in useful later as well, if you are planning in the long term for the dog to sleep in your child's bedroom.

Put up a poster in the kitchen with the house rules applicable to the dog, so everyone is clear as to what is expected.

Make sure you show the dog its bolt-hole, which should contain chews and robust, dog-safe toys. Let the dog explore its new home and garden on its terms for the first couple of days. It is inevitable that the dog will be under some stress and will need time to adjust to its new environment and routine.

The dog collar

It is best to ask the breeder beforehand to introduce a soft collar to the pup as soon as possible. Some breeders use coloured collars on all the litter, so they can identify which pup is which. Introducing a collar is a gradual process that needs to be built up, so the pup gets used to it. At first, let the pup get a good sniff at it; play with the pup with it in a calm way for a short while. Put the collar on the dog for brief periods of time, such as at feeding time, when the dog is at its happiest. When they are not bothered about wearing it, you can leave it on. Especially with boisterous pups, make sure it fits correctly – not too loose and not too tight. The rule is that you should be able to slip two fingers between the collar and the dog's neck. If the collar is transferred from the cuddly dog, it will have the headshot picture of your child attached. As with the cuddly dog, the child will understand that the real dog belongs to him or her.

Introducing the dog lead and harness

Follow the same principles for getting the dog used to the harness as you did with the collar. Only when the pup is used to the harness, and tolerates it without any notice, can you introduce the lead in a similar way. Remember to allow the pup to sniff and explore the lead with you before you try to attach it. When you attach it, let the pup run around with it, ensuring it doesn't become caught in anything. This is enough for a first try.

Next, try to get your puppy to sit, reward him with a treat and, when he is calm, attach the lead again. Because the lead is attached to the harness, the pup is less fazed by it.

When you are training the pup or older dog, you need to introduce the lead attached to the collar in the same gentle way you introduced the collar and harness.

Walking with your dog

As the dog is adjusting to its new home, keep the dog in the back garden for the first two to three days. Then build up, with adult walks only, on familiar routes, so the dog is socialised to its new home and surrounding environment. You will know when the time is right and the pup or more mature dog is ready to walk with the child. The dog must be able to walk at a controlled pace, not pulling; it should be obedient and have acquired all its socialisation skills.

Introducing the child to walking with the dog is a delicate and gradual process. Start to practise in the safety of your garden. Walk around the garden with the dog, perhaps with an older child, in a relaxed and calm manner. Progress to going for very short walks with the older child on a familiar route. When you feel the dog and disabled child are ready for walks together, again practise in the garden, and progress as you did with the older child to short familiar walks outdoors.

Using a crate

If you are using a crate, this should be the dog's bolt-hole. It should be a happy, safe and secure place for the pup to retreat into. The main objective with the crate is to reduce unwanted chewing when you are not there at night time and when you have to leave the pup alone.

When you are home and able to supervise the pup, leave the crate door open so the pup can wander in and out on its own terms. You introduce the concept of the crate to the pup in a similar way to introducing the collar – in a gradual and relaxed manner. Wean the pup into being in the crate with the door closed for short periods and gradually build up. For example, when you are taking a shower, and for similar small periods, you can leave the pup alone in the crate. This will help alleviate any anxiety for the pup by preventing it from associating the crate with you leaving it alone.

Don't encourage learned behaviour with the pup: you don't want it to think that barking or whining is the trigger that gets it out of the crate. It is vital that the crate is never used as a form of punishment for the dog. Remember to implement your strategies, and use signs that the child understands, so everyone leaves the pup alone when it is sleeping. You can start to wean the pup out of the crate at around six months of age, when its teeth are more developed and chewing behaviours are under control (when it sticks to chewing its own dog toys and chews like Nylabones).

When weaning from the crate, begin by leaving the door open when you are leaving the pup for shorter episodes; then build it up. If any chewing behaviour returns, then continue using the crate as you did when the pup first arrived until the problem is resolved.

Helping your dog bond with the family

Your pup or older dog coming home is a delicate time for them. Remember that dogs are descended from wolves; they have a natural fear of the strange and unfamiliar that, if not addressed, can lead to the dog being stressed and retaliating to protect itself.

Thankfully, dogs and puppies are very sociable. However, puppies need strategies and sufficient time to allow them to know and bond with all the family. There is a very brief window of socialisation opportunity for a pup: the first 12 weeks of their development is the most crucial. By 16 weeks, the window for socialisation is virtually closed. When puppies are taken to their new home, they are right in the middle of their socialisation stage, and that is why they can move in and learn to settle with their new family.

Once the puppy is vaccinated, it's essential to get him or her out and about to be exposed to all elements of the weather, street noises, cars, buses, horses, police and fire engines and all that the outdoors brings. More importantly, the pup must be phased into greeting and meeting other dogs.

To help the puppy cope better when you first take it home, you may want to use products on the market that are a chemical copy of dog-appeasing pheromones released by the mother dog from her mammary area after the birth of her puppies. These pheromones contribute to the attachment process between the mother and her offspring. They come in diffuser form, as sprays, collars or tablets, and replicate the mother's pheromones. They help by comforting and reassuring puppies and adult dogs that are in stressful situations like:

- rehoming

- going into kennels or boarding

- being alone

- being exposed to loud noises (like firework night and thunder)

- travelling in the car.

Most important of all, they can help the dog focus better when training and learning socialisation skills.

Your breeder or vet can best advise you, but using these products can make a real difference to the well-being of the dog and the transition of coming to their new home.

Being a responsible owner

Now you are a dog owner, there are important legal responsibilities you need to be aware of. The Control of Dogs Order 1992 states that any dog in a public setting must wear a collar and tag with the name address of the owner on it.[33] It is now compulsory to have your dog microchipped.

Under the Clean Neighbourhoods and Environment Act 2005,[34] you must not allow your dog to foul footpaths or public places. Local authorities have the power to fine dog owners if they do not clean up after their dogs. Dog faeces can carry disease that can affect humans, farm animals and wildlife.

Be aware of the Countryside Code[35] and the Scottish Outdoor Access Code,[36] which provide guidelines on how you can safely access rural and similar areas with your dog.

A major benefit of being a dog owner is the enjoyment of taking your dog for walks. You have to be mindful, though, that it is everyone's right to enjoy the outdoors: share these areas in a respectful manner with others that don't have dogs. Dogs can be a problem for land managers and visitors to the countryside if not kept under proper control. If not obedient and complying with the handler, dogs can worry or injure farm animals and wildlife and upset other people. Therefore, you must keep your dog on a short lead (the recommendation is no more than two metres long), especially when you are near fields where there are cows, sheep or horses. Cows can be frightened by dogs; they may react badly and panic, causing injury to themselves or damaging property. They may be aggressive towards you and your dog. Sheep are a bigger problem with dogs and should always be avoided. Dogs can worry sheep in a way that can contribute to the death of a sheep as well as unborn lambs. Under the Animals (Scotland) Act 1987,[37] a farmer in some cases has the right to shoot your dog if it is worrying animals.

You also have to think about areas where ground-nesting birds are breeding and rearing their young, particularly from April to July. Keep your dog on a short lead and be mindful of places where birds are nesting, such as moorland, forests, grassland, loch shores and the seaside. Remember, some reservoirs and streams are used as public water supplies, so don't let your dog swim in these waters.[38]

Caring for Your Dog

Canine Health and Learning Opportunities for the Child

This chapter summarises what you need to know in order to take care of your dog and keep it healthy and happy. It lists common precautions you need to take, including keeping your dog away from foodstuffs (like onions, chocolate and many other things commonly available in the average household) that are actually poisonous to dogs. In this chapter, you'll find information on:

- the question of neutering

- grooming your dog and conducting a physical examination

- feeding your dog, including information on how you can use this task as an educational tool for your child

- establishing a toilet routine for your dog

- exercising your dog and the importance of playtime for your dog

- how to tell if your dog isn't well

- vaccinations and visiting the vet

- the most common ailments and dangers to the dog's health.[39]

Some information regarding neutering[40]

If you have sourced a puppy, you will have to think about neutering. There are many thoughts in the canine world regarding the pros and cons of neutering. The best advice I could give is to seek guidance from your vet.

All working dogs are neutered at around six months of age, because of the anti-social problems that otherwise arise and because working dogs must always be obedient and well behaved in public settings. I would be led by the working dog world's policy of neutering all dogs that will be working with a disabled child or person.

There are other reasons why neutering is in the best interest of the dog, apart from preventing unwanted pregnancies. There are many health and behavioural benefits to having your dog neutered. If the testicles are removed, then the dog won't be prone to testicular cancer because the risk has been removed. In female dogs, heat periods or seasons usually occur twice a year and last about three weeks. During this time your dog will be a magnet to the advances of unneutered dogs it comes across. In both sexes, the urge to mate can lead to roaming, potentially leading to your dog being permanently lost, getting into fights, being injured or being involved in a road accident.

In females, spaying involves removing the ovaries and uterus under a general anaesthetic. While this prevents seasons, it also removes the occurrence of life-threatening uterine infections and reduces the risk of developing potentially fatal mammary tumours later in life. In males, neutering or castration involves the removal of both testes under a general anaesthetic; this can help control excessive sexual drive and some behavioural problems.

It is also worth remembering that a neutered dog won't be stolen for breeding purposes.

Forewarning your child about your dog's operation

When you decide to go through the neutering process, you need to involve the child and give them some explanation so they don't give the dog stress and added discomfort during the healing process. I used the neutering stage with Henry as an opportunity for Dale to take care of his dog and show empathy. Neutering may feel like too complex a concept to explain to your child, depending on their comprehension. In Dale's case, I felt it was better to tell a white lie: I explained that Henry had a very sore tummy and needed the vet (dog doctor) to fix it. I involved Dale with the visits to the vet to drop Henry off for his operation and to collect him (the latter with the head cone on, which really amused Dale). Dale understood that his dog was sore because he helped give Henry his pain relief medicine and he saw where the vet had 'fixed' Henry's tummy. Because Dale knew to leave the dog alone when it slept, the healing stage of the neutering process was really straightforward, with Dale being unfazed throughout.

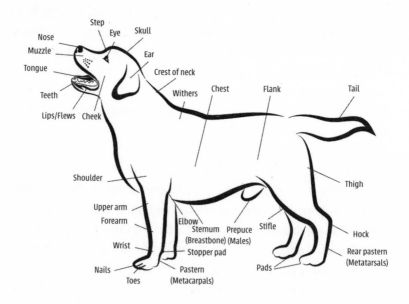

Anatomy of a dog

Grooming

A regular grooming routine for your dog is important and serves many purposes. *Grooming the dog is a great way for you and your child to bond with your dog.* Your dog should enjoy and look forward to the experience. It is also a great opportunity to give your dog a general health check – you may detect a wound, lump, fleas or dirty eyes or ears.

If you use a grooming table, get your dog to place its front paws on the table first, so you can lift the hind end the rest of the way without hurting your back. Ensure the dog is in a comfortable position so you and your dog can enjoy the time face-to-face. A grooming session should only take around 10 to 15 minutes. Rubber surfaces are best, so the dog does not slip.

First, examine the ears for dirt or infection and clean as needed. Check the eyes and clean away any accumulated matter; look for redness, swelling or excessive green/yellow discharge. Examine the dog's mouth and teeth and check for broken teeth and tartar build-up. Tartar can cause gum disease and expensive dental surgery.

There are various dog grooming brushes on the market. While you can use the standard brush from the transitional kit, you will need other brushes suitable for the type of coat your dog has.

Ear cleaning

Breeds of dog that have loose ear flaps are more prone to having dirty ears or ear infections due to poor air circulation. If your dog's ears are dirty, they will have brown oily dirt in them. Signs of infection are redness of the skin and a strong odour. Your vet can help you with maintenance and can advise on ear-cleaning solutions to use. A normal healthy ear is clean and dry.

If you need to clean the dog's ear, put the solution in the ear, hold the ear flap closed so fluid will not leak out, and then massage the ear for about a minute. Once the entire ear area is bathed, clean out with cotton wool balls. Never use Q-tips as these can cause damage. Your dog may not enjoy this experience as there may be some discomfort, but try to make your dog as relaxed as possible throughout. Use treats to reward them for their patience.

Nail trimming

Your dog's nails will need to be trimmed at times but, if it walks on pavements a lot, its nails will be naturally worn down. An easy way to tell if your dog's nails need trimming is if you can hear them clicking on a hard wood or tile floor. Many people don't feel confident about cutting their dog's nails, worrying that they may cut them too short or cause damage; a dog groomer or vet can do them instead.

Bathing

Your dog should be bathed at least every four to six weeks. Bathing your dog too often will dry out the natural oils in the skin and can damage the coat. Undoubtedly, using a dog groomer is best as they have the expertise and all the necessary equipment – and take all the mess involved. If you have a Golden Retriever, a dog groomer can trim the hairs between the pads of the feet and thin out the tail and neck area. Some dogs don't like bath time, so take your time and praise and reward them accordingly.

Avoiding the head area, soak your dog with warm water from the neck downwards. Try to eliminate any shaking by placing a hand on your dog's ear. Care should be taken to avoid water getting into the ears and eyes. Rinse thoroughly, ensuring all soap residue is gone, towel dry and allow your dog to shake. You should always provide your dog with the opportunity to toilet.

If your dog goes swimming in the sea, then salt water needs to be rinsed out of its coat.

Care of the dog's teeth

It is important to take care of your dog's teeth. Nylabones or toys they chew on can help keep their teeth clean, but it is recommended you brush your dog's teeth at least twice a week with dog toothpaste.

Do not use human toothpaste, as it can make your dog sick. You can use a normal toothbrush or one that fits over your finger (available from a pet store).

Physical examinations

The benefits

Physical examinations are a very important part of caring for your dog and have added benefits. They help establish a bond and a level of trust between you and your dog. Regular examinations also help desensitise your dog to being physically handled (especially important when it attends the vet). They allow you to be vigilant and pick up any abnormalities which could become serious health problems. To be aware of what's abnormal, though, you need to know what is normal for your dog. Regular physical examinations will help you learn this.

As well as ensuring your dog is in the best health, regular examinations also help your child to desensitise to and be prepared for visits to the doctor or dentist. This is an exercise that can become an educational tool, supporting your child through the dog.

How to conduct a physical examination

As with grooming, this should be a pleasurable experience for your dog; it should be done in a calm, relaxed manner, when your dog is sleepy, to make it easier for you and your dog.

Make a note of any markings that are particular to your dog, to prevent you mistaking them as abnormal in future examinations. Look for discharges, inflammations, rashes, cuts, lumps, bumps, dandruff and broken teeth and nails. A green discharge generally indicates an infection is present.

Examine your dog in a relaxed, non-forceful manner, but be thorough as it is easy to miss small cuts and abrasions. Observe your dog's reaction throughout; watch for any flinching or recoiling when you touch any body part, as not all injuries are visible to the eye.

Examine your dog in a logical, hygienically appropriate sequence so your dog becomes familiar with the routine. Look at the eyes, ears and mouth as described earlier. The nose should be clean and free from dry, crusty build-up and abnormal discharge. The feet between the toes should be free from knots, redness and lick-staining. Check nails and pads. The dog's skin shouldn't be red, nor have hairless patches. Walk your fingers over the entire dog to check for lumps, scratches, bites and parasites. Check the abdomen as well as the genitals and anus for any lumps, bumps and skin changes.

Your dog should remain relaxed, responsive and comfortable during health checks.

What are you looking for during a physical examination?

Take a note of the overall appearance, behaviour and attitude of the dog. You need to know what is normal for your dog if you are to notice the abnormal.

Monitor abnormal behaviour that may indicate health issues, like the dog shaking its head or scratching its ears, which could mean there is an infection. Another example is if the dog drags its rear end along the floor – this could mean its anal glands are swollen and need attention. The dog's anal glands are where the dog's natural scent secretion is stored. In some breeds, these glands can become engorged and need manually emptying – with caution. The vet can empty them so they don't erupt and lead to infection. The dog dragging its rear end along the floor can also be an indication of worm infestation or something hanging in the lower rectum, like blades of grass or remnants of something the dog has been chewing, like blankets.

Look out for any signs of the dog limping or sensitivity to touch, light or sound.

Start at the top of the dog and work your way down systematically. Always start with looking at the head first and the genital and anal area last, to maintain good hygiene. If you find an issue with any area, be careful not to cross-contaminate other healthy areas. Maintain proper hygiene by washing your hands after health-checking your dog.

Head
Look at your dog's overall appearance; note any lumps, bumps or changes.

Eyes
Your dog's eyes should be bright and clear, without any squinting. A brown or white discharge is usually normal as the eye is functioning as it should to rid itself of dust and dirt. A green discharge may need attention as it could mean inflammation or infection.

Ears
The ears should have a slight amount of wax build-up on the pinna (the outer part of the ear); this shows the ear is functioning properly. Note any redness, offensive smell or excessive discharge or build-up of wax; these may be signs of an overgrowth of yeast or an ear infection.

Mouth and teeth
Gums should be pink and moist, not red or bleeding. Look for any fractured teeth and tartar or calculus (hardened dental plaque) build-up. Note any missing teeth.

Skin
The dog's skin should be in good general condition, with no noticeable bumps or lumps. Take a note of any loss of condition of the hair, coat and skin, for example whether it is dry, flaky or oily, and the size and placement of any hair loss. Look for hotspots (pyoderma), any redness, pustules, oozing or fleas, etc.

LEGS

The dog's legs should look healthy, with no noticeable bumps or lumps. Look out for swelling or tenderness or heat in certain areas differing between each leg.

FEET

Pick up each foot and check each pad, the spaces between the pads and the condition of the nails. Check for any cracks or lacerations, redness, moisture, odour or foreign bodies in the spaces between the pads. Check the nails are not torn, cracked or too long. The dog's nails should clear the floor when the dog is standing normally.

GENITAL AREA (MALES)

In the male, note any swelling of the prepuce or abnormal discharge from the penis. A small amount of whitish discharge is normal in many dogs. Check the testicles for symmetry and check the condition of the skin. They should be relatively symmetrical and smooth.

GENITAL AREA (FEMALES)

The vulva should be clean and smooth without any discharge, unless the dog is in season. The crease around the vulva should be clean and dry, not moist, red or smelly.

ANUS

Check the dog's anus is clean and dry and that there are no sores nor redness or swelling.

Feeding time – and opportunities for children to learn

Now you have your dog, the process of using it as a facilitator can begin, as you create a routine for the dog that is conducive to the child's routine. Feeding time is an important part of the day for the dog; it is more than just putting the bowl down and allowing your dog to eat. This is a great time for your child and dog to connect and can also be used to do some obedience and tolerance exercises with the dog.

Most Labradors and Retrievers will devour their food quickly. If your dog doesn't finish its food, do not leave the bowl for the dog to graze on and complete later; it will learn to eat all of its food at the next feed.

I always feed my dogs in the morning and in the evening, as it is better for the dog and provides more learning opportunities for the child. In the case of working with a disabled child, consider getting him or her involved with feeding the dog only in the evenings when there is less family chaos. Siblings could feed the dog in the mornings. This gives you time to work with a disabled child and makes sure siblings are also included in looking after the dog.

Feeding time for the dog is an immense learning opportunity for the child, with all its associated language and the many steps involved in the entire feeding process. Think about all that is involved with this activity alone:

- It teaches the child early responsibility skills, and language, as the dog is waiting patiently and eagerly.

- The child washes their hands and fills up the bowl with the right amount of food, learning early numeracy ('one scoop, two scoops').

- The child has to learn to cope with all the sensory issues involved, like the smell and texture of the food and the noise of the food hitting the metal bowl.

- It helps the child understand sequencing, while improving hand and eye coordination and fine motor skills.

- It teaches empathy towards the dog, as the child begins to learn that the dog has needs like they do.

This is an opportunity to show and teach the child what they can do, rather than be negative and tell them what they can't do. If you are patient and relaxed with the child throughout, while giving lots of praise, the child should, over time, learn this complex skill of feeding their dog independently.

The dog's feeding time is a great opportunity to address all of the triad of ASD impairments simultaneously.

It has been scientifically recognised that there are 30 steps involved with an autistic child learning how to properly brush his or her teeth, so the numerous steps needed to feed their dog must seem insurmountable to the child. You want the child to learn to wash the dog's bowl when the dog is done eating and learn the skill of refilling the water bowl to place in the dog's raised feeding table. Mastering this skill is more enticing and challenging for the child, because most children with autism love anything to do with water.

This is why, during feeding time, you want to ensure that the dog is trained to sit and wait – to allow the child time to prepare the food at their own pace.

The feeding table

A raised feeding table makes negotiating all the steps involved so much easier for the child than haphazardly having the food and water bowls lying on the floor. (On the floor, they could be ignored by the child and people could walk into them, causing constant spillages.) A feeding table is a prominent and practical place that allows the child to see when the water needs to be topped up; and it's easier for the child to do this because the table is a fixed height and has compartments for the bowls to go in. Placing the bowls in the compartments will help the child improve spatial awareness problems. The dog's feeding time improves proprioception problems for the child too.[41]

As discussed earlier, the feeding table aids the dog's digestion and comfort when eating, while reducing the risk of reflux or aspiration of the stomach contents to the dog's lungs. Aspiration of water or food particles can cause problems like chest infections or pneumonia for the dog. The risk of this happening increases when the dog gets older.

The dog having its own feeding table reinforces the message to the child that eating at a table is more socially acceptable. Just as the dog eats its meals at its table, the child should eat his or her dinner at their table.

I remember the vital lesson Dale taught me: he understood and learned via the dog first and was then able to transfer these skills to his own experience.

Learning new words
You can vary the dog's treats to help the child to learn new words. For example, try dried sausages for the dog and then, once the child has learnt the word 'sausage', change to small pieces of chicken. Use anything that is suitable for the dog's diet and increases the child's vocabulary at the same time. Beware of the dog gaining weight, though – this must be monitored very carefully. As the dog wears a harness every day, this is a good guide as to whether the dog is gaining too much weight.

The feeding routine
With the dog in the 'sit and wait' position, the child can prepare the dog's food with the parent guiding them. Ensure the dog waits by holding it by the collar. When ready, the child can place the bowl in the dog's table and stand beside it. The child (if verbal) or carer should give the command 'eat' and the carer should blow twice on the whistle, allowing the dog to race to the bowl. Try to progress to the child blowing the whistle, as this is a great mechanical exercise for the child to learn – one that could encourage speech.

Using the whistle in this way will also encourage the dog to learn recall when the whistle is blown, as the dog will associate the whistle with getting food. The dog responding to the verbal command allows the child to learn the power of communication and, more so, that communication works!

While it goes against what most dog experts would advocate (that the child and family should eat first), I always ensured Dale fed his dog before he ate. This was because, initially, it took ages for Dale to learn all that was involved with feeding time for Henry. Also, after being fed, Henry would patiently lie at Dale's feet under the dinner table content with having a full stomach. This meant that when opportunities arose to eat in public places in outdoor cafes, Henry was used to being under the table – just as any guide or assistance dog is trained to be when in public places. It also helped prevent Dale sneaking food off his plate to give to Henry – Dale understood that Henry was full because he had given him his dinner.

I got Dale to feed Henry twice a day, morning and evening (half his daily food allowance in each case, to prevent him getting fat). It is vital to prevent the dog becoming overweight as it causes serious health problems, could shorten their life and, more importantly as a facilitator dog, inhibit the dog's ability to work and respond. Feeding the dog twice a day allows a double learning experience for the child. However, remember to limit the dog treats the child gives to the dog and, when the daily allowance is used up, teach the child 'finished' or 'no more' (whatever words the child is familiar with). Put the daily treat allowance into the dog's cupboard, so the child understands when the allowance is used up for that day.

Important points to note!

- Never let your child interrupt the dog while it is eating.

- Do not allow your dog to play or run around in the hour before or after a meal, as this could cause bloat and other serious health problems.

- Teaching your dog not to steal food or beg at the table is teaching him or her good manners.

- Never feed the dog titbits – only those used as a reward. If you do, you are encouraging the dog to beg for food and, especially at family mealtimes, the dog will sit and stare at you, salivate, bark and even paw you.

- If your dog attempts to take food and you witness it, vocally get its attention and give it the command 'leave!'

- If the dog has stolen food and you discover it after the event, do not shout or respond in any way, because you have missed the moment to correct the dog. Instead, take measures so the dog can't access food lying about or accessible on worktops.

- If the dog has stolen food, cut back on its meal portion as weight can pile on very quickly.

Toilet routine for the dog

When Henry arrived in Dale's life we were really struggling to teach Dale to understand how to be toilet trained. However, because of the process of training his puppy, there were lots of reinforcement opportunities for teaching Dale – so much so that, within a couple of weeks, Dale achieved full toilet control. By repeatedly demonstrating to Dale how the dog used its special toilet, Dale learned the concept of using his own toilet with Henry by his side. The dog being rewarded for successful toileting helped Dale understand the meaning and value of his reward. Taking hygiene steps, such as regular handwashing when dealing with the pup's toilet issues, helped increase Dale's understanding of the importance of toilet hygiene. This was so successful that, in the years that followed, Dale was able to clean up Henry's toilet area himself, which we used to call 'the poop patrol'.

To use the dog as a facilitator to help the child with any toileting issues, you need to learn how to establish a toilet routine for the dog, as relieving your dog regularly is best for its welfare. Try to get your dog to use the allocated toilet area in your garden as much as possible, even before you go out for walks, so you don't spoil public pathways and communal areas. To get the dog to use the designated area, you need to train them via the lead with the command 'toilet'. Give the dog a food reward when it has succeeded with lots of upbeat praise like 'good dog!' This may take a few days or even weeks to achieve, but the result is well worthwhile in the long term. If your dog decides to run around in the garden rather than focus on the toilet, then use the lead to reinforce what is expected of it.

Generally, dogs urinate every two to three hours and usually defecate at least twice a day. Always allow your dog to relieve itself as soon as you are up in the morning and the very latest you go to bed. With good training you shouldn't need to relieve your dog during the night unless it has an upset stomach or urine infection that means it can't control its normal pattern. Remember, dogs are creatures of habit, and if you allow it to toilet during the night the dog will expect this thereafter. A good toilet routine will be more easily established in conjunction with a good feeding routine because eating causes the gut to be stimulated and the dog will usually go to the toilet after feeding times.

Important toilet times for the dog are:

- first thing in the morning

- last thing at night

- immediately after each meal

- before and after walks

- after waking from a sleep

- after a play session.

To support the child's learning, you can buy dog toilet themed board and similar games. A popular one is called 'Doggie Doo'. If you Google the name, you will find it and other such games. 'Doggie Doo' is a very basic family game and lots of fun; it helps reinforce the issues around toileting, particularly bowel motions. This game could really help alleviate anxieties the child has around the defecation process, an area that children with autism have severe problems with. There are free dog toilet games online, from popular dog charity sites, and dog PC games that cover the subject.[42]

When accidents occur inside the home

Do not punish the dog in any way if it has an accident. You will traumatise the dog and just be wasting your own time and energy.

Do not use ammonia-based cleaning products as urine contains ammonia and this will attract the dog to continue using the same spot. Instead, use diluted vinegar and water or bicarbonate of soda and water to remove the smell. Review whether you are providing sufficient opportunities for your dog to relieve itself.

Finally, remember that, for toilet purposes and its emotional well-being, a dog must not be left alone for more than four hours at a time.

Exercising the dog

Exercising your dog is a very important part of the daily routine, together with a balanced diet, for maintaining good health and weight management. It is also a great way to have your child interact and bond with the dog. Daily walks are a good opportunity for the entire family to get out and enjoy the well-being benefits of the outdoors. Creating a twice-daily walk routine for the dog is great for motivating your child to access the benefits of the outdoors and increase their social skills by doing so.

As with feeding time, you can alternate walk times with siblings, but ensure your child remains the 'master' of the dog. I used to walk Henry with Dale after evening dinner, as it gave Dale something to focus on and helped him relax and prepare for settling down for the night. There was the added benefit of meeting other dog walkers and the interaction that would bring for Dale, because he had Henry with him and Dale thought he was in charge.

If you can access an enclosed area or safe park, you can let your dog have free time off the lead to play fetch or you can throw a ball for the dog with the child. Remember, your dog is a facilitator for your child at all times when they are together, so use walks and off-lead time to bathe your child in all the language involved and everything that is going on around them while you walk. My evening walks with Dale and Henry would be around a mile, but it could take ages (sometimes an hour or two) to walk because I used every opportunity en route to teach Dale what was within his environment and why. A good example was when Dale attended an autism-specific unit 20 miles from our home for his schooling. On our evening walks with Henry we would pass the local school. I would always remind Dale that this was where the local children went to school and that one day he could maybe go to the school like the other children.

If you stop to think about all that you meet and see while walking outdoors, there is a wealth of educational opportunities to talk about with your child while you are with your dog. When I could, I would involve Henry in the teaching, saying things like 'Dale, one day Henry and me will collect you from this school, and you can walk Henry home'. Because of what Henry taught Dale, he did walk Henry home from his local school.

Dale also liked it when people stopped to admire and pat Henry. This interaction was the catalyst for a lot of engaging with strangers as well as improving Dale's language.

On walks, although I would toilet Henry in the garden beforehand, there would be occasions when I would need to pick up a deposit. From the first time this happened, I would pick up the poo but Dale would put the bag in the bin. Bear in mind that, if your child has really bonded with the dog and believes the dog belongs to him or her, he or she will be very motivated by all that is involved with the dog. Using the dog as a facilitator, consider how attending to the dog's needs can have a positive impact on your child's future independence. While it may take years for a disabled child to master the skill of poop scooping, it is better they are involved with all the needs of the dog, in any way they can be, big or small, as this will increase the child's own independence in the long term.

During these evening walks, apart from pointing out things to Dale, I had mapped out the route for Dale and Henry in every detail. We would stop at every kerb, wait…no cars…we go! Dale very quickly would be the one directing Henry at every kerb. On every walk, I taught Dale why we stopped at a certain lamppost to cross the road (because it was the safest place to view traffic, etc.). Because the walks were done in a slow-paced, fun and relaxed way via Henry, Dale was confidently walking Henry on the same routes independently by the time he was 10 years old.

Dale would do things for his dog that he didn't do before Henry's arrival. I thought Dale would never gain the skill of putting rubbish in the bin but, with the necessary task of putting Henry's poo bag in the bin, Dale achieved the domestic skill immediately thereafter. Another example of this (which demonstrates the usefulness of the transitional kit) was when Henry got wet on walks. Dale learned to dry his dog with the towel and hang it up afterwards, which taught him to hang up his own coat.

As well as using the dog as a facilitator to teach Dale all Henry could, Dale's partnership with his dog very quickly became a real friendship. Dale would treat Henry as a human counterpart – with the advantage that Henry didn't come with all the social baggage and pressure a person would.

This is why using the dog as a facilitator is such a powerful educational tool for your child. How you use the tool, though, is critical to success.

Another useful aspect of visiting the park with your dog and child, if you can let the dog off the lead, is showing your child that the dog likes and needs to play and interact with other dogs. This is an opportunity to show your child that, like their dog, he or she could have fun, play and interact with others.

Finally, exercise is a great reward for your dog and an excellent stress reliever – and a tired dog is a good dog!

Playtime

Just as children need to play in order to develop and to maintain their well-being, so do dogs!

Keep play activities for your garden and outdoors, as it is safer and lets the dog and child burn off energy, and express themselves to the fullest, but under adult supervision. This will reinforce the message that play is outside; inside the home is where the dog can relax quietly with a safe dog toy or bone while the family watches TV or takes part in other activities.

Toys are an essential part of your dog's life. It is natural for a young dog to want to mouth and bite, so they need suitable toys and chews to play with. Soft toys are needed as well as hard ones; they should be checked regularly to make sure they have not perished too much. That's why I really like the Kong Wild Knots Teddy, because it serves as a soft cuddly, but has a robust rope-knotted skeleton. Dale liked that his dog loved cuddly toys and, as Dale grew out of some of his own cuddly toys, he didn't think twice about donating them to Henry, as long as they weren't too big. For Dale, this was a nice empathetic way of recycling his soft toys, teaching him that as he grew older things would change and sometimes you need to move childhood things on.

There is an abundance of dog toys available on the market, but the safest and most enjoyable I have found for my dogs is the Kong; this is why I feature it in the transitional kit. As mentioned before, a Kong is hard-wearing and good to give your dog when it is left unsupervised or alone. As well as food-filled Kongs from the freezer, you can rub Marmite or similar inside the Kong to give your dog something to focus its attention on rather than getting into mischief or missing you. Whatever you provide for your dog, do not give it an old household item, like a shoe or slipper, as a toy. Dogs, like a child with autism, will take ownership of these items literally and, thereafter, all shoes and slippers in the home will be sought as a toy to chew.

Never give your dog real bones no matter how hard you think they are. Larger-breed dogs like Retrievers and Labradors have very strong teeth and jaws and there is a real risk they can splinter off fragments of bone that could get stuck in a dog's gullet. Many a dog has been killed by this or needed emergency surgery for obstruction in the dog's small or large gut. Instead, look at the Nylabone range of bones and chews, which are virtually indestructible (although they do perish and need to be replaced). Nylabones are made from really hard nylon, which dogs like to chew on, and are great for cleaning the dog's teeth as they chew. Treat balls can be filled with treats for the dog to roll around the floor – with the reward of a treat being dislodged.

Beware of over-feeding your dog; decrease the daily food allowance if Kongs are given frequently.

Health

How do you know if your dog isn't well?
Sometimes, your dog will not feel well – but how can you pick up when this is occurring? The two most common signs that something is wrong are:

- loss of appetite

- loss of energy.

Your dog will usually devour its food but, if something is wrong, he may simply give the food bowl a sniff and walk away. Also, you will note when your dog isn't excited about the prospect of a walk; if he doesn't want to get up and see you off, as you indicate you're going out, then something is not right.

If you have done all you can to meet your dog's welfare needs and taken the necessary preventative measures to maintain its health, and either of these two scenarios occur, you have to consult your vet.

Visiting the vet

A visit to the vet can be a traumatic situation for your dog, as it may associate the visit with a previous bad experience. There will be lots of distractions, scents and other animals, so you must try to make the visit as positive and relaxed as possible. Controlling your dog's excitement or behaviour may be a challenge, so you need to gain some control and maintain obedience; try getting it sitting at the door before you go and then lying down while you are waiting to see the vet. Don't allow your dog to visit other animals, unless given permission to do so, as this may upset other animals, even more so because they are sick or injured.

Most vets will want to inspect your dog on the examination table. While your dog is on the table, make sure it is as comfortable as possible and ensure it doesn't fall off or slip. Reassure and reward your dog with treats, if allowed, when they are behaving well on the table and during the examination. While your dog is being examined by the vet, you may need to help as much as the vet asks you to, because your dog will trust you and feel calmer with you there.

Your dog may have to be held tightly so the vet can do a thorough health check. Talk to and praise your dog throughout and continue to use treats if this helps keep your dog calm and coping with the vet's check-up.

Vaccinations

Your vet is the best person to advise you on which vaccinations your dog needs and when. To this day, there are still dangerous diseases that affect dogs in the UK and rabies can still be transmitted to humans. Vaccination, if kept up to date with boosters, can protect your dog for life!

Puppies should be vaccinated at around six to eight weeks old, with a second vaccination given a few weeks later to complete the primary course. Just as with some human vaccinations, immunity can decrease or stop responding; this is why your dog needs to attend the vet annually for a check-up and vaccination boosters.

Your vet will also advise and provide your dog with the necessary medications against common conditions like distemper, hepatitis, parvovirus and parainfluenza. You will also need to give your dog preventative medications for the control of common intestinal parasites like roundworms and tapeworms.

Fleas

Fleas alone can contribute to causing your dog endless hours of torment, including bites, itching and hotspots. Fleas are also notorious for being carriers of tapeworms. The best way to avoid having to treat your dog's hotspots and rashes with various disinfectants and creams, or having to constantly medicate your dog to rid them of tapeworms, is to eliminate the fleas that cause the problem in the first place. Various sprays, powders and monthly oral preventatives are available from pet stores, but are best sought from your vet. Your vet is the best person to advise you on which treatment will be most effective for the environment you live in.

Ticks

Ticks are more common in rural areas, especially if you like camping. They embed their heads into your dog's skin to access the dog's blood supply. Once the tick becomes engorged with blood they look like a little brown pimple on your dog's skin.

Ticks can cause serious diseases by transmitting bacteria and microbes when they come into contact with an animal or human. It is best to protect your dog from tick bites by using a year-round flea and tick treatment. Ticks are common in woodland, grassy and heath areas, and can also be found in your garden if you live in an area with wildlife. Ticks are common where there are lots of deer or sheep; they are more prevalent in spring and autumn, but remain active throughout the year. Ticks don't fly or jump; they climb or drop onto your dog's coat when it has contact with an area, such as long grass, that the ticks are living in.

Always check your dog and yourself for ticks following a walk and remove them immediately (see 'How to remove a tick safely from your dog', below, for instructions). Ticks look like very small spiders; they are egg-shaped, are blood suckers with eight legs, and can vary in size from 1mm to 1cm. Their bodies become larger and darker as they fill with their host's blood.

FIVE SIGNS YOUR DOG HAS TICKS

- *You find a tick in your home.* You may come across a tick on your bedding, carpets or floor; you or your dog would have brought this into your home. Be vigilant and don't assume this is a one-off – do a closer examination of your dog.

- *Your dog has a fever.* Following a tick bite, your dog may develop a mild or high-grade fever; it may pass in 24 hours or it could last for days or even weeks. Signs of fever include generalised weakness, loss of appetite, shivering or unusual panting. Fevers can be a sign of other sicknesses and symptoms, but think 'tick contamination' and check your dog for these parasites.

- *Unexplained scabs.* An embedded tick may cause your dog to excessively nip, lick or bite at the bite site. If this behaviour occurs and you find scabs on the area, conduct a closer examination.

- *Excessive head shaking.* If your dog constantly shakes its head, this could indicate that a tick has burrowed into the canal of the ear. Ticks like to hide in warm, damp places and will crawl from the ground to areas like the dog's ears, groin or under the front legs. If the head-shaking behaviour persists, then get a torch to look carefully into your dog's ears and conduct a full examination.

- *You feel a small bump.* If you feel a bump when petting your dog, this is a real sign of a potential tick bite. Immediately part your dog's fur and get a closer look. Brushing your dog will also remove them.

How to remove a tick safely from your dog

As ticks carry diseases, the sooner they are removed, the better the outcome and the less chance there is of the dog contracting a tick-related disease. Removing them is a delicate and tricky process! You need to be careful not to squeeze the tick's body or allow its head to get stuck inside your dog. If you squeeze the tick there is an increased risk of expelling blood back into the dog, which will increase the risk of infection.

Ticks should always be treated and killed first with an insecticide like Frontline or similar. After 30 minutes, the tick can be safely removed using tweezers or tick-removal devices. Remember the insecticide may only stun or paralyse the tick, so it must be fully removed. Remove them in a twisting action to ensure that all of the tick, particularly the head, is removed. Pinching the skin and popping it like a pimple is recommended. After you have removed the tick, give the bite area a good wash.

Why you should protect your dog from ticks

Ticks are well known for passing infections from one animal to another. They feed by biting an animal and feasting until they are gorged on the host's blood. This could take several days and, when they have had enough, they simply drop off. More importantly, ticks are capable of transmitting diseases such as Lyme disease and Babesiosis.

Always check your dog's body for ticks when you return home from a walk. If you live in an area where ticks are prevalent, it is better to prevent tick infestation by using a tick treatment that either repels ticks or kills them if they attach. Spot-on treatments, tablets and collars can be used. Read the instructions carefully as some treatments are specifically for dog use only and could be dangerous for cats and even kill them.

WHAT IS LYME DISEASE?

Lyme disease is a bacterial infection that can have a serious effect on your dog. The infected dog becomes quite depressed-looking, with associated loss of appetite. They may develop a fever, lameness with swollen and painful joints, and swollen nodes. This is a case for an urgent visit to your vet, so that they can start treatment with suitable antibiotics.

People can catch Lyme disease from ticks just as dogs can. Symptoms of Lyme disease include a circular rash, muscle and joint pain, and generalised fatigue. If left untreated, the disease can develop into other conditions such as viral-like meningitis, facial palsy, arthritis and nerve damage. Lyme disease can be treated with antibiotics if caught early. Remember to tell your doctor you have been bitten by a tick. Be vigilant abroad, as ticks in Europe can transmit a number of serious diseases.

WHAT IS BABESIOSIS?

Although extremely rare in the UK, the tick that can cause this serious disease has been found in southern England and on the continent. The first case in which a dog was infected with and treated for Babesiosis in the UK was reported in March 2016.[43] Babesiosis is spread by the bacterium Babesia, which can be spread by ticks. The incubation period is two weeks, but some pets are not diagnosed with the disease for months or even years after transmission.

If your dog is suffering from Babesiosis, it will become quite depressed-looking, with pale gums, a swollen abdomen and associated fever. The dog will lose its appetite and its skin may become a yellowish colour. If any of these symptoms occur after walking your dog in a high-risk tick-contact area, contact your vet immediately and alert them to possible tick infestation in your dog. Sadly, a dog has died after contracting the disease in Harlow, Essex.[44] The best way to avoid a tick-borne disease is to avoid being bitten in the first place.[45]

Intestinal parasites

The first step to knowing whether your dog has an intestinal infestation is to know the difference in appearance between a normal stool and one that is not. When cleaning up after your dog, if you notice the stool is not as solid as usual, or it is covered with mucus or streaked with blood, you may need to take a fresh sample to the vet to have it examined under a microscope for parasites. The following will be some of the 'critters' your vet will be looking for.

ROUNDWORMS

Adult roundworms live in the dog's intestine and may grow seven inches long. The female roundworm can produce up to 200,000 eggs per day. These eggs can live for months or years in the soil, and can be transmitted orally to your dog due to it stepping on an infested area and then licking its paws. The worms can appear in the dog's stool as wiggling white worms.

WHIPWORMS

These usually grow to about two to three inches long and the adults attach themselves to the walls of the dog's large intestine. Infestations are usually small, with the female laying a small number of eggs, which makes detection more difficult. The dog becomes infected by coming into contact with the eggs in heavily soiled areas. Signs of whipworm infection are loss of weight and diarrhoea.

HOOKWORMS

These are quarter- to half-inch worms that attach themselves to the small intestine of mostly puppies and young dogs. A general area can be infected by dogs passing eggs through their faeces. Stools tend to be bloody or wine-coloured diarrhoea. Anaemia, weight loss and progressive weakness are signs of infestations in older dogs.

Tapeworms

The primary cause of tapeworm in dogs is fleas. The flea will harbour the immature tapeworm in its intestine and, when the dog chews an infested area on their skin and swallows the flea, the tapeworm larvae will attach itself to the small intestine of the dog and grow to its adult size, which can be one inch to several feet long. At the adult stage, the tapeworm will release egg packets, which are visible as quarter-inch rice-like segments around the dog's anus or on the dog's stools.

What to do if you suspect your dog has intestinal parasites

With all parasitic infestations, the most important point to remember is not to panic! Your dog doesn't have an alien living inside it! Simply collect a sample in a plastic bag and take it to your vet for identification so that you know what type of worm you're dealing with. In most cases, the problem will be simple and painless to cure. You may find it helpful to take a photograph of the infested stool, perhaps on your mobile phone: your vet may be able to identify the type of worm if it is obvious and visible.

Lungworms

Another parasite you need to be aware of is lungworm, which, if undetected, can be life-threatening for your dog. While the garden is a great happy environment for your dog, there are many risks for the dog's health lurking within it. Lungworm, known as *Angiostrongylus vasorum*, can be present in slugs and snails and be carried in frogs and foxes if they are prone to being in your garden. If your dog eats any of these or comes into contact with the parasite then you can have a very ill dog on your hands. Lungworm cases are now on the increase and becoming more widespread in many parts of the UK. The dog becomes infected by eating the infective larvae from the hosts or it can be spread by larvae being present in the slimy trail of exudate that snails leave behind. Infected larvae can be found in puddles or the dog's outdoor drinking bowls, or on the dog's garden toys.

The dog is infected with adult worms in the heart and pulmonary arteries, where they lay eggs which hatch into larvae that pass into the airways of the dog's lungs. Subsequently, the larvae are then coughed up and swallowed and are then passed via the dog's stools. Slugs and snails then swallow the larvae and that increases the risk of transferring the parasites to other dogs.

THE SYMPTOMS OF LUNGWORM INFESTATION

It is important to remember that the symptoms of lungworm infestation can mimic other health conditions in the dog.

Breathing problems and coughing, or the dog tiring more readily, can be due to the dog's lung capacity being compromised with the worms. Other symptoms may include poor blood clotting (where minor wounds bleed excessively), unexplained nosebleeds and bleeding into the eyes and gums. The dog would show signs of anaemia with paleness noted around the eyes and gums.

There could be behavioural changes noticeable in the dog, such as seizures, spinal pain, weight loss and loss of appetite with diarrhoea and vomiting. Any breed at any age can become infected; with early diagnosis and treatment, though, the dog can make a full recovery.

If lungworm is suspected, your vet can prescribe a suitable treatment that can encompass the eradication of many other parasite infestations at the same time.

Canine heartworms

Since the year 2000, with the introduction of the Government's Pet Travel Scheme, pet owners of dogs and cats can take them to EU countries, and some specified non-EU countries, and return without the need to put their pets into quarantine. The pet must be microchipped, and it is compulsory that the dog is vaccinated against rabies. When this has been done, your pet can be issued with a Pet Passport. Animals can travel from 21 days after their rabies vaccination. Before you travel with your dog, it must also have veterinary treatment for tapeworm. There are other potential treatments required depending on where you are travelling with your dog.[46]

If you take your dog abroad to a country that has mosquitoes, be aware they can carry the risk of infecting your dog with heartworm. When an infested mosquito feeds on a healthy dog, it deposits infected larvae onto the dog's skin which then burrows into the dog. Over the next three to four months, the larvae will develop and eventually penetrate a vein which will enable the larvae to lodge themselves into the right side of the dog's heart. In the heart, the life-cycle is completed; here they can grow into 250 mature adult worms around four to 12 inches long. If left untreated, the dog experiences congestive heart failure which is life-threatening.

Treatment depends on the geographical area in which the dog was infected. Before you can treat the dog, a blood sample must be obtained to determine if the larvae are in the bloodstream. Your vet can treat the dog with a suitable wormer.

Vomiting
Do not give your dog food or water if it is vomiting. You may find your dog vomits after eating grass or they may cough up phlegm; both of these symptoms can be fairly typical for most dogs. Monitor and don't become alarmed.

Poisoning
Most signs of poisoning will occur quickly or present over a few days. If you think your dog has come into contact with a poisonous substance then take it to the vet immediately.

Chocolate poisoning
Many people feed their dogs chocolate without realising the potentially harmful effects it can have on dogs. Chocolate contains the

drugs theobromine and caffeine (of the drug class methylxanthines); these are toxic to all pets, especially dogs. Only a small amount of chocolate (unsweetened baking chocolate or dark chocolate being the most dangerous) needs to be eaten by the dog for the poison to take effect (approximately half an ounce per pound of body weight).

Signs of chocolate poisoning include vomiting, hyperactivity, excessive urinating, rapid breathing and general weakness. Seizures can occur. While rare, death can occur, usually due to the adverse action of methylxanthines on the heart.

Care should be taken at all times to prevent your dog having access to chocolate, especially during Easter and Christmas. Most dogs will scavenge or help themselves to any chocolate left lying around. So, keep all chocolate out of the reach of your dog. That includes chocolate decorations on the Christmas tree – I would avoid using these, as our first dog Henry managed to get access to mine once, leaving the empty foils hanging on the tree as evidence. Advent calendars with chocolates in them are another danger. I'm embarrassed to have lost count of the number of Amy's chocolate advent calendars our dog Thomas has managed to consume over the years, as his 'high jump' improved to access the calendars.

Don't be fooled into thinking that wrapped chocolate presents, under the tree or hidden in cupboards, are safe. Again Thomas has conquered them all – even a wrapped box of Ferrero Rocher in my wardrobe was consumed by Thomas, with just the plastic splinters of the box and a few gold foils left on the floor as evidence. Such are the lengths a dog will go to for chocolate.

Not surprisingly, dogs like chocolate as much as we do. Dogs can sniff out chocolate 300,000 times better than we can, such is the extraordinary power of their noses.

If your dog does have a helping of chocolate, it would be advisable for you to estimate the amount of chocolate eaten and telephone your vet who should be able to determine if the dose was sufficient to cause any problems.

Common canine poisons in the house and garden

From the point-of-view of looking after your dog, a 'poison' is any substance that, if your dog comes into contact with it, will have an unwanted damaging effect on your dog's health. I advocate that you treat your dog in your home and garden as you would a mischievous curious toddler – one that has no sense of danger, but has a great urge to explore many things with their hands/paws and mouth.

The potential poisons that could harm your dog are not dangerous chemicals like cyanide, but commonplace things in the home and garden, such as plant leaves that can cause skin irritation or simply smoke from a cigarette. When researching this subject, I was shocked to learn of the vast range of everyday things in our homes, obvious and not so obvious, that could have a serious harmful effect on a dog. Dogs can be exposed to the dangerous effects of poisons through skin contact, substances getting into the dog's eye, inhalation and through envenomation (via a bite or sting). Sadly, the most common occurrences of poisoning involve dogs eating something that's poisonous to them.

The most crucial advice of all is…if you suspect your dog has come into contact with poison, or been poisoned, see your vet immediately – time is of the essence. Do not try to make your dog sick, as this could do more harm than good.

If you can, tell your vet what the source of the poison may be. Include the product name and the list of ingredients that may be involved. If possible, take the poison source with you to the vet and tell the vet:

- how much of the poison the dog has been exposed to

- when your dog was in contact with the poison

- how your dog being unwell has manifested and what their symptoms are.

If you are in any doubt, do not wait for your dog to become affected or unwell before you seek advice. Time can save your dog from damage or even death! Remember to protect yourself from the risk of contamination too.

Risks of poisons in the kitchen

You may be surprised to learn about the range of human food that is dangerous to your dog, so be careful if you like to give your dog a treat. We now know the risk of poison to our dogs from chocolate, so only give the recommended few dog treats and use canine-friendly chocolate.

ONIONS (ALLIUM SPECIES)

The onion family (onions themselves, garlic, leeks, shallots and chives) contain a substance which can damage red blood cells in dogs, causing life-threatening anaemia. Signs can take a few days to manifest; they include stomach problems, lethargy and the dog becoming sleepy, with dull, weak or rapid breathing. Poisoned dogs may also have discoloured urine. Therefore, ensure your dogs don't eat cooked foods that contain these vegetables (e.g. onion gravy, onion bhaji, etc.).

RAISINS (FRUITS OF THE *VITIS VINIFERA*)

Grapes, raisons, currants and sultanas are all toxic to dogs – particularly the dried versions. It is not known why, nor how much is poisonous to dogs. Some dogs can eat large amounts and not be affected, while others have ingested a small amount and been very unwell, with serious stomach problems or kidney failure, up to three days following contamination.

Kidney failure could be indicated by decreased urination, or the dog may show as being unwell, with increased thirst. Prompt treatment by your vet is necessary.

Bear in mind the wide range of foods that contain this type of fruit, such as hot cross buns, Christmas cake and pudding, fruit cake, mince pies and stollen, etc.

XYLITOL

Some sugar-free sweets and gums, like chewing gum and nicotine replacement gums, some medicines and some brands of peanut butter contain an artificial sweetener called Xylitol, which can be poisonous to dogs. It can cause an unnecessary drop in the dog's blood sugar levels, to dangerous life-threatening levels. Larger amounts can lead to liver failure. Again, your dog would appear weak and tired; he or she may collapse and develop seizures.

Other poisonous things in the kitchen include:

- alcohol
- blue cheese
- raw bread dough
- large amounts of sugar and sweets
- macadamia nuts
- mouldy foods.

(Cooked bones are not poisonous but can splinter, causing mechanical damage and gut obstruction.)

Therefore, just as you would poison-proof your home to protect a child, you need to do the same for your dog!

In your cupboards

Cleaning products are undoubtedly an unpleasant taste to dogs, but the brightly coloured packaging and interestingly shaped bottles give the impression they are toys for the dog to play with, just as a child would.

All of these items should be locked away, just as you would do to protect a child.

Chlorine-based bleaches

Dogs can come into contact with these by chewing the containers or drinking from recently cleaned toilets. Although diluted with the toilet water, bleach can still cause excess salivation and stomach problems. If the dog swallows bleach, it can cause corrosive injury to the mouth or gut. Another danger is damage to the eyes. Bleach should never be mixed with other cleaning products.

Laundry detergents and similar products

Many of these products contain chemicals that can cause salivation and stomach problems if licked or drunk. If your dog vomits following exposure to these products it will look frothy or foamy. This will increase the risk of aspiration into the lungs leading to breathing difficulties.

Liquid-form capsules or tablets are highly concentrated and are very attractive to children and dogs. These can cause extreme stomach upsets that can lead to dehydration if untreated. They can damage the dog's eyes through direct contact.

Oven, drain and other caustic and corrosive cleaners

These substances can cause tissue damage and injury to the eyes, skin and surrounding mouth area. They can cause salivation and stomach problems, ulceration, chemical burns and difficulty breathing or swallowing.

Other items to be mindful of the damaging effects of include:

- dishwasher tablets
- dishwasher salt
- kettle descalers
- metal polishers.

In addition to all the other preventative measures (such as locking kitchen cupboards), protect your dog by making sure the toilet seat is always down and the bathroom door closed.

The medicine cupboard

Dogs, like children, are more likely to access drugs if they are left lying about the home rather than being safely locked in the cupboard. Do not leave tablets lying about while you retrieve a drink as dogs can grab them in an instant.

Most importantly, remember that dogs are not like humans – their metabolisms and digestive systems are different to ours. Therefore, your dog should never be treated with human medications – only those specifically prescribed by a vet.

Ibuprofen and other non-steroidal anti-inflammatory drugs (NSAIDs)

NSAIDs are used to manage inflammation and pain in humans and dogs, but NSAIDs for humans, such as ibuprofen, diclofenac and naproxen, are different to the ones given to dogs and can make them unwell. They can interfere with the dog's gut, causing stomach upset, with ulcers developing, leading to blood in their stools and vomiting. Kidney disease can occur within days, preceded by inappropriate urination and increased thirst. Some NSAIDs can cause fits in dogs.

Oral contraceptives

Unfortunately, these are the most common tablets consumed by dogs; fortunately, though, they are of low toxicity, and large amounts consumed are unlikely to cause any harm other than mild stomach upset. Some oral contraceptives may temporarily disrupt the oestrus levels in bitches.

Paracetamol

This widely used analgesia can cause vomiting, brown gums, increased heart rate, changes in breathing, swelling to face and paws, and delayed liver failure that may not be present for several days. These symptoms are typical of an anaphylaxis reaction and the dog must be taken to the vet immediately to receive adrenaline. Paracetamol is found in many over-the-counter medicines, in combination with other drugs (especially caffeine).

PSORIASIS CREAMS

These often contain vitamin D derivatives which are extremely toxic to dogs. The dog can be contaminated by licking off cream recently applied to humans, as well as by licking or chewing the tube of cream. These drugs enhance the re-absorption of calcium from the bone, leading to increasing the absorption of calcium from the gut. This causes a condition known as hypercalcaemia which is an excess of calcium in the blood.

Signs of the poisoning could occur six hours afterwards (but could be delayed) and include weakness, profuse vomiting and diarrhoea, with excessive thirst. As calcium levels rise, this can cause muscle spasms, seizures, heart problems and kidney failure, and cause the lungs and gut to be calcified!

Other common items found in your medicine cupboard that can harm your dog include:

- anti-depressants

- aspirin

- blood pressure medications

- diabetes medicines

- heart medicines

- sleeping aids.

Again, keep these locked up and be aware that many people carry medicines around in their bags – when at home, don't forget to keep bags, etc. out of reach from your ever-inquisitive dog.

In your garden

The garden may seem like a pleasant and safe place for your dog to play in, but it is important to be aware of the hazards that can exist there.

Note: Your dog should only be in your garden with supervision. If you are in the house, then your dog should be with you.

There are numerous plants to be found in the garden that are harmful to your dog. Some are very poisonous, while others can cause mild tummy upsets. Plants also vary in their attractiveness to dogs – a bush can sit in your garden for years without being disturbed, but a sudden fallen acorn or conker could cause immediate attraction. Deciding what to keep in your garden will depend on the toxicity of the plant and how curious your dog is.

FUNGI (WILD MUSHROOMS AND TOADSTOOLS)

There are literally thousands of types of fungi in the UK. They vary dramatically in shape, size, colour and how toxic they are. Many are easily distinguishable, but it is very hard to identify most wild mushrooms. Some are safely edible while others are very dangerous – and it is virtually impossible to know which is which.

Signs of poisoning to the dog can vary a lot, depending on what type of fungi is ingested by the dog. Signs may include an upset stomach, blood in the stools or vomit, neurological effects such as hallucinations or seizures, and kidney or liver failure. The type of fungi eaten will determine the onset of the effects, whether sudden, 10 minutes after ingestion or days and even weeks later.

If your dog does eat fungi, take it to the vet immediately with a sample of the mushroom wrapped in paper or a paper bag – not plastic! Take a note of the area where the fungi was found. Was it in a grassy or tree stump position, for instance? This may help the vet to identify the origin of the fungi that has made your dog ill.

Spring bulbs

Incidents of poisoning from spring bulbs are more likely to occur in autumn when they are planted or in spring when they are due to flower. The most common culprits are daffodils; these cause vomiting, stomach upset and excess salivation. Other symptoms include the dog becoming very sleepy, wobbly on their legs or collapsing. Symptoms can become more serious with seizures and changes to heart rate, body temperature and blood pressure. Dogs can become ill if they eat daffodils or drink water from a daffodil vase.

Tulips

Toxins in tulips can cause irritation to the mouth and gastrointestinal tract, resulting in drooling, vomiting and diarrhoea. Serious cases are rare, but effects can include heart and breathing problems.

Spring crocus

These are low toxicity but may cause a mild stomach upset if eaten. Don't confuse these with autumn crocus which flower in autumn and can cause serious stomach upset, kidney and liver problems, and bone marrow depression.

Other poisonous plants to be aware of include:

- apricots

- asparagus fern

- various berries, including lantana berries

- poinsettia

- privet

- wisteria

- castor oil plant

- buttercup

- wandering jew

- chrysanthemum

- ivy

- sago palm

- paspalum

- peaches

- rhubarb leaves

- nutmeg

- nerines

- jonquils

- spider lilies.

General symptoms of poisoning include vomiting, lethargy and diarrhoea and, in some cases, there will be evidence of contact allergy.

TOADS

Toads secrete venom from skin glands that can be poisonous to dogs that bite them. They are more common in warmer months and can be found by your dog after rain or at dawn or dusk. The venom can cause irritation in the mouth leading to pain, salivation and pawing at the mouth. In severe cases, it can lead to behavioural changes in the dog such as wobbly legs with associated disorientation and anxiety, increased breathing and heart rate changes, and seizures.

Toads commonly eat slugs and snails and could therefore be a source of lungworm for the dog.

Other items in your garden that can be a source of harm for your dog are:

- acorns

- compost or mouldy foods left out to feed birds

- conkers

- foxgloves

- large amounts of apple seeds

- pesticides

- stones from the prunus species (plums, cherries, etc.)

- yew.

In your garden shed

Substances that could be harmful to dogs and children are usually stored in the garden shed or garage. Nevertheless, many dogs, being scavengers and playful explorers of areas open to them, are at high risk of poisoning from the contents in these places. We use many chemicals in our garden without realising their toxicity to our pets and to the environment they are used in.

Garden chemicals are all too often the cause of major illness or death in dogs.

Please read the instructions carefully and be aware of the dangers and hazards involved with a particular chemical. Where possible, try to use an organic or non-toxic alternative. Where this is not possible, restrict your dog from the area that's affected or has been treated.

ANTIFREEZE

Care should be taken with all types of this substance, but particular caution is needed with those that contain the chemical ethylene glycol. As the word 'glycol' implies, this chemical is sweet to taste and tempting to dogs, but it can be fatal if ingested!

Therefore, antifreeze must be stored in secure containers away from animals and children. When using antifreeze, keep your dog well away as it may mop up any spillages.

Effects of poisoning may appear as vomiting, diarrhoea and lethargy and the dog may behave as if it is drunk! If intervention following exposure doesn't occur, the dog may appear to have recovered but there is the risk of kidney failure to follow. Therefore, prompt treatment by a vet is necessary immediately following poisoning.

Herbicides (plant-killing chemicals)

The type and toxicity of chemicals used to kill plants vary. Common cases of poisoning in dogs occur when they have brushed up against, chewed or licked recently treated plants, or when dogs have accessed the chemical containers. Symptoms of poisoning vary dramatically depending on the type of chemical ingested. Again, be aware of signs of vomiting, dehydration, blood in the vomit or stools, ulcers in the mouth, breathing difficulties, and heart, kidney and liver failure.

Rodenticides (rat or mouse killers)

These substances are designed to be appealing to mice and rats and are unfortunately attractive to dogs as well. This type of poisoning is the most common cause of dog owners seeking veterinary care in cases of poisoning. Rodenticides vary in type and many can do real harm to your dog.

The most commonly encountered rodenticides are designed to be consumed by the rodents over a period of time. These will interfere with the dog's blood-clotting mechanism and can cause episodes of bleeding. The dog's haemorrhaging may not always be external; poisoned dogs can show signs of lethargy, weakness, lameness or bruising. Other substances in this family of chemicals can cause vomiting, excitement, changes in body temperature, seizures and also gastric obstruction.

SLUG BAIT

Slug bait pellets are very appealing to dogs as they look similar to dog treats. Again, they vary in types and toxicity. They contain a substance called metaldehyde that is extremely toxic to dogs. Ingestion of these causes tremors, twitching and seizures, which can last for a few days. The risk of poisoning is increased during warm and wet weather, when slugs are common, and gardeners are most likely to use this pesticide.

Other items stored in garden sheds and garages that are harmful to dogs include:

- creosote

- fertilisers

- fuels

- gloss paints

- insecticides

- water-proofing sprays

- white spirit.

General poisons

BATTERIES

If a battery is chewed or punctured by your dog it can cause chemical burns or, in rare and extreme cases, heavy metal poisoning. If they are swallowed whole, they are less likely to leak their contents but the size of the battery itself can cause serious gut obstruction, which will require surgical intervention.

If you suspect your dog may have swallowed a toy or object, look for signs of obstruction: persistent vomiting, lethargy, being off their food, not able to open their bowels or finding it difficult to defecate.

Small batteries lodged in the throat or gut can produce an electric current which can damage the surrounding tissue.

CARBON MONOXIDE

This is a very poisonous gas that has no colour, taste or smell and can be produced from gas fires, faulty boilers or heaters that are used in poorly ventilated areas. If inhaled in enough quantity, it can cause a range of non-specific clinical signs with the dog being sleepy, vomiting or showing changes in its behaviour, breathing and heart rate as well. Carbon monoxide is an extremely poisonous gas to humans as well as dogs and other pets. Poisoning from this gas is best prevented by fitting a carbon monoxide detector in homes where gas appliances are used.

POTPOURRI

This is made up of various dried plants and flowers. If your dog ingests these it will, at the very least, have vomiting and diarrhoea. The toxicity of the potpourri depends on the plants and flowers it contains. Identifying the content's origins, though, is difficult as they are usually artificially coloured before they are dried. Potpourri has hard items, like cones or bark, which can cause throat or gut obstruction if swallowed. These can become dangerous, causing breathing difficulties or intestinal obstruction requiring surgical intervention.

CIGARETTES AND SIMILAR NICOTINE-CONTAINING PRODUCTS

If ingested, these products can all cause vomiting, increased salivation and tremors, and may interfere with the dog's heart rate, blood pressure and breathing. Swallowed nicotine patches may cause prolonged effects due to the slow release nature of the product. Swallowed e-cigarette refill bottles or vials may cause sudden toxicity after lying in the gut for a while.

Some nicotine gums may contain Xylitol (the artificial sweetener mentioned previously), which is very toxic to dogs. It can trigger a quick and serious drop in the dog's blood sugar levels. In some cases it can cause liver failure.

Poisons out and about

ADDERS

Adders are the UK's only native poisonous snake and can be found in a wide range of different habitats. Adders hibernate in winter and emerge in spring, when the risk of a bite is at its peak. These snakes love to bask in the sun, and curious dogs that come across them are often bitten around the face, muzzle and front paws.

Indications that your dog has been bitten occur rapidly; you might see small puncture wounds, swelling, bruising, pain, lameness, salivation, vomiting, increased temperature, bleeding and changes to the dog's heartbeat, blood pressure and breathing.

You should take your dog to the vet immediately and leave the bite itself alone.

Do not apply a tourniquet and don't attempt to suck out the poison, as this will make matters worse! If you come across an adder in your garden or while out for a walk with your dog, it is better to avoid them; adders are protected and it is illegal to harm or kill them.

BLUE GREEN ALGAE

This type of algae is found in many types of water body across the UK – in ponds, streams, lakes and estuaries. These algae produce toxins which can be harmful to humans as well as dogs. The types of chemical secreted by the algae vary and can have a wide range of adverse clinical effects, including vomiting and diarrhoea (blood may be seen in both), lethargy, effects on the heart and blood pressure, twitching, breathing difficulties, liver and kidney impairment, and even death, soon after the actual exposure!

Obviously, dogs are exposed when they swim in such waters or drink contaminated water. Infected water may appear a different colour or you may see coloured algal blooms appearing on the surface of the water or growing close to the shore. It is difficult to know if the waters are toxic without testing them. The amount of algae present varies throughout the year, but is more common in the hot sunny weather that we get around mid-to-late summer.

Seasonal Canine Illness (SCI)

The origin of this illness is unknown, and may not derive from a poison, but it affects a small proportion of dogs that are walked in woodland between August and November. Dogs display a range of symptoms such as sickness, diarrhoea and lethargy that all manifest 72 hours after your dog has walked through woodland. SCI was first recognised in 2009 after similar cases were emerging in the Sandringham Estate and Thetford Forest in Norfolk, Sherwood Forest and Clumber Park in Nottinghamshire, and Rendlesham Forest in Suffolk.[47]

Other dangers

Fireworks and dogs

It is recognised that around 80 per cent of pets are scared of fireworks. It is normal for dogs to have fears, and many, such as mild firework worries, can be managed with pheromone diffusers like Adaptil. The infuser should be in the same room as your dog's bolt-hole from two weeks before until two weeks after firework night. If you don't address your dog's fear of fireworks, then it could progress to becoming a more serious noise phobia.

Preparation before firework night is essential so your dog can survive unscathed. Adapt the dog's bolt-hole, so it is more comforting and secure, by putting in lots of blankets for your dog to bury itself in. You can also include one of your old unwashed pieces of clothing or a woolly jumper, so your dog can smell your scent which will comfort and reassure him or her.

The objective is to reduce the amount of noise entering the bolt-hole or hide-out room from the outside; ensure windows are closed, curtains are drawn and blinds shut, so the dog doesn't see flashes, etc. and that the room is dark.

Make sure the dog's food and water bowls are near and that it has emptied its bladder well before fireworks start. Have a filled Kong from the freezer handy and make sure that your dog has special chews and toys in his or her bolt-hole as well; these will help reduce tension. It is not unusual for dogs to be uninterested in food when they are anxious, so don't get concerned if this occurs.

You can mask the noise of the fireworks by putting on rhythmic music or the radio or TV. Keep the volume at a loud but comfortable level. If your dog is used to using a bolt-hole, then it will be familiar with this on firework night. Ensure the room's door is kept open so your dog can access the rest of the home and can wander around if it desires.

If your dog is particularly scared, your vet may prescribe medication; follow the instructions for this carefully.

When the noise of firework night begins, lead your dog to their bolt-hole or safe place and encourage them to stay there. You will be tempted to try to reassure and soothe your dog, but this will reinforce the message that there is something to be scared of – and the dog may perceive your efforts as a reward for being scared. In addition, your dog may begin to believe that you are the only one that can alleviate its fears; this will cause the dog more worry if you are not about when there is a sudden noise like a police siren or a firework going off.

Ignore your dog when it is frightened and reward and give it attention when it is relaxed. Your dog may respond well, and be in a happy mood, if you play lots of active games it likes, and it sees that you are not worried. If your dog doesn't respond to playing games, then lead it to its bolt-hole or safe place instead.

Finally, many dogs can be treated using behavioural methods called desensitisation and counter-conditioning. Specially made recordings of fireworks can be used to train dogs not to react to the noises they fear, and a CD with instructions can be obtained from Sounds Scary.[48]

Heatstroke

Although the climate in the United Kingdom doesn't lend itself much to the chance of your dog suffering from heatstroke, it is better to know how to prevent your dog being at risk. Heatstroke is caused by over-exposure to heat. Try not to exercise your dog in excessively hot weather. Never leave your dog shut in a closed car on a hot day. The same applies to a dog being shut in a non-ventilated room for a long period of time. Beware of the signs of heatstroke if your dog is over-excited in hot weather.

General progressive signs of heatstroke include:

- your dog becoming restless and distressed

- excessive panting with profuse salivation

- the dog being unsteady on its feet and lacking normal coordination

- the dog may have blue mucous membranes.

A dog may finally collapse or go into a coma, or even die, as a result of heatstroke.

As heatstroke progresses, your dog will feel increasingly hot to touch. The rising body temperature of the dog can have devastating effects on its brain and, if left untreated, will lead to death.

As soon as you discover your dog is suffering from heatstroke, remove the dog from the source of heat.

Cool the animal immediately but, to prevent it going into shock, do not cool the dog down too quickly. If possible, take the dog's temperature at regular intervals, because the dog will have poor body temperature regulation.

Ways to cool the dog include:

- running cool water from a hose pipe continually over the animal

- putting the dog into a cold bath, ensuring cold water is continually added

- placing cold wet towels all over the dog and changing them frequently.

If your dog doesn't respond to cooling methods, then you should transport it to your vet, ensuring that you keep the dog cool during the journey.

To prevent your dog from suffering from heatstroke it is important that:

- your dog always has access to fresh cold water

- you do not leave the animal confined in a small room without adequate ventilation

- you never leave your dog in the car on a warm day unsupervised.

Wasp stings

Wasp stings are alkaline and should be treated with an acid substance like vinegar to neutralise the sting. Wasps don't leave their stings behind, so there is nothing to be removed.

Bee stings

Bees usually leave their sting on the skin, so these should be carefully removed. Remove the sting using tweezers or by gently scraping the area with a flat edge like a credit card. Bee stings are acidic, so should be removed with an alkaline substance such as a bicarbonate of soda solution.

Caution! Any stings to the dog's face, throat or mouth area are potentially serious as any swelling can impair or prevent breathing. Affected animals should be closely monitored and, if any breathing difficulties arise, the dog should be examined by your vet as soon as possible.

Bloat

Gastric dilation and torsion of the stomach is a true medical emergency that requires immediate veterinary attention. It is caused by a build-up of a large amount of gas in the dog's stomach. It involves bloating (dilation) and twisting (torsion) of the stomach. It is not unusual for the dog to get a mild case of bloat if it over-indulges. If you suspect your dog has a mild case of bloat you must carefully monitor it.

Symptoms include:

- the dog makes several unsuccessful attempts to vomit

- the dog's abdomen is bloated and feels like a drum

- breathing is distressed

- the dog appears severely distressed and may even be in shock

- the dog may stretch its front legs into what looks like a play bow.

Possible causes include:

- swallowing large amounts of air while eating or drinking

- exercise before or after feeding.

PREVENTING BLOAT

- Avoid excitement at feeding times.

- Do not feed one hour before or after exercise.

- Do not allow large amounts of water immediately before or after exercise.

- Feed soaked or wet food.

If your dog tends to gulp down its food, then using a raised feeding bowl and table which gives the dog an elevated position to eat from will greatly reduce the amount of air your dog swallows.

Remember, a raised feeding table is easier for the child to navigate as well.

Minor cuts or grazes

Simple cuts or grazes can generally be attended to at home. Clean the affected area two to three times a day using warm salty water or antiseptic. Do not use Dettol, Savlon or tea tree oil, as the dog will lick it off, and this can cause vomiting. Ensure the infected area is then dried.

Meaningful Dog Commands

How a modified set of dog commands helps both children and adults

This chapter shows you how using a modified set of commands for your dog can be extremely beneficial for a child, especially for a child with autism or sensory processing difficulties. By demonstrating how communication works with the child's dog, you can provide the child with many perfect learning opportunities. This modified set of commands is also extremely useful for adults with ASD or similar processing difficulties.

I remember so well, day in and day out, trying to get Dale to say a single word. Trying to get him to understand what this word meant was a daunting task; progress was at a snail's pace. I knew I had to be consistent with a single word, say it in context, show him the meaning via a picture, and the power of the word with the action. For five years, myself and Dale's teachers worked this way to try to give Dale some key words that would give him a platform towards meaningful language. But it wasn't until I could do this via Henry that Dale learned basic core language and he could understand more what this language meant.

Every day, using the dog as a facilitator, Dale could hear and see what a single word like 'sit' meant because Henry would comply when the word was used. When Henry arrived, Dale still couldn't grasp the concept of toilet training despite my own and his school's efforts. Within a few weeks of Henry's arrival, Dale literally learned what the word 'toilet' and the associated process meant – because he had repeatedly heard the command 'Henry, toilet' while we were house-training the puppy and had seen Henry performing the act on a regular basis. The puppy being rewarded for doing the necessary enabled Dale to understand and triumph over his own toilet needs.

In 1993 when I trained Henry, I knew I had to adapt the core dog commands so they would be meaningful to Dale as well as to the dog. By doing so I've created a meaningful platform of core words for the non-verbal child, so every day the child witnesses how communication works!

I also felt that, by avoiding over-training Henry with too many commands, I would leave scope for dog and child to naturally bond and develop together. Many organisations in the working dog world can train dogs to comply with around 60 commands. For the child with autism or sensory and processing difficulties, though, this many commands can overload and therefore confuse them. I understood I couldn't bombard Dale with too much language via Henry; only concise, meaningful language would give Dale the best chance of learning to communicate effectively. Using basic training commands for the dog, I wanted Dale to be the person who, in the long term, would be commanding Henry. I wanted Dale to learn that he was Henry's master, and that it was Dale who Henry needed to look to for his needs, to play with or get a treat or affection. I knew that this would enhance the bond between Dale and his dog and that, maybe one day, Dale would be able to transfer all he learned from Henry to being able to look after himself.

To achieve all this, I modified basic dog commands, with associated hand signals, so that they would be meaningful for Dale and the dog. I recognised that the teaching approaches used for an autistic child were literally the same as you would apply to training a dog. A gentle, constant approach, with lots of rewards, praise and opportunities for repetition due to the dog's regular needs, was perfect for both boy and dog.

Think how a child with ASD learns in the first place. They learn by seeing, hearing, and doing the act, with lots of repetition; *they learn in a literal way.*

With all this in mind, I ensured that any learning via the dog was educationally and socially relevant to allow the child to progress. I didn't want the child to learn a word or action via the dog that they would have to be untaught as an adult. A good example is the practice of tethering the child to the dog for road safety reasons: How would you progress to untethering the child as they get older? What if you didn't need to tether the child in the first place? The way the child learns road safety via the dog should be compatible with and socially appropriate for adult life.

A child first learns to communicate non-verbally by pointing; a child with autism might do the same by taking the adult by the hand to direct them to what they want. The majority of children with autism first learn to speak by echoing what they heard (known as 'echolalia speech'). The child learns to repeat what they heard, in the same tone, sometimes in context, sometimes out of context (the latter being 'delayed echolalia'). The first time a child attempts to say a single word he or she will echo what they've heard. The child that points has the ability to echo words as well; pointing itself is a pre-verbal gesture and should be encouraged with the spoken word from the adult. These two areas of non-verbal communication are the first building blocks towards the child obtaining language. Therefore, the tone in which we speak to the child and dog must be positive and rewarding. Dogs can only learn to think about one thing at a time; the same is true for children with autism. Both need the same constant praise and rewards. Both need repetitive and consistent language in order to understand the function and meaning of language.

If exposed to persistent negative responses, the child, just like the dog, will become confused about what is happening or what we are expecting of them. The child will communicate their confusion via tantrums, leading to communication breakdown. If the child is overloaded with language, he or she will compensate by shutting down – and the opportunity to be able to speak in the first place is gone.

Dale's teachers and I used Makaton sign language to give him the foundations for verbal language and the vocabulary of about 12 words he gained at age five. I used Makaton hand signals and adjusted some core dog commands that enabled Dale to develop his language. This was the reason that, within weeks of Henry's arrival, Dale's vocabulary soared. Henry became a meaningful third teacher and facilitator for Dale, because everyone involved, including the dog, were on the same page. Because Henry was a dog he was less intimidating for Dale. Henry's facial expressions, body language and behaviour were easier for Dale to decipher than the complex bombardment of signals human faces were throwing at him. As Dale told me, 'Henry's face only had slight changes with his expressions, so I understood them.' Dale confirmed the eminent dog psychologist Daniel Mills' research findings – that a dog has only five recognisable facial expressions.[49] When he was 19, Dale drew Henry's four facial expressions for me: happy, excited, worried and content. Dale omitted the snarling, angry face because 'Henry was a Golden Retriever'.

Nowadays, in the field of autism, scientists have recognised the need to reduce facial expressions and non-verbal body language to the minimum, together with using a basic tone of voice and familiar vocabulary. Since 1998, Professor Kerstin Dautenhahn and her team at the University of Hertfordshire have been developing Kaspar, a child-sized, humanoid animatronic robot used as a social mediator to help children with autism engage, interact and communicate with human counterparts.[50] Kaspar has minimal facial expressions and basic language. The research team has found that Kaspar acts as a social and educational facilitator because he provides a safe and predictable tool for the children – just as Henry did for Dale. The scientific animatronic world has taken this theory and expanded the range of robots to include both human-like and animal-like friendly robots (dinosaurs and monkeys, to name a few). Just as the children are happy to interact with these robotic intervention tools, Dale was comfortable communicating with Henry, because it was on his terms with no verbal or social pressure from Henry.

I knew it was essential for all the dog commands to be meaningful to the everyday language the child heard or used. I am convinced that this consistent platform of language used with the dog is a major reason why children with autism are able to learn new language via a dog. I knew the importance of not having too many verbal commands for Henry and not bombarding Dale with too much language via the dog. Keeping the dog commands to the minimum, and making them meaningful to children, allows them to adopt the same words.

In the long term, these minimalist commands will help the child use the commands themselves with their dog and, in a sense, become the master of the dog. If the child does take ownership of the dog and cares for it, then they can progress to transferring the same skills to looking after themselves. This will allow the child to work towards their own independence via the dog rather than being dependent on the dog.

The modified commands described in this chapter enable the child to learn via the dog in a literal way: the child hears a command and sees the dog complying. There are lots of opportunities for repetition every day. *This is exactly how a child with autism learns.*

Using meaningful dog commands also facilitates involving siblings with the disabled child and the dog. The disabled child should learn the pleasure of sharing their dog with others, and that sharing as a social skill is good for positive social relationships. There are many strategies you can implement to allow siblings to be involved with the child and the dog. This is another important role of the cuddly dog transition kit, as it creates opportunities for a lot of sibling inclusion before the real dog arrives.

There are some key pointers on dog training in the following chapter, 'The Principles of Dog Training'. For the benefit of the child with autism or those with processing or learning difficulties, below are the adjusted core dog commands to demonstrate to the child how good communication works.

Before you start...

When you're working with the child, your tone of voice has to be correct to mark or praise a desired behaviour or response. This approach is the same when training and working with the dog. Using a positive tone of voice, the words 'Good' and 'Yes' will help child and dog learn simultaneously.

Note: The rule of saying the child's name first, so they know you are addressing them, is the same for the dog. In these examples, I've used the name Rover for the dog.

The core dog commands

Rover...toilet

This command will prompt the dog to relieve itself regularly in a socially acceptable area in the garden or when out for walks. This is more socially correct for the dog and family and allows the dog to have a daily routine; in turn, this will help create an improved routine for the child.

Using this word will help the child that's not toilet trained, as they witness the dog's toilet behaviours and learn what this word and process means. Using the same word for the same process for both dog and child will avoid confusion for the child. Using the dog as an educational motivator will help the child make more sense of this difficult problem. Together with the use of social stories, it will make toilet training the child more meaningful and less stressful. To achieve this, it may be helpful to have the dog with the child in the toilet until toilet training is established. The child could be weaned from having the dog with them via other diversions like music or the cuddly dog being in the toilet instead. I'm aware that using the real dog in this way has been successful in toilet training many children. (Toilet training for the child is discussed in more detail in the chapter 'How to Use the Dog as an Educational Facilitator'.)

Rover...stand

All dogs need to stand still for grooming, while you put on their leads and, more so, for continuity of training (because, from a standing position, the dog will naturally sit).

Rover...sit

The '*sit*' command is used with a hand signal – a pointed finger directed towards the floor. Parents can use the same language and hand signal for a child. A parent will know when the time is right to begin using the word on its own for the child; the hand signal can be discontinued for the child and continued for the dog only, to allow the child's communication to progress.

Always give lots of praise to both when they comply: 'Rover... good boy!', 'Dale...good boy/good sitting.' Verbally praising the dog and child regularly increases their motivation to learn and boosts the dog's and the child's confidence and self-esteem.

Rover...down!

This command is used with a hand signal – the flat right hand out showing a downward movement at the dog's eye level with a firm but good tone of voice.

The dog needs this vital command because, in the down position, the dog is under the adult's full control in a relaxed way. It's needed for good social behaviour outdoors, on or off the lead. All assistance dogs are taught to lie under the table and be almost invisible. Having the dog in the down position or under the table is good control, but is also helpful for the child, encouraging them to eat their own meals appropriately at the table, creating happy and relaxed meal times. Getting the child to feed the dog before their own meals will help him or her bond with the dog and encourage the child to eat up his or her own dinner.

If you are using the Picture Exchange Communication System (PECS) or pictures as visual aids to let your child know where they are going or what will happen, it's important to continue using these strategies until it's apparent that your child understands via the dog. Using pictures that include the dog will help the child make sense of going to familiar places like the park or tell them why it's time to leave (for example, because the dog needs its dinner).

Note: You can use the command 'up sit' when your dog is in the down position and getting ready to move forward. Use the hand signal with an upward movement.

Rover...stay

The child learns what the word 'stay' means when they see this regularly. The accompanying hand signal is a flat hand with fingers pointing towards the ceiling/sky (like a traffic policeman's hand signal to stop traffic). This command is usually given when the dog is in the down position and is required to stay there for a longer duration. 'Stay' is the dog's anchoring command; the dog should not move until you give them another command.

Rover...wait

This is a temporary command usually used in conjunction with the 'sit' or 'stand' commands. This command is essential for road safety for the child and dog. It is also used to indicate that another more formal immediate command is coming. You can use this command when you want your dog to wait before going through a door, at the kerb edge, at feeding time and when the dog is going in and out of the car.

Rover...stop

The dog will stop at the kerb or any time required. This command helps the child to understand road safety. For preference, try to teach the dog to stay in the 'stand' position at the kerb. Through daily repetition with the child and dog, on reaching the kerb, you reinforce that everyone needs to stop: '*Stop* (to both dog and child)…we wait…no cars…we go!'

Rover…go! (Or let's go!)
Use this command to move forward.

Rover…down…stay
A dog can help divert a child who's having a challenging tantrum, reassuring him or her and enabling the child to reach resolution quicker and be calmer as a result. Using this command, a dog can be trained to lie next to the child to pacify and divert them, as they stroke its fur, etc. If the child has bonded well with their dog, challenging tantrums can decrease in frequency and be resolved quicker when using the dog in this manner.

This command can also be used as an 'emergency button' when you need to focus on the child's behaviour in public places without the distraction of the dog to deal with as well.

Rover…go play
All dogs need free time to allow them to relax, play and exercise off the lead.

The child will like having his or her own coloured lead which is attached to their dog's harness; the adult's or handler's black lead is attached to the dog's collar, giving them full control of the dog. When it is time for the dog's free play, the dog should be in a '*sit and wait*' position while the adult lead is removed. The focus for the child is the removal of the child's lead, together with the child seeing and hearing the command 'Rover…*go play!*' Seeing this regularly, the child will eventually learn what the word 'play' means. More importantly, the child will start to understand that all play has a beginning and an end. On successful recall of the dog, the child's lead is put back on first, then the adult's. This will let the child know that play has ended and it is time to go home.

Rover...fetch

Used for the game of fetch, this command will show the child what the word 'fetch' means. Until the child's comprehension and language increases, it would be helpful to ask the child to 'fetch' their coat or shoes, etc. In this way, via the dog, they understand what the word means.

Rover...come!

As a tool for helping the child to learn, this command is one of the most effective and powerful of all the dog's training commands. To maintain a safe environment for the dog and child, you need both to come to you when required. Using this command with the dog allows the child to learn to copy the process of the dog's recall.

Recall for the dog should be practised in the safety of the back garden first, gradually progressing to outdoors in a quiet park. (In Alberto Alvarez-Campos's work using this programme, children who were not tethered to their dog chose to stay with their dog at all times.)

Using the dog recall command also allows you to teach the child that positive body language is good communication. All children with autism need clear warnings before an action or change in routine occurs. Teachers in the field use many different warning techniques to inform the child that an activity is coming to an end. Recalling the dog is a superb opportunity to teach the child that you want him or her to 'come' to you. Here, good body language and social timing are imperative. Both dog and child need to know you are calling them ('Rover...come', 'Dale...come'). Kneel down to the dog's and child's eye level: you want both to see open and welcoming body language. With both arms wide open, repeat the 'Rover...come' and 'Dale...come' calls. Remember the six-second rule for the child before repeating the command.

You can use a whistle (two toots) to reinforce the command to the dog to return, as the dog will associate the whistle with a food reward, as described below under 'Rover...eat!' In the early days, until good recall is established, the child and dog could be rewarded with a treat for coming back. The way you lure a dog to look at you, and remain focused on you, in order to receive a treat is the same for the child. Here is your opportunity to encourage the child to give you eye contact as well, by holding the child's treat nearer to your adult eye-level.

The positive body language involved in the recall of the dog provides immense motivation for the child and parent to unite with a big rewarding hug. Giving the dog lots of praise for recalling will be adequate reward for the dog in the long term.

Rover...eat!

To encourage bonding of the child with the dog, parents should teach the child from the outset to be as fully involved with the dog's needs as possible, from the moment the dog arrives. However, this has to be done in a relaxed way, allowing lots of time for the child to be involved, so the learning experience is motivating and engaging for them. For the child with autism, feeding time for the dog is a great opportunity to address all of the triad of impairments simultaneously!

With the dog in the 'sit and wait' position, the child prepares the dog's food, in their own time, with the parent guiding them. The food is placed into the dog's raised food bowl while the dog remains in the 'sit and wait' pose (vary the time from four to 18 seconds). With the carer holding the dog's collar, the child places the bowl into the dog's feeding table and stands beside it. (Alternatively, they can place the food bowl between their feet.) The child then blows the whistle twice and gives the command 'eat!' If the child is non-verbal, the carer can give the command. The dog will associate the whistle with its signal to eat and with receiving food. This routine reinforces the recall command for the dog, as described above.

Rover's tired (for the child only, as described below)

A serious problem can occur during the child's bonding process with the dog if the child hugs and overwhelms the dog too much, not allowing it any time out. This is why there is a real dog bed included in the transition kit, which is transferred to the real dog when it arrives. Using the cuddly dog and bed from the transition kit, parents teach the child that, when the dog is sleeping on its bed, the child must leave the dog alone, reinforcing the message that 'Rover's tired!' The child is shown a picture of a sleeping dog or their own dog, learning this is the time they must leave them alone. Dale told me the visual use of the cuddly dog bed along with the picture of a contented sleeping Golden Retriever which I used before Henry arrived helped him understand that his dog needed to rest or sleep.

Rover...car! (the word 'car' is used for the benefit of the child)

Proper behaviour of the dog when entering and exiting a vehicle is very important. For safety reasons, you do not want your dog barging into or out of your car or running about. The dog should be in a static position, a 'sit' or 'stand', while you ask the dog to 'wait'. When you are ready for them to get in or out of the car, tell them 'OK...car!' Remember to always direct everything via the dog first. So, the child sees the dog safely in the car, encouraging them to copy the dog and calmly join it in the car.

Rover...off!

All dogs may jump up due to excitement, but this anti-social and potentially dangerous behaviour needs to be discouraged. Therefore, the dog should be trained not to jump up on people. Use the command 'Rover...off!' The same command is used if the dog jumps on the sofa or bed, etc., assuming you've decided this is not for your dog. (Be mindful that it is all or nothing with this rule – otherwise the dog will get confused about what's expected of it.)

Rover...leave!

On hearing this command, the dog should pay attention to you and leave what it was doing and work with you, regardless of the distractions in its environment (other dogs, cats, birds, food on the street, scents, etc.). Praise the dog for complying! This command ensures good manners from the dog.

Rover...bed!

This is the command to use when you want your dog to go and lie down on their allocated bed (the dog's safe and quiet place) to sleep for time-out. The child is taught not to touch the dog at all in this bed or designated rest area, and to leave the dog alone while it is resting or sleeping. The dog learns to use this bed area when it wants to be left alone.

Using the same word 'bed' for the child and the dog will help both learn when it's bedtime. Many dogs for children with disabilities sleep in the child's room, as the dog calms the child so they tend to sleep better.

Rover...quiet!

If the dog barks with excitement and the child becomes excited, use the command 'Rover...*quiet!*' Dogs that are allowed to bark uncontrollably are anti-social and must stop when told. The child also learns what the word 'quiet' means.

Well-trained dogs should only bark occasionally with excitement and during play. It is still essential that the child understands this is the dog's language and they are not put off their dog because of the occasional bark. The dog barking could be a useful cue to help the child understand the dog's needs. For example, I taught all of our dogs to bark at the back door to let us know they wanted out for toilet purposes. I also taught our first Henry ('Henry One') a '*speak*' command, using a hand signal as well, at which Henry would let out one almighty bark. I used this to allow Henry to verbally confirm when Dale had done well with anything, for example, eating all his dinner, drawing a nice picture, etc. Dale used to enjoy seeing Henry's approval of anything he did in this manner.

Rover...heel

This command is used when the dog is walking on your left side. It means that the dog should be walking nicely without pulling, with its shoulder beside your knee. It can also be used to bring the dog into position if in a static position. You can reinforce this command by patting the left side of your lower leg to show the dog what you mean.

Note: When walking with your dog, keep the lead loose. A tight lead causes counterforce pulling, causing the dog to be unbalanced and not relaxed; therefore, the dog is not working with you.

Steady!

This is used when the dog is on the lead and is starting to get ahead of you and is pulling, either when walking or going up and down stairs, etc.

OK!

This is the command to use to tell the dog to take a biscuit or treat gently from an open hand.

Give!

This command is used to encourage the dog to release an object from its mouth, usually during play like a game of tug!

Summary of core commands

- Toilet.
- Stand.
- Sit.

- Down!
- Stay.
- Wait.
- Stop.
- Go!
- Down…stay. (Emergency button.)
- Go play.
- Fetch.
- Come!
- Eat!
- Rover's tired. (For the child only.)
- Car!
- Off!
- Leave!
- Bed!
- Quiet!
- Heel.
- Steady!
- OK!
- Give!

The Principles of Dog Training

WITH ALBERTO ALVAREZ-CAMPOS

Dog psychology

Dogs and humans are similar in some ways and drastically different in others. Both are emotional and social creatures that desire contact with each other and members of their own species. Where we differ is in the intellectual form. Humans are able to plan, organise and study concepts, whereas dogs tend to be more reactive! Dogs live in the here and now. Whatever is in front of them is the most important thing to them at that particular time. They don't wake up in the morning and think to themselves 'What am I going to do today?' This is beyond their mental capability. However, dogs have some intelligence and many can be very bright and sharp. Their brains just do not have the intellectual capacity to work at the same level as ours.

Keeping this in mind, you must remember when you are working with dogs that they are simply dogs. They are not little humans. They cannot be negotiated or reasoned with. They are unable to speak or understand the complexities of our spoken language or the reasoning behind our human society. Dogs are unable to comprehend the concept of equality. The key to developing a long and productive relationship with your dog is understanding and accepting your dog for what it is.

Respect

Your dog's respect and understanding is something that should not be expected. It must be earned! The way you handle yourself and the expectations you have of your canine companion will be critical in developing and maintaining your dog's respect and understanding.

All the wonderful skills you and your dog have learned will mean nothing if the dog has its own agenda and is not under your control.

By adhering to the simple rules outlined in this chapter, you will be able to leave the lasting impression on your dog that you alone are the leader!

Confidence

At first, confidence is something you may not readily display when handling your dog. However, it is important that you act as if you know what you are doing. Your dog will respond and interact better with someone who takes charge.

Perseverance

A marksman doesn't hit the target every time and, initially, neither will you. Do not let yourself feel frustrated, impatient or discouraged when things don't work out as planned. Keep trying. If you do, the rewards will far outweigh the effort. This will send a strong leadership signal to your dog – that you are not a quitter and that success is the only option.

Be positive

Your dog will neither respect nor follow a negative leader. A positive attitude is infectious and will definitely motivate your dog to work more effectively. Remember, if you do not think you can succeed, you have already lost.

Consistent expectations

Be consistent with enforcing your wishes with your dog. This will send a very clear message to the dog, showing it what you as the leader expect of it at all times. It will also eliminate any confusion on the part of the dog as to where it stands in your relationship. As you train your dog, you will begin constructing a 'rule book' of regulations for yourself and your dog to follow. Like the rules of any game or sport, if the rules are continually being changed, the system will break down and both players will become frustrated and confused.

Be assertive

Give commands to your dog in a firm, assertive tone of voice. A command is not a question. If you ask your dog, you will be giving it the option of completing the command or not. The command does not have to be loud, but should be given as though you expect the command to be completed immediately at a standard you deem acceptable.

Do not repeat commands

If you take the time to get your dog's attention before you give it a command, the need to repeat the command will be eliminated. Repeating commands in a weak tone of voice is a definite sign of poor leadership. After a period of time, the dog will tune out of your voice and not execute the command properly. You are better off starting the command structure from the beginning by being sure your dog hears the command, rather than repeating something they will never hear. Tips on how to get your dog's attention are given in the command structure section, later in this chapter.

Display the proper body language and show leadership

Dogs rely heavily on body language to communicate with each other. Therefore it is important that you display a leadership posture that your dog will recognise. You don't want to indicate insecurity or indecisiveness by exhibiting body language such as slouching, hanging your head, pointing or showing uncertain facial expressions. Sit up straight, stand tall, hold your head high and move like you know what you are doing and what you want to accomplish. This will send a message to your dog that you are the leader and it is the follower.

Do not chase your dog's attention

Your dog's hearing is around five times more acute than a human's; their sense of smell is approximately 40 times more sensitive. Unfortunately, despite dogs having these remarkable senses, people still have a tendency to try and put themselves in the line of the dog's sight by leaning over the front of the dog's face to get their attention. It is your dog's responsibility to know where you are at all times, not the other way around. Demand your dog's respect and work on improving your attention-getting skills, so your dog will spend more time focusing on you rather than the environment around it.

Reward your dog for good effort

At one time or another you may have worked for a boss who only conveyed negative feedback or belittled your maximum effort. This negativity does not empower a subordinate to excel or even consistently perform their duties.

Your dog is no different. Dogs are not machines. They need something positive from you to motivate them to repeat the command responses and to learn new ones. Be a positive leader and make the environment in which your dog works one in which they are happy and enjoy working. The dog should not be allowed to deviate from the rules you have outlined for it, but it's important that the dog knows it has done well within those guidelines.

At times, dogs will simply want to be dogs and do the things that dogs do. They can be selfish and self-serving and show concern only for their own pleasure, rather than the task at hand.

Take responsibility for making your partnership work

- Do make your dog move if it blocks your path on a floor or stairway, etc – even if you are able to step over it. You are the leader, not the dog!

- Do teach your dog that everything belongs to you – the toys, the bowls, the bed, etc. You should be able to clean, move, handle or remove any item at any time; the only exception is the dog's food bowl while it is eating.

- Do give commands only if you can follow them through.

- Do praise your dog warmly and quickly, but don't overdo it.

- Do be firm, but loving.

- Don't allow your dog to mouth or bite you.

- Don't leave your dog unsupervised with children or anyone who cannot maintain leadership over it.

Positive reinforcement

In order for your dog to have the motivation and willingness to be a facilitator dog and do his job, it must receive a paycheque for its hard work. We receive money and the occasional kind word. For your dog, it is the reward of a pat on the chest, a rub under the chin and a kind tone of voice when they have done well. Treats are a powerful tool in offering a positive message for a job well done. Once the dog fully understands the training and the expectations of his job, though, it should be weaned off treats – to the point where its only need for reward is from you, either physically or verbally.

As you train your dog, you will begin to learn the sequence and command structure for handling your dog, when it is necessary to give a correction and when to praise your dog. It is important you follow the sequence and develop your timing each time you work with your dog.

Remember your dog should be praised every time it has responded well to anything you have asked it to do. If you praise your dog immediately following a desired outcome, it is likely that the same behaviour will be repeated by your dog the next time you ask.

As you and your dog develop into a strong team, and your dog's understanding and respect for you grows, you will find you will be using more positive reinforcement than negative reinforcement.

Motivation and praise

A motivator is something that increases the likelihood that your dog will perform and repeat a command response. Just as the child with autism focuses and learns better if they are motivated, this applies to the dog also. When it comes to developing and maintaining the dog's working skills, it is so much easier if the dog enjoys what it is doing. Consistently rewarding your dog for the correct responses will reinforce favourable behaviours.

When to use motivation

It is impossible to give a detailed list of all the situations in which motivation can be used. However, there are two rules of thought about when motivation can be useful:

- *At the conclusion of a command.* When your dog has correctly completed a command, it should be rewarded – or some sort of positive reinforcement should be given – to let the dog know it has done well.

- *Immediately after the command is given.* There will be times, particularly early on in the relationship with your dog, when the dog will be a little unsure about whether it is responding correctly to your command. You might need to reassure your dog by telling it 'Yes' (i.e. 'that is what I want') and, as long as the dog is trying, continue to motivate it.

Types of motivation
FOOD REWARDS
To most dogs, food is a very powerful motivator. However, because of the poor timing associated with the delivery of the treat and the distracting smell of it for your dog, just using food rewards all the time is impractical. There will be times during and after the dog's training that it may be useful to use a food reward, but it should always be your goal not to rely on treats as the primary form of motivation.

A good tip regarding food rewards is that they can be changed to motivate the dog better. Training dog treats (a low reward) can be used to get the dog to comply initially with what you want it to do, for example *sit!* When teaching the dog to respond to the recall command, you can upgrade the food reward to something that will be more enticing for the dog – like cooked chicken or liver pieces. This will be more motivating for the dog as the food reward is a higher grade (a high reward).

PHYSICAL PRAISE
Most dogs love to be touched and will view physical interactions with people as a reward for a job well done. Physical praise can vary from a light scratch behind the ears to a play session on the floor. As with all types of reward, the amount of physical contact will be determined by where you and the dog are and the level of the dog's accomplishment.

Verbal and emotional praise

As you progress through your training, you'll find that emotional praise will be used more than other forms of reward as you also progress in getting the timing right. A smile with a positive tone of voice or a welcoming body posture will convey the message to the dog that it is on track. It will be to your advantage to 'get silly' from time to time when praising your dog.

Your dog will be a master at reading tone of voice and body language and you will be able to send clear messages of approval to the dog quickly and effectively.

The timing of rewards

The timing of the reward is critical to the dog making the association between what they have done and the praise they are receiving. Issue the reward immediately on completion of the dog's task so that it knows it has performed the correct behaviour.

Variety

Dogs can become easily bored if the praise they receive is stale or repetitive. If the dog is continuously hearing just the words 'good dog, good dog', after a while, the praise will lose its shine and the dog will stop making an effort to comply. Vary your praise to keep your dog interested and coming back for more!

The effect of the dog's personality

Dogs, like people, have their own individual personalities and temperaments. Some are hyperactive and easily motivated; others are calm and reserved and will require more enthusiasm to motivate them. As you get to know your dog better, you will quickly learn what level of motivation it will respond to.

Think about the environment you are working in with your dog – start in low-level distraction areas first, like your back garden. If indoors, make sure there are no distractions like the television being on, or intrusions like too many people or other dogs.

Conclusions on motivation

It is impossible to outline every situation you will encounter with your dog and recommend a course of action you should take regarding motivating your dog. This is something you will discover for yourself. By following these guidelines, though, you can establish a starting point for the types and levels of motivation available to you.

As long as your praise is sincere and you are genuinely excited about the accomplishments of your dog, you will be communicating the appreciation your dog needs for it to continue to repeat the desired command responses.

Corrections (negative reinforcement)

A correction is defined as giving the dog a negative response or slight discomfort that will be enough, in the present situation, for it to change its behaviour (negative reinforcement). Examples range from a leash correction to something as subtle as not praising the dog. Well-delivered negative corrections are short and to the point – the dog will know immediately that it has made the wrong choice.

Deny the dog what it wants and it will often stop what it is doing!

While you are training your dog there will be times when the dog will behave in an inappropriate manner, and it will test you by showing a lack of responsiveness to your commands by displaying unacceptable behaviour.

As highlighted at the beginning of this chapter, dogs view the world in a different way from humans. You must change the way you deal with your dog when it comes to teaching it right from wrong. Your goal is to teach your dog that, when it does well, it will be rewarded and it will feel good. If the dog steps out of line and misbehaves, it will not be rewarded and it will feel bad!

There are many varied views amongst dog trainers as to what types of correction are ethically the most effective to use on your dog. Ethically, you want to get this right – especially when in the public eye with your dog.

You can adopt good verbal capabilities for commanding your dog; therefore, it is better that your dog learns and responds to your voice correction only.

Verbal corrections

I use two verbal corrections, 'no' and 'leave it', which are both useful for the child to witness being used with the dog. These verbal commands do not inflict discomfort as a physical correction would. They can be very effective when given in a firm tone of voice and coupled with a physical correction (if possible).

- 'No.' The dog immediately stops whatever it is doing.

- 'Leave it.' Prevents the dog from sniffing, scrounging for food, and licking or touching people, food or other dogs.

Training collar corrections

Here is some guidance on how the right type of collar or device can be used to give the dog a quick stinging sensation, without the need for pulling or a tugging motion which could lead to resistance from the dog.

Many in the dog training world use the Martingale-type collar. This is half chain, half flat collar material and, if used properly, can be very effective in correcting the dog.

Haltis are similar to bridles that are used on horses. They compensate for a lack of arm strength during corrections. These collars control the dog's head and, with proper use, greatly magnify the effect of leash corrections because the dog's head is under control, not the neck.

Rules for using correction

- *Correction must be objective.* Dogs have a tendency to become fearful of a person who exhibits anger or negative emotion towards them. It is important to not show any negative emotions or anger when you correct your dog.

Rather, administer the necessary discipline in an emotionally controlled and calm manner; otherwise, the dog may become quite fearful of you.

- *Apply the proper amount of correction.* Dogs, like people, have their own personalities and physical characteristics. Some dogs are passive, while others are assertive. Some have a very high physical sensitivity and require a firm hand. When administering a correction, it is important that you apply just enough correction to stop the undesirable behaviour – no more and no less.

- *Time the correction appropriately.* Because dogs are reactive animals and live in the here and now, corrections must be given during the undesirable behaviour so that the dog knows what it is being corrected for. The dog will then associate the inappropriate behaviour with the unpleasantness of the correction you gave them and will be less likely to repeat the behaviour in the future.

- *Praise the dog after corrections.* Dogs will find the discomfort of correction an unpleasant experience. However, you do not want to see this negativity continue once the dog is behaving appropriately. By praising the dog once they have been corrected and they have responded well and complied, we are discouraging what we don't want and encouraging what we do want. It is important to keep the dog positive, as this will maintain a responsive working attitude.

- *Corrections should be given quickly.* People are capable of holding grudges and seeking revenge and some take legal action when dealing with each other in regards to emotional issues and discipline. Luckily, dogs are not this way at all. We must therefore issue corrections quickly and decisively – and then move on.

Conclusions on corrections

Corrections are an effective tool for you to use with your dog to help it understand what your expectations are and that the rules in your 'rule book' must be adhered to.

You must exercise good judgement and not overuse correction when handling your dog.

Command structure

I have used a three-step command structure to train my dogs:

1. Get the dog's attention by using its name.

2. Give the command.

3. Praise the dog for complying.

This is a vital part of the way you will interact with your dog, from now until its demise. It's important you give your dog the commands in the proper order, with the right tone of voice.

Getting your dog's attention

In order to begin the proper command structure, you must first learn how to get your dog's attention. Dogs have very acute sensory perception. In the wild, prior to domestication, the dog needed these senses to survive. Although your dog may no longer need these senses to detect an enemy or hunt and chase prey, these senses have remained within your dog's being.

It is your task to keep your dog's attention, and keep it focused on you rather than the environment around you. This is very important when giving the dog a command.

There are four different types of stimuli that will attract your dog's attention:

- *Movement:* All dogs have an instinctive 'prey drive'. Dogs have a natural temptation to chase things. Movement tends to be the prominent stimuli to activate this instinct. Birds, cats, balls and other dogs are some of the distractions out there that are moving around, competing for your dog's attention. You can use movement to your advantage. Waving your hand in the dog's face or wiggling the leash are some ways movement can be used to achieve your dog's focus.

- *Odour:* Right from a puppy's first breath, its sense of smell is one of its most powerful senses. A dog's sense of smell is around 40 times more sensitive than ours; they can pick up scents you do not even know exist. When your dog is sniffing around, getting its attention and keeping it is going to be quite a chore at times. If you have a handful of treats, you will have no trouble getting and keeping your dog's attention for most of the day. However, you will have to sacrifice mobility and timing in your handling, so it's best to focus your energy on mastering the use of the other three stimuli to get your dog's attention.

- *Sound:* Although dogs are capable of hearing a much greater range of sounds than humans, they are also very selective in their hearing. There are countless sounds you may use to get your dog's attention, like whistling, clicking your tongue or changing the intonation of your voice. These sounds can very easily be ignored or 'tuned out' by your dog if the sound becomes repetitive or annoying. It is necessary to become quite creative with the sounds you use to see whether or not the dog is responding.

- *Touch:* Dogs love to be touched. This enjoyment goes back to their pack animal characteristics – each individual interacts with the other individuals within the pack on a physical level. A tap on the top of the dog's head, a scratch behind the ears, using the leash to pop the training collar, or gentle pressure on the Halti collar, are all excellent ways to get your dog's attention before issuing a command. Make yourself more interesting than whatever else is going on around you and you will have your dog's attention.

In most cases, getting and keeping your dog's attention is half the battle on the road to a successful command response. It is important to display a proper leadership posture when giving your dog the command.

Giving commands and praise

Here are some simple rules for giving your dog commands:

- *Give the command quickly.* Because of the reactive, movement-to-the-moment nature of your dog, you only have a small window of opportunity to give a command once you have the dog's attention. Once you have contact with the dog, give the command immediately, before it has a chance to be distracted.

- *Do not ask.* Give the command in a firm and assertive tone, as if you expect it to be carried out immediately. If you give the command in a passive tone of voice, as a question, you are giving the dog the option of either completing the command or rejecting it. Tell it, don't ask it!

- *Use intonation, not volume.* Dogs, like people, are able to distinguish the emotions in your tone of voice when you speak to them. In other words, it is not what you say; it is how you say it. By giving the command in a firm assertive tone, at low volume, you will achieve the same desired result as if you were to yell the same command.

- *Do not repeat the command.* There should be no reason to repeat the command if you have made the effort to get the dog's attention first. Your voice will become background noise if the dog does not know that you are giving the command directly to it!

- *If you give the wrong command, follow through.* At times, you will make the mistake of giving the dog a different command to the one you meant the dog to perform. A good leader will not confuse the dog by changing midstream. A good leader will follow through with the incorrect command first and then execute the desired command on the second try.

- *Do not pat the dog while you are giving a command.* If your new companion is sitting nicely beside you and you decide to give it a '*down*' command, you will make it a bit more difficult for your dog to pull itself away from all the affection to perform the '*down*'. Leaning over and putting yourself face to face with your dog will have the same effect.

- *Do not mix commands.* A '*sit down*' or a '*jump up*' command combination is very confusing for your dog. Which command do you want? You are fully to blame if the dog does not finish your request properly. Make a mental note of which command you want your dog to perform before you give it.

- *Each command given must end with a release command,* for example '*OK*' or '*forward*'. Once a command has been given it is very important that you are the one that decides when the command is over, not the dog! If the dog is allowed to decide, the duration of its obedience to your commands will become shorter and shorter until the dog will not hold the command for very long at all.

- *Follow through.* After you have your dog's attention and have properly given the command, the final step in the command structure will depend on how the dog responds. The dog will either respond positively to the command and comply or respond negatively and reject your command. Either way, it is necessary for you to respond in a consistent manner.

- *Reward the dog if it responds correctly.* It is very important that when the dog does well it is rewarded for the effort. Praise for a correct response can vary from verbal encouragement, for example '*good dog*', to a brisk rub on the neck or a small treat. Try to match the level of praise with the feat the dog has accomplished. If the dog has just executed a '*sit*' which it has done successfully hundreds of times before, a quiet verbal '*good boy*' should be an appropriate reward. If you are teaching your dog a new task and the dog completes it correctly for the first time, a more exuberant physical reward is in order. As time passes and you get to know your dog, you will be able to judge at what level the dog should be rewarded. The important point is the dog receives something positive.

Social behaviour

It is very easy for the dog to learn bad habits and not so easy to re-educate it. Your dog will require guidelines and consistency – this will help to avoid confusion.

It is important you set the boundaries from day one!

It is a good idea to show the dog how to behave rather than allowing it to learn how not to behave.

Do not allow your dog to dictate, initiate play or seek attention. If your dog nudges you or barks at you for attention, you would be best to ignore it. Two minutes later, when your dog is no longer seeking attention, you can initiate the play, so it is when you say and not when your dog says.

Note: The leash is not just for use when walking your dog. Use it to encourage your dog to '*down*' by your side whilst you are relaxing and watching television. The dog can have a toy and learn the correct way to behave. This is relaxing for both you and the dog.

A word about your dog jumping up

Jumping up is a favourite way for your dog to show it is happy; it is also a way of them trying to attract your attention. Jumping up should not be encouraged – it may knock someone over.

People saying 'hello' to your dog, particularly visitors to your home, can encourage it to jump up. When this happens, your dog begins to believe that everyone who arrives at your home is coming to see it. Your dog will learn to anticipate and expect a fun time when your friends visit, and its exuberance will become more uncontrollable as it gets older. Basically, your visitors can easily teach your dog how not to behave!

To help your dog stay calm and learn how to behave around visitors, do not allow anyone to greet it in a high and excited tone of voice, no matter how happy they are to see it. Instead, they should ignore the dog at first and, only when it is calm, greet it in a calm and quiet manner. Providing something else for your dog to focus its attention on other than your visitors is also a good idea.

Putting your dog on its lead can also aid with the control of over-excitable behaviour.

Excitability

Over-excitability creates lack of control – you lack control of your dog and your dog lacks control of itself; jumping up, mouthing, biting and chasing will all become more of a problem.

- Excitability should be controlled and anticipated.

- Games should be stopped before over-excitability takes over.

- If your dog's level of excitability does get out of control, you need to put it on its lead or confine it to a calm room for a short period of 5–10 minutes until it is settled.

- You should never chase your dog to catch it; this will only heighten excitability and you reward your dog by playing chase. You would be more likely to gain success by being excited and running in the opposite direction to encourage your dog to chase and follow you. (This is particularly useful if your dog escapes and is in danger from the road.) Your reaction would be to chase, but your response should be to run away.

To get control of your dog you can either:

- walk out of the room and ignore it; if there is no audience, then it will calm down much quicker, or

- be encouraging; crouch down at its level using a pleasant voice and body postures and a toy or food to achieve a response to 'come'.

Clicker training

Clicker training is a method of positive reinforcement training that rewards the dog for the behaviours we want instead of punishing behaviours we don't want.

The clicker is a small plastic box containing a metal plate which, when pressed (always just once), makes a clear click sound. When the dog does what you want him to do, you 'click' and give the reward of a treat. So with the click sound, the dog learns the concept of 'well done' and that a treat is coming.

The benefit of the clicker is that it makes a consistent sound at the instant moment the dog complies with the behaviour you want. The dog learns to associate the good behaviour with the click and the reward treat, so this encourages the dog to repeat the positive behaviour.

Three clicker rules to remember

- Always reward with a treat after a click, even if you have accidentally clicked. The dog must associate the click with having done well.

- Only click once and then give the treat reward.

- Keep clicker training sessions short – around 5–10 minutes – as they should be fun for you and your dog.

Playing with your dog

It is through play that your dog will learn about its strengths and weaknesses. Your dog must never learn that it is mentally or physically stronger than you or any member of your family.

It is important that you initiate games like fetch or hide and seek and stop them on your terms. Don't just wander off leaving your dog in possession with the toy, as this will give the impression it has won. It is important your dog never learns it has an automatic right to maintain possession of a toy or that it is permissible to snatch a toy from the handler. The aim of the game is to teach the dog to take and release the toy on command. You should win possession of the toy more often than your dog. However, remember that if your dog never wins it will get bored and give up and will not enjoy playing the same games as you.

Once you decide to end a play session, take the toy away and put it out of your dog's reach.

Chase-related games and wrestling with your dog should be avoided as they teach it to bully and play bite. Children are particularly good at teaching the dog to perfect these undesirable skills.

Games and children

- Both dog and child must learn respect from one another. The key to success is fun with control; avoid over-excitability.

- Wrestling games should be avoided, as the dog will play with your child in exactly the same way it would play with another dog. These games can often be rough and children can get hurt or easily frightened when games get out of control.

- Excitable and enthusiastic children can easily over-excite a young dog, resulting in rough play. The child will normally come off worse in any exchange of this behaviour.

- Anything fast moving will encourage chase and excitability in your dog – that includes children running and screaming.

How to Use the Dog as an Educational Facilitator

T his stage of the programme is about education and working towards the best possible independence for the child, using the dog as a facilitator.

Working with the dog and child at home, and including your child's school, will allow the dog to be an educational motivator. An indirect approach with the dog will increase the child's learning and make it more fun and meaningful. All children learn better if play and fun are included in the learning process. You want your child to be empowered by the dog and take real joy in being the dog's master. We want the child to be able to work towards commanding, handling and looking after all the dog's needs themselves to the best of their ability. The repetitive opportunities that attending to the dog's needs brings will enable the child to transfer similar skills to themselves. This will be achieved if it is done at the child's own pace because the child will see communication working as demonstrated through their dog!

Due to the learning achieved with the transitional kit, your child will now be familiar with accessing the dog's cupboard and so should be able to fetch their real dog's items when needed.

The first few weeks – bonding and seeing the first benefits of using the transitional kit

The first few weeks of this part of the programme are devoted to creating a routine for the dog and child. During this time, your child will begin to get familiar with the dog's daily needs and being the dog's 'master'. The fun way you used the transitional kit will have helped this transition.

While you want to include siblings when possible, it is vital that everyone knows that the child is the dog's master. The dog will then bond more with the child, and he or she will learn that the dog depends on him or her for its needs. This will help give the child a real sense of ownership of their dog and a sense of responsibility for fulfilling its needs. To reinforce this, encourage your family or visitors to ask the child if they can pat the dog. Use the same approach when the opportunity arises in public places, enabling your child to take responsibility for the dog at all times while he or she indirectly learns to engage and interact with the new people encountered when out and about with the dog.

If the dog has been properly socialised prior to being partnered with the child, then the bonding process will be seamless. Before Dale got Henry, as luck would have it, the breeder, Val, had a nephew, Robert, who was the same age as Dale. Val allowed Robert to handle the pup, feed it treats, etc. as Dale would; this was a real factor in the almost instant bonding that occurred between Dale and Henry. Val knew the vital rule and implemented it with Robert: always direct everything via the dog first!

To help you use the dog as an educational facilitator for your child, make use of the child's obsession and favourite colour, as introduced with the transitional kit. Again, while it was luck that Henry was named after Dale's favourite train, with the real dog now in the home, we could connect all the components of the programme together. As Val's mother said, 'Well, if he loves Henry

the dog as much as Henry the train, we'll have no problems there.'
How right she was!

In a sense, with Stages 1 and 2 of the programme completed, and Stage 3 being implemented, you are putting together the different parts of a jigsaw to form the whole picture – a meaningful, successful partnership between the dog and the child or adult.

Such was the success of all the transitional work I did with Dale before Henry arrived that we had all bonded already with our gorgeous bundle of joy. The puppy rapidly became a major part of the family. I will never forget how myself, professionals and many others witnessed, almost instantly, the way Dale had been transformed – from a lost and lonely child into a happy little boy who at last had a friend to give him a sense of purpose. Our home came to life in a sense we had not known before Henry arrived and began to work his special kind of magic.

By day two of our pup arriving, we as a family knew we couldn't carry on without Henry. It was not lost on me that, of all Dale's obsessions, like Mickey Mouse and the wonderful Thomas the Tank Engine, with Henry I now had the most amazing living educational resource I had ever known. I embraced all that Henry could facilitate for Dale.

To get the greatest potential from our dog, I made the decision to allow Henry to have the run of the house; nowhere would be out of bounds, not even the sofa or any beds – especially Dale's! Just as I used the cuddly dog to teach Dale about the dog's body parts, he could now do this with the real dog and transfer his learning to pointing to his own eyes and ears, etc.; this assisted his learning at school.

Using Henry as a facilitator day-by-day taught Dale to take care of his dog; I ensured he was involved with all aspects of looking after his dog. Although Dale had practised and thought it was fun playing with a cuddly dog, with Henry in our home, Dale's motivation and focus increased – he would do anything for his dog. I used Henry as a facilitator with a holistic approach: no daily event or detail of caring for the dog was lost.

Feeding the dog – opportunities for learning

Feeding time was a great learning opportunity for Dale. Using Henry to motivate Dale, I trained Henry to '*sit and wait*' at feeding times at his special allocated cupboard (where all his things were kept, especially his food and treats). Henry patiently waiting at the cupboard, with the occasional loud bark as a prompt, motivated Dale into learning the feeding process. Previously, at his own mealtimes, Dale showed no desire to wash his hands; but he would wash his hands before going through the sequence of feeding Henry. The potential for learning new language was immense, as was numerical learning (counting 'one scoop, two scoops', etc.). Dale even washed the empty food bowl afterwards and replenished the other bowl with water for his dog.

Many children, particularly those with autism and disabilities, can be notoriously bad eaters; seeing Henry devouring his food and treats on a regular basis taught Dale to gain the same behaviour. Eating to grow to be 'big and healthy' was reinforced, as Dale witnessed his dog get bigger as time went by.

Henry taught Dale another abstract social rule – the concept of greed! I put a strict daily allowance of dog treats in Henry's cupboard, for Dale to give to Henry on his terms. (Again, this reinforced Dale's sense of ownership and autonomy with his dog.) When the treat allowance had been used up for the day, I taught Dale to tell Henry, 'Henry, no more, don't be greedy.' It was pleasing to see Dale glow with pride as Henry reluctantly walked away from his cupboard.

The feeding process helped Dale grasp the concept of sequencing and the skill of being organised. The fact that Henry needed three meals a day in the beginning lent itself to a wealth of learning opportunities for Dale. Incorporating all the teaching involved at Henry's mealtimes meant it could take around half an hour to feed Henry. It enabled learning for Dale, addressing the triad of impairments of his autism simultaneously!

The scope for enhancing Dale's language skills and improving his fine motor skills was endless. I would break down Henry's mealtime feeding process into minute steps:

'Dale, open Henry's cupboard door.' Then…

'Dale, what do we need next? We need his bowl', etc.

To help increase Dale's comprehension, as this precedes spoken language, I would talk in a basic, concise way and try to be at Dale's eye level while emphasising the word I wanted Dale to learn. Once Dale appeared to understand, I would prompt Dale to respond. So, when pouring the food into the bowl, I would say 'Dale is pouring the food into Henry's bowl and now we add some…' and Dale would say 'water'.

Throughout the entire process, poor Henry was ready to burst with anticipation, but he never moved from his *'sit and wait'* position until the command 'Henry, *eat*' was given by Dale.

Henry very quickly became king of the household, and Dale thrived on it. Because we used Henry as a facilitator in the widest sense, Dale came to see that Henry's needs were similar to a person's – and he treated the dog as such. Dale would even tell Henry when the dog's favourite TV programme was on. (I had positively manipulated Dale into believing it was *Ready Steady Cook*, because Henry loved anything to do with food!)

Improving the child's fine motor skills

Dale's motivation to learn via Henry was undoubtedly due to the strong bond Dale had developed with his dog. It encouraged Dale to start to draw and, very quickly, Dale progressed from having a palmar grasp when holding a pencil to developing a tripod grip, albeit with the aid of a special rubber grip on the pencil.

It wasn't surprising that Dale's first ever attempt to recreate an image was a drawing of his dog, with its water and food bowl by its side. This first picture from Dale was proof that he needed the right motivation to draw in the first place and, in addition, it showed that he understood Henry's physical needs as well. The dog in the picture had a big smile on its face, which showed me that not only was Henry happy that his needs were being met but Dale was very happy with his dog!

A dog theme was used to teach Dale early writing skills, with resources allowing Dale to draw a straight line to connect the dog to its bone, take the dog to its kennel and so on. Other educational resources used to teach him to write included joining the dots to make dog pictures, and dog-themed reward stickers (used in his school). As little as three weeks after Henry had arrived in our home, professionals were commenting in Dale's progress notes that he'd had a particularly happy spell and was mixing well with other children – and that all of his skills were showing progress.

It was so rewarding, back in 1994, to see Dale's response to Henry. The results very much confirmed the research of Marine Grandgeorge and her colleagues,[51] which showed that, after the age of five (as Dale then was), pets can trigger positive social behaviour in children with autism. There is an abundance of research showing that having a pet – especially a dog – can and does have an incredible positive impact on our physical and emotional well-being. Given the nature of autism as a disability, this rings very true! No matter what, to me, one thing was apparent – involving Dale in the minutiae of Henry's care was getting results.

Learning personal hygiene

While I used both Dale's obsession and his favourite colour to help with the learning process, there was another strategy that enhanced progress. It was essential to 'think out of the box', especially when it came to addressing Dale's autism. By now, I had learned the power of directing daily life activities – absolutely everything – via the dog first! So much so that, one day after Dale and Henry had a mud wrestle in the garden, the only way I could get Dale into the bath beyond his normal bath time was to get Henry in first – then Dale followed.

This tactic worked in addressing all of Dale's personal hygiene issues. Regularly grooming and brushing Henry reduced Dale's anxiety and sensory issues around getting his own hair brushed. Although Dale's hair brush was the same style as Henry's soft wooden brush from the transitional kit, Dale soon progressed to tolerating a normal brush and comb. Dale was fortunate that an excellent autism practitioner and teacher, Maureen, worked on all the transition strategies needed to take Dale for a haircut.

Again, involving Dale in taking Henry to the dog groomers helped Dale learn the importance of good grooming. I brushed Henry's teeth with Dale looking on and, when we visited Henry's vet, Nigel, Dale would be involved in examining Henry's teeth. This reduced his own anxieties regarding the dentist and helped Dale look after his own teeth.

Throughout my amazing journey raising two children with autism and facilitating their love for animals to help them, I have never had a problem with a vet, dog groomer or pet shop owner. They have all embraced using my children's love for animals to help me teach both of them. Dale was often Nigel's veterinary assistant, rather than the veterinary nurse, while Amy has taken her obsession with all things equine as far as she can.

Finding a whole new social world

In a way, Henry himself became Dale's new obsession. Given the wealth of Henry's needs and quality of life, the scope for using Henry as an educational facilitator was virtually endless and Dale's social world could be expanded in many ways. In a way, Thomas the Tank Engine became almost redundant, as I could introduce

Dale to dog stories, cartoons and movies as Dale's love for all things canine grew. This was so successful that the release of the first ever *Beethoven* movie (about a large St Bernard dog) was the catalyst for getting Dale into the cinema for the first time, albeit with the right autism approach to the screening. This was the ice-breaker, allowing Dale to enjoy going to the cinema thereafter.

I had learned how to use the power of the dog. I didn't waste any opportunity to use Henry to teach Dale even the most basic of skills. Even the simplest of events could be used to good advantage. For instance, when Henry had outgrown his collar, Dale was involved in choosing a new one. All children learn better when they are empowered and given choice. Going through all the steps involved in getting Henry a new collar was again a vast learning opportunity for Dale. What size was best? Should it be a buckle- or clip-type collar? What colour should we choose? Dale would have to try the collar on his dog and, as usual, pet shop owners encouraged Henry to be with Dale in their shops.

Today, the big pet stores encourage owners to bring in their dogs. This provides a massive new world of learning for our children, via the dog and its world. Being able to grasp the concept of Henry growing out of his collar helped Dale understand how he himself grew out of his shoes and needed new ones. Again this is an opportunity to use the cuddly dog as a teaching tool – I put Dale's wellington boots and shoes on the cuddly dog before Dale wore them. Maureen, Dale's teacher, also played mock shoe shops with Dale and his peers at the pre-school language unit.

A whole new social world had opened up for Dale; we would take him to dog shows and let him see dog agility events that took place locally. The opportunity to meet and greet new people with his dog served to increase Dale's interest in his dog as well as dramatically improving his social skills.

How the dog can assist with toilet training

For three years, I tried to teach Dale the concept of toilet training. I implemented all the right strategies to try to help Dale be successfully toilet trained but, no matter what I did, he didn't seem to understand. While the dog can be used to help facilitate success in this area, it is essential the right approach is initiated: a detailed child-centred toilet plan, tailored to the child's disability, has to be implemented first. Thereafter, the dog can augment the process. Below is an example of a toilet plan for the child with autism that can also be used for any child.

Achieving continence for the child is the interaction of two processes:

- *Physiological maturation:* The child has the ability to sit/walk/ dress with maturation of the bladder and bowel.

- *Understanding and social awareness:* The child can respond to basic instructions and has good self-esteem and motivation. The child displays the desire to imitate and identify with peers and has self-determination and a desire for independence.

Recommendations — the toilet training plan

Toilet training for any child is a daunting experience. For a child with autism or those with a learning disability, the process is confusing, and many children have a real fear of the toilet environment itself, let alone the impact sensory issues have on the physical processes of toileting.

- All children with delayed toilet training should be assessed to exclude underlying problems and offered an individual toilet plan and treatment programme.

- Treatment interventions should not be delayed due to the child's disability. Waiting for the child 'to be ready' is not appropriate.

- Long-term use of disposable products should be avoided and perhaps stopped altogether.

- Early intervention appears to be the essential key.

The younger the child is when a toileting plan is introduced, the more successful the outcome. This is because there will be less chance of fixed behaviours being developed. Identify a settled time in the child's and family's life and choose a date to start the toilet plan. To help motivate the child, the night before the plan starts, think about having a little celebration with a special cake and make a fuss about disposing of or putting away pull-ups. I did, as many parents do, put a pull-up in a big envelope and address it to the 'nappy or pull-up fairy', care of a grandparent's address. The child should be involved with this, allowing a concrete farewell to the nappy. Many parents do the same when it is time to stop the child using a dummy.

A couple of weeks before the nappy send-off, start to read the child toilet training storybooks and introduce the child's own real toilet social story. There is an abundance of toilet training story books available on Amazon and similar sites. You can also use a PECS (Picture Exchange Communication System) behaviour strip, which shows the sequence of the toilet routine, and put it on the bathroom wall so the child can clearly see it. When planning the bathroom environment, beware of processing difficulties for the child – 'less is more', so think about the environment from the point of view of the child trying to process information.

The toilet plan has to be adhered to by all parties involved with the child. The use of motivator awards for the child is crucial. Remember to use the child's obsession in any way. I used chocolate Thomas the Tank Engine lollipops and made dog sticker ones for Dale. For Amy, I bought horse stickers and covered chocolate pieces with kitchen foil and placed a horse sticker on them.

Consider the bathroom environment: it should be a calm happy place with no nappies or pull-ups on display. Make up a toilet routine social story, using real pictures. You can incorporate the dog, reinforcing the message about where the dog goes to the toilet and where the child has to go.

Always warn the child when it's toilet time and use the appropriate communication symbol the child is used to (PECS or Do2learn, etc.). The toilet plan should be adhered to wherever the child is, especially at the child's nursery or school.

Many children like it if you blow bubbles while they are sitting on the toilet, or you could read them a story or play their favourite music or nursery rhymes.

Allow the child to sit on the toilet for as long as they are happy to do so. If the child can sit on the toilet then they are halfway to achieving the process!

The child has to experience having an accident in order to learn from their mistakes. That is why you should put normal pants on the child first, then the pull-up, if you want to use them initially, so the child gets the experience of when they are wet. Alternatively, you can get thicker towelling-type underwear on the internet (or, as I used to do, put two pairs of pants on the child), to help absorption at the same time as giving the child the sense of being wet or soiled.

When accidents occur, the child should be attended to and changed in the toilet. Try to get the child to sit on the toilet with the lid down to put on their clean pants; put a towel on the lid, so they don't feel the shock of the lid being cold. When the time is right, progress to doing the changing while the child sits on the toilet with the lid up, if he or she will tolerate it. This will give the child practice sitting on the toilet with no pressure to perform!

There are adult toilet seats on the market that have a built-in child toilet seat, so the child doesn't experience anything different when they get bigger.

Allow your child to take a favourite toy with them. I used to have a selection of Dale's and Amy's story books to read to them. The bathroom door was decorated with pictures of their favourite characters. I put up a dog poster for Dale and, when I was toilet-training Amy, she had a poster of a horse on the bathroom wall.

Use a toilet symbol to prompt the child to go to the toilet. I feel a picture of the child's actual real toilet works best. Put a picture of the child on the toilet cistern or the wall, so the child knows what is expected of him or her.

If the reward is a chocolate lollipop, put it out of reach but where the child can see it, so he or she knows they will get it if they pee or poo in the toilet. I used to put the chocolate reward high up on the inside of the bathroom door, so the child could see the reward when they were sitting on the toilet.

A child refusing to poo in the toilet is a common problem. Using visual resources, we need to convince the child that poo belongs in the toilet! Use your drawing and imaginative skills to do this. I made a poo character with a sad face, with a big arrow showing it belonged in the toilet!

Getting the child to play in the toilet and flush the toilet for fun will reduce sensory problems and reinforce the importance of flushing! With Dale and Amy, I used pellets of Henry's dog food, one at a time, to give them something to flush; both shrieked with laughter as each food pellet disappeared down the u-bend.

A good tip is to put a little toilet paper in the loo first; this gives boys something to aim at and it is easier to see success. It also prevents the child being put off by cold splashes occurring. There are also target markers, etc. available on the market that give boys something to aim at.

Let little boys stand or sit to pee – whatever comes naturally to them. Sitting at first is probably easier; then progress to standing. Children learn better seeing the peeing process first, then doing; use a sibling for the child to copy!

Soiling problems

You need to differentiate between 'overflow', which is soiling associated with underlying constipation, and encopresis (a normal stool in an inappropriate place). The latter is a common problem with children with autism, which may be related to:

- toilet refusal or fear

- learned behaviour

- underlying behavioural issues due to the child's lack of understanding or immaturity.

I feel the best way to address this, if possible, is to involve the child in the cleaning up and proper disposal of the poo. The adult can put the poo in the toilet, to reinforce the message about the right place it should go. The child can flush it away and wash his or her hands afterwards. Any success with the child should always be rewarded with upbeat verbal praise. This is what is known as a 'low reward'. Leave the 'high reward' (chocolate or similar) for when the child uses the toilet to pee or move their bowels, as this is the ultimate goal!

Patience, persistence and consistency are crucial with all children. However, with a child with autism, achieving toilet continence is a long-term educational objective. This could mean anything from months up to a couple of years, but it can be achieved!

Night-time control — managing bed-wetting
While you are working to establish day-time continence, you could use pull-ups, but with real pants next to the child's skin, for night-time. (Of course, remember to protect the mattress.)

How to use the dog to augment the child's toileting plan
Thinking out of the box when you use the cuddly dog can contribute to making the toilet process more meaningful for the child. To start introducing the child to wearing pants, put a pair of the child's pants only on the cuddly dog to show the child that it is good to wear pants and that they get changed regularly, at least once a day. If all is well, you can involve the child in play with the cuddly dog's pants, letting him or her choose a pair and put them on the cuddly dog.

I also used changing the cuddly dog's pants to teach Dale and Amy the concept of days of the week, since this was a daily occurrence. Nowadays, it is easy to find children's pants that have the days of the week on them; more importantly, though, use a different colour or pattern of pants each day to show which day of the week it is.

If your child doesn't show much interest in using the cuddly dog this way, create a small washing line in the bathroom and encourage the child to put up the corresponding day's pants on the washing line.

Once you have implemented an achievable and child-centred toilet plan, you can use the real dog to augment the process, to help make toileting time for the child a positive and happy experience. Involving the real dog can help calm the child, as well as increase the child's confidence with toileting issues. Having a dog poster in the bathroom will help the child like having the real dog in the bathroom with them. You can entice the dog either to 'sit and wait' beside the child or be in the 'down, stay' position. Rewarding the dog with lots of verbal praise, as well as the child, will help increase the child's self-esteem and will add to the success of the toilet process.

Another useful strategy is to try to synchronise the times the child accesses the toilet, the same as you do with the dog. Let the child see the dog toileting first. Although your dog is now completely house-trained, it's helpful to use the dog to help reinforce the reward process for the child by allowing the child to give the dog a treat when it has been to the toilet. This will help the child understand what they have to do to receive their special reward, as well as helping you achieve voiding patterns for the child. (Be careful not to overfeed the dog with treats, though, as this could cause it to put on weight.) When the time comes and the child has achieved continence or understands their own reward process, you can wean the dog off the dog treats towards verbal praise only. This tactic worked very well with Dale – the penny dropped for him immediately when he saw Henry the puppy getting a chocolate drop for doing the necessary. Having witnessed this, Dale, on successfully using the toilet, put out his hand to me and said 'Choccy drop'.

Initially, having the dog in the bathroom with the child will help reinforce positive toilet behaviours for the child, but you must be mindful of the dog's welfare! If Dale or Amy accessed the toilet during the night, they understood that Henry would not be there because he was sleeping (as they should have been)!

This is a vital rule to remember at all times: when using your dog as an educational facilitator, make sure it gets enough time out from its role as a facilitator, with rest, walks and play periods. This is the crux of this programme!

Once you are confident that the child has learned the skills needed, you can gradually remove the dog from the process. On saying that, I found that Dale and Amy spontaneously started to go to the toilet, not even thinking about having the dog present. Such was the success of all the strategies in their individual toilet plans and the newfound confidence they had obtained via Henry.

Thinking out of the box when using the dog to help toilet train the child will reap many benefits. Alberto Alvarez-Campos told me about a seven-year-old child with autism and mobility problems; the child used the handle on the dog's harness as a support when walking to the toilet with the dog. This child's toileting issues were resolved in a few weeks.

The internet has an abundance of information on toileting advice for all children, as well as specific guidance for children with disabilities. As children with autism learn in a visual and literal way, there is an admittedly graphic but superb resource cartoon on YouTube called 'Tom's Toilet Triumph' (go to YouTube and type in 'Tom's Toilet Triumph'). There are also specific links and guidance on achieving continence with a child with autism.[52]

Should your child sleep with the dog in the bedroom?

Many parents have had great success getting their child settled, and sleeping better, by allowing the dog to be in the child's bed or simply in the room. Some parents have discovered that their child's sleeping habits improve, with many children sleeping through the entire night. The warmth and pressure of the dog may give the child increased comfort. Temple Grandin, autism spokesperson and Professor of Animal Science at Colorado State University, devised a 'squeeze machine' (based on her knowledge of securing cattle for vaccinations, etc.) that she used to help herself be calm and relaxed in times of acute anxiety.[53] The therapeutic, stress-relieving pressure of the machine could be echoed by the dog lying next to the child, providing pressure with its peaceful rhythmic breathing.

However, the majority of families prefer the dog to lie on the floor next to the child's bed rather than being in the bed with the child. This may be the answer for many children; not everyone will be comfortable with the dog being in the bed beside the child. The child can still hear that the dog is present, due to its breathing, especially when it is in a deep sleep.

The main things to remember are:

- you must be comfortable with and confident about the child being alone with the dog

- you must treat the process as a major transition.

All dogs need to settle into the family home first and must still have their bolt-hole for during the day, for time-out and naps, etc. The dog being in the child's room at night-time should be phased in gradually.

As soon as our second Henry was toilet-trained, at around 10 weeks old, he slept in Dale's bedroom. Sometimes he slept on top of Dale's bed; sometimes he would choose to sleep in his own bed in Dale's room. Dale was 16 when this happened – Henry was allowed to sleep with Dale at this stage because Dale knew how to meet Henry's needs, including when to give Henry toilet breaks.

Dale loved Henry being snuggled beside him on the bed and sofa; he confirmed he loved all the positive sensory things he got from Henry – the softness of his fur, the weight and pressure of Henry as they slept back to back, the rhythmic breathing of Henry's chest rising and falling and the comforting sounds of Henry's deep breathing. The dog seems to give the child a sense of security, and the practice increases bonding between the child and dog.

When introducing your dog to your child's room, it is important that you take your time – do not rush things. If you are not fully confident that the child and dog will do well together when left alone in your child's room, take things slowly until you have complete confidence. You may start by having the dog in the room for short periods. You can use a child gate to allow the dog to stay in the child's room for a short time while you observe and supervise the two! Some parents allow the dog into the bedroom when the child has gone to sleep. Experiment with what works best for your child – in the end, you will find the positive results that work best.

Remember your dog should be offered a toilet break at around 10 or 11 at night (or later, if possible) and again at the earliest possible time in the morning whenever adults are awake.

I used to read Dale a story at bedtime, sometimes a dog-themed one, with Henry lying beside Dale on the bed. I found that Dale was more relaxed and interested in the story because he thought Henry was listening too. Henry was very comfortable being with Dale in his room and, if Henry wanted out for a change of scene, he would sit at the door or let out a loud bark. Dale would comply and let him out. Henry wasn't trained to do this – it is a good example of the many little spontaneous positive things that went on between Henry and Dale due to the bond between them being so strong!

Improving social skills

There is no doubt that using Henry as a facilitator improved Dale's social skills. With the establishment of a daily routine for Henry, Dale's routine was virtually the same. Such was the bond between them that I treated Henry as a human counterpart for Dale.

Henry helped reinforce positive social rules for Dale. Every night, Dale would say good night to his dog – saying the same to us would follow. The same happened with 'good morning', 'good afternoon' and 'good evening' – Dale transferred this practice to saying the same to us and others. This also helped give Dale a better concept of the time of the day.

Out and about with the dog

When you are confident your dog is trained to a safe and obedient level, with no negative behaviours, you can start to introduce dog walks and outings with your child. Start with very small walks, to create success, and then build up until parent, child and dog are in harmony. After you have had some successful outings with the dog and child in tow, it is time to decide if you want to place an autism sign on the dog's harness. This is very much a personal choice; remember, you will be disclosing your child's condition to the public.

You can obtain patches (check the internet) that say 'autism' on them and then sew these onto the dog's harness so that members of the public are aware of the dog's role.

However, it is crucial to remember your legal obligations as a dog owner. The public should be aware that the dog is not a registered assistance or therapy dog, but a pet, albeit a special pet, just like any other dog in public. You need to inform any person wanting to pat the dog or interact with the child, so they are aware of the situation. Your legal responsibilities and indemnity remain the same as those for any pet dog.

Check the situation out with your dog's insurance company, because having an autism sign on the harness, for example, may throw up some problems and you need to be sure you're not compromising your dog's insurance cover.

Having said that, there are plenty of social opportunities for your child to engage with others when out and about with the dog. If you have used the dog as I suggest with its harness on, and the child's lead and dog collar with a toy attached, this will look interesting and appealing to those you meet in public places where dogs are allowed, particularly play parks. Your child's dog being presented in this unique way will immediately let the public know that the dog's role is to help your child.

Many people, seeing the dog out in public, will want to approach you to pat the dog, just as they would any other dog. This is a good time to follow the advice of Autism Assistance Dogs Ireland,[54] by encouraging the public to ask your child's permission first.

The general public, seeing the unique way the dog is presented, have lots of visual clues to help them engage and interact more effectively with the child. The dog reflects the child's personality, giving anyone engaging with them something to talk about. Members of the public can see the child's coloured lead with its matching collar, with the child's picture, showing them the dog belongs to the child. People can also see the child's favourite picture or toy that depicts their obsession or current interest; this lends itself to interaction and meaningful language between the child and the person engaging with them. Via the dog, the public learns a lot visually about the child's specific autism, which enables positive interaction with the child. Interacting in this way allows the child to learn literally, with lots of repetition, as different members of the public engage with them and talk about the dog and how it is presented.

Road safety with the child and dog

The autism-friendly dog commands described earlier in this manual will help parents keep the child safe when they have to cross busy roads. The dog should *'stop and wait'* at the kerb; when it is clear, *'no cars...we go!'* With the opportunity for lots of repetition, the child hears meaningful language and sees the dog complying. This will help keep them safe and, over time, the child will learn the same concept.

The child being with the dog also helps reduce bolting behaviours. The majority of children with autism have bolting behaviours – and no sense of danger. They are easily distracted and tend to wander off. My experience and that of others in the assistance dog world suggests that many children tend to stop bolting around the age of 10. When Alberto Alvarez-Campos placed autism assistance dogs with Spanish children, working via the charity PAAT, none of the children were physically attached to their dogs; all had had detailed transitional phases and Alberto found the children wanted to stay with their dogs.

This programme aims to avoid attaching the child to the dog; if attachment is needed, it is done as a last resort and only for a short period until a safe routine with the child and the dog is established.

If your child has bonded well with the dog, you will witness signs that the dog has a calming influence on the child that lowers his or her anxieties when out and about with the dog. Your dog can be used to help reassure and divert the child during a tantrum, enabling the child to reach resolution quicker. If the child is distressed, get the dog into the *'down and stay'* position lying beside the child so that he or she can pat the dog and use it as a diversion.

It is possible to train the dog to put its head on the child's lap. However, I found the dog naturally gives the child eye-contact, snuggles beside the child and remains calm – which in turn calms the child, especially as he or she can pat the dog, etc. This was the case with Dale – Henry spontaneously learnt to respond to Dale's upset due to their strong bond.

What to do when the dog can't be with the child

You will need to decide upon strategies for those times when the dog is not able to be with your child, such as at school and accessing supermarkets, etc. At school, Dale's teachers used dog stickers and dog-themed library books to allow Dale to maintain his link with Henry. Dale naturally incorporated Henry into his school work in any way he could, through social stories and other related school work. I put a laminated picture of Henry with Dale on his school bag, which pleased Dale. When we went shopping and Henry needed to stay in the car, Dale would take Henry's blue lead with him as a positive connection with his dog.

In a way, the lead acts as a comfort blanket and gives the child something positive to focus on and fidget with, keeping him or her calm during shopping times, etc. Many children with autism like to play with long ropes or similar items, so the dog's lead is perfect for this purpose.

You want your child to have security with or without their dog.

A note about assistance dogs going into the child's school

A vital aspect of this programme is promoting the independence of the child, so that the dog does not need to be with the child at all times. While a courtesy visit to the child's school with the assistance dog or well-trained facilitator dog can, with appropriate planning, be beneficial, I do not advocate the dog being with the child full-time at school. You want to promote independence via the dog, not dependence on the dog!

If there was a case for an assistance dog going to school with the child, the dog would require full supervision at all times. This would impose unacceptable levels of stress on the dog and teachers. Other children may not adjust to the dog and you would have to seriously consider children with dog allergies and/or phobias. This programme aims to give the child the opportunity to be away from the dog for a period of time, so that the child can engage in other activities and programmes that support independence from the dog.

Having said that, I have to mention an internationally recognised initiative whereby specially trained dogs are taken into mainstream and additional support needs schools to encourage literacy skills in children. There are many different canine reading scheme programmes across the world but, in all of them, the calibre of trained dog is on par with an assistance dog. In the UK, the Kennel Club provides information about dogs going into schools to encourage and promote children's reading.[55]

One organisation, the Bark and Read Foundation, provides grant aid to charities that send dogs into schools as reading volunteers.[56] These grants help working dog charities and volunteers to provide specific services to reach children and young people who can benefit from being involved with reading with dogs.

Another charity, the Canine Concern Scotland Trust, provides opportunities for reading with dogs in schools and libraries in Scotland as part of their Therapet programme.[57] Their aim is to encourage young readers who lack confidence in reading to come along to one of their regular sessions. Instead of reading to a person, children can read to a Therapet dog; the dog will listen to the child and not judge them, allowing him or her to relax, gain confidence in their own ability and improve their enjoyment of reading.

I found these same benefits with Dale when I read him a bedtime story, with Henry lying beside him on the bed or on the sofa, and when we were doing Dale's reading homework. Dale's school reading scheme, the Oxford Reading Tree scheme,[58] is used in 80 per cent of schools and, as luck would have it, features a big Labrador-type dog called Floppy. The books from the range cover many first experiences suitable for helping a child with autism, such as: At the vet, At the doctor, Going to the dentist, and many more.

Involving the dog when reading – or doing any activities with the child – will help the child focus and be motivated to learn. This lets you indirectly work with your child on language and story comprehension. I used to include Henry when reading with Dale. I would show that Henry was interested by giving the dog a picture from the book to sniff at; he would respond by waggling his tail, which Dale really liked.

Reading with dogs

Colum Scriven from Doggy Chillin,[59] an organisation I have had the pleasure of collaborating with, describes below the pleasures and benefits of reading with dogs. Doggy Chillin enables primary school children access to reading with dogs. Some of the children have autism and other types of disabilities.

Reading with children is a delightful experience. I remember reading the early Harry Potter books to my son, Sam – I was just as interested as he was in the story. I would imagine the nature of the characters and develop a voice to match them. Needless to say, Harry's voice was exactly the same as mine. Later, as Sam grew more confident with his reading, he would read ahead and didn't want nor need our regular bedtime reading session. I had to balance my disappointment in missing out in that shared experience with the knowledge that he was finding enjoyment in his own ability.

For children who are low in confidence or have an aversion to reading, the question is how to bridge that transition between being read to and reading themselves. There has been a growing body of interest on the internet which suggests that children who read to a dog are less anxious than if they read to a human. The dog is non-judgemental and doesn't correct the child if they make a mistake. Often a dog will lie down when the child reads to it, which can have a calming effect on both child and dog.

I set up Doggy Chillin Community Interest Company (CIC) in 2016 as a social enterprise that, amongst other aims, wanted to safely introduce a dog into the classroom as a way of reducing stress in the pupils and encouraging them to become more involved in the lesson. We got the opportunity to pilot a reading programme in a primary school with children who were low in confidence or were reluctant readers. Being a Jan Fennell-trained Dog Listener, my concern was for the safety of the dog as well as for the children. Bringing a dog into a classroom can make it anxious, as it needs to know who will protect it and make any decisions if there is a potential issue. The experience can also be stressful for children in the room, especially for those who have a fear of dogs. Before we start any programme, we teach the children about the importance of giving personal space to the dog and when to make appropriate eye contact. We talk about how their energy levels will affect the dog and that, if they're calm, the dog will be calm. Finally, we explain when to call the dog over and how to know if they can pat it or not (or read to it). In that way, when we bring the dog into the classroom for reading, the children understand the rules of engagement. The dog then calms down, which creates a calm, therapeutic environment to learn in.

The classroom we worked in had an informal atmosphere; the children sat on cushions, with the dog often at their feet. The younger ones, aged four and five years of age, would often come in small groupings. As they got older, the school reduced the size of the groups, until pupils of around 11 years of age had one-to-one sessions. The pupils would bring along their class reading book or could choose from one of our stock of books. We would also give the children the choice of being read to by a Doggy Chillin staff member (there was always one present with the dog), or them reading to the dog or a mixture of both. Catherine, a highly experienced teacher who designed the programme, made the decision on whether to support or prompt the child whilst they read.

The school's priorities for the reading programme were:

- to reduce anxiety

- to boost self-esteem

- to promote enjoyment of reading.

Bringing a dog into the learning environment immediately relaxed the children. The staff noticed that the children, even those with Attention

Deficit Hyperactivity Disorder (ADHD), were much calmer when they returned to their classes. Children who were anxious about reading were keen to come to our classes, mainly because of the novelty of having a dog present. Teachers reported that they had seen pupils behave more confidently and be more willing to read out loud in class or take a more active part in lessons. At the end of the nine-week programme, teachers reported that over 90 per cent of the pupils who took part were less anxious about reading. Nearly 80 per cent of the pupils appeared more self-confident and, more importantly, over 90 per cent enjoyed reading more. The pilot was deemed a success and was featured on a local TV channel.

Amongst the different groups of pupils were some with ASD. They would be treated no differently, though some children were more apprehensive about having a dog in the room. In those cases, we would keep the dog out of the way at the back of the classroom and offer the child a cuddly toy dog to hold instead. By not pushing them and allowing for the child's natural curiosity to take over, we usually found that the child would want to pat the dog by the end of the course.

In one instance, at the start of the course, a pupil with ASD went home in tears after they felt trapped in the classroom when I was standing by the exit with my dog, Jenna. The child's parent wrote to the school saying that they still wanted their child to continue with the sessions, in the hope that it would overcome their child's fear of dogs. The next week the class teacher set up some screens in the room for the same child to sit behind. As the pupil could hear the process they were still part of the lesson. The following week the teacher offered the child an iPad to take photos of the reading sessions with the other pupils – all done from the safety of the screens. The next week the pupil came out from behind the screens, still keeping their distance from Jenna, and showed us the photos they'd taken. Each week the pupil would get a bit closer or spend more time away from the screens. In the penultimate week, the student actually joined the group, but sat farthest away from Jenna. In the final week, the pupil sat on a bean-bag with the others only a foot away from the sleeping dog. Just as we were ready to go, the pupil asked permission to pat Jenna. Following our normal rules, the pupil called Jenna over and stroked her on her back. It was a first for them and an incredible step in overcoming a deep-seated fear.

With children with ASD, we found that they had the same responses when a dog was brought into the classroom: much calmer when they were around the dog, improved self-confidence and an increase in enthusiasm for reading.

Catherine and I were sad when we came to the end of the course, as it was such an enjoyable experience. We're hopeful that we'll be invited to go back to the same school and be able to take the programme into other ones. My son is a grown man now and regularly encourages me to read whatever climbing book he is currently engrossed in. I still get a lot of fun from reading some brilliant children's stories out loud, and the reading project has meant that I've had to dust down some of my old voices. I am also quite convinced that Jenna sighs in delight, and snuggles deeper down into a cushion, when she hears the opening lines of one of her favourites.

Colum Scriven

Using the dog as a positive diversion for the child

The dog's ability to calm the child can be used to reassure him or her and divert the child from the trigger of a tantrum. Equally, the dog can be used to encourage the child to move on if they become fixated on something when they are outdoors. On walks with Henry, when Dale stopped to study a car hubcap, I would get Henry to 'sit and wait' while Dale would naturally leave Henry's lead on the ground. I learned to allow Dale a few minutes to explore the hubcap but, to get him to move on, I used the tactic: 'Dale… look…Henry is waiting for you, he wants to keep on walking.' Or: 'Dale, Henry wants to go home for his dinner.'

I never picked up Dale's lead, but waited until Dale did. Many a time, Henry 'waiting' for Dale allowed us all to move on again without any upset to Dale.

Other opportunities for using the dog as a motivator and facilitator

Another useful activity you can introduce with the arrival of the dog is creating a photo album. You can include photos of the dog getting bigger and passing milestones, like birthdays and Christmas, etc., just as the child would. To give Dale a concept of getting older, I made an album showing him as a baby and pictures of him getting older with each birthday that arose. I did the same with Henry, who would get the age-corresponding candle in a plain muffin or cupcake, which Dale would eat or share with Henry. Dale would go to the butchers shop with me to buy Henry a juicy steak for his birthday. These initiatives taught Dale all the necessary social skills these activities brought with them, as well as helping Dale cope with the associated transitions that he used to find upsetting.

You can create and show at leisure a photo album of the child and dog growing up together, and enjoying all the activities that life brings, in a fun and relaxed way. This photo album will help the child understand the concept of themselves and the dog getting older; at the same time, you are working towards Stage 4 of this programme with the dog – letting go!

I involved Henry at all life events for Dale. For instance, at Easter Dale would make something special for Henry and put in some dog-safe chocolate drops. For Halloween and Christmas, Dale would make Henry a card and he would choose and buy Henry's Christmas present. Doing this helped Dale cope better with the different occasions each year brings. Nowadays, it's easy to get fancy dress costumes and accessories for dogs that can be used for special events.

Having access to the internet allowed Dale to expand his language and knowledge of all things canine. I remember sitting with Dale as we looked at lots of Google images of dogs dressed up, some wearing different hats and funny costumes; doing this helped increase Dale's vocabulary.

The dog story books available taught Dale so much in the way of values and social skills. There are too many to mention all of them but a favourite of Dale's was a story about a dog that had bad breath (the dog was called Hally Tosis). This story encouraged Dale to look after his teeth better. Dale also enjoyed the array of participation dog games available. One such game, called 'Fleas on Fred', gave us lots of opportunity to address the triad of impairments of Dale's autism simultaneously. It was a team game and allowed Dale to learn all the social skills of turn-taking and team participation. Another useful participation game that helped reinforce toilet issues (as well as good social behaviour with dogs) is called 'Doggie Doo'. This is a basic game of turn-taking and reinforces the need to clean up after your dog.

Another new social aspect of the dog world that Henry opened up for Dale was dog agility shows. I sometimes took him to local dog shows too. Dale enjoyed the spectacle of these events. He loved being amongst people who, like him, loved dogs. He got to see many other breeds of dog and saw how clever they could be. Such was the inspiration Dale gained from doing this that, when he was 16, he was able to teach Henry Two (our second Henry) to fetch – under strict control and exceptional obedience. He also trained Henry to weave in between Dale's legs.

I've heard of many instances of people with Asperger syndrome, learning difficulties, depression and other types of disabilities being able to do dog agility activities with their dogs. The impact on their conditions has been positive and has made a real difference to their quality of life. I did think of Dale doing dog agility with Henry, but Dale had so many extracurricular activities going on, there simply wasn't the time! For anyone wanting to explore the possibilities of accessing dog agility there is a wealth of information about it on the Kennel Club website.[60]

You can also expand the use of the dog as a facilitator by finding out whether there is a dog-walking club in your local area. While I was carrying out research for this manual, I stumbled upon a great article describing how a teacher called Beth Temple Thurston taught young adults with ASD (age 16 plus) at the NAS Broomhayes School in Devon. Beth was one of the founders who piloted a dog-walking programme with the primary aims of getting the students to appropriately handle and interact with dogs and to see if the students could tolerate being with the dogs. As Beth says, 'The response from the students and the dogs was astonishing. It was as if the dogs, my own two reliable friendly family pets, understood the students' needs and adjusted their behaviour accordingly; still friendly, but more calm and patient than usual.'

Beth noted that the dogs provided focus and stimulation for the students. There were some students who had dog phobias, but their tolerance quickly increased as they switched on to the dogs' behaviours; some students were happy to pet the dogs and to hold leads to walk with the dogs, while some walked with dogs that were off the lead. These dog walks with adults on the spectrum were so successful that parents could subsequently go for leisurely walks on the beach, etc. with a son or daughter no longer afraid of or avoiding dogs.

Beth explained the impact of the new focus the dogs gave some students in the community like this: 'Many negative behaviours were abandoned, and they were able to cope with a variety of situations with less staff intervention than usual, providing increased dignity and independence.'

Beth found that the dogs provided a vehicle, like a facilitator, for helping those on the higher-functioning part of the spectrum to develop a number of skills. Some students learned to communicate with the dog while giving it clear commands, speaking assertively to gain the dog's attention. The students also developed empathy for the dogs, tuning into the dog's needs by giving it praise and affection to help reinforce its good behaviour.

Such was the positive impact the dogs had on the students that they were able to take part in the Appledore Dog Show. The students were surrounded by different varieties of dogs, and lots of people, and took turns showing the dogs, answering judges' questions and keeping the dogs focused. One of the dogs in the team, called Grommet, won best in show.

The dog-walking programme was such a success that some of the students went on to work towards gaining a nationally recognised accreditation scheme certification in animal care; this would allow them to gain work experience in placements within dog shelters and in similar environments. It was heartening to read a few of the students' comments showing the impact the right dog could have for adults on the autistic spectrum:[61]

We take them for walks, give them baths. I like Grommet when she's feeding, catching balls and to stroke. (Jasmin Ellis, age 16)

What I like about dog walking is getting exercise and fresh air. I like learning about Grommet's sense of smell and watching Grommet find pieces of cheese. (Charlotte Thomas, age 16)

Introducing the concept of letting go!

It is hoped that you will have many years – at least 10 – with your dog. The reality, though, is that dogs, like humans, can pass on and leave us at any time, for any reason. While I was in Ireland researching this programme with Autism Assistance Dogs Ireland, one family lost their autism assistance dog within six months of having it in their lives. Therefore, it is important that the concept of bereavement and death is addressed for the child at the appropriate time.

Parents know their children best and they need to decide when the best time is to introduce the concept of Heaven and bereavement to a child. Of all the transitions a child with or without autism must face, coping with loss and bereavement is easily the most emotionally challenging. It wasn't long after Dale got Henry that his beloved Granny Madge suddenly passed away. Because of the strong bond Dale had developed with Henry, my biggest fear was how Dale would cope without Henry in his life. I really worried that Henry's demise would cause Dale to regress.

The sudden loss of my mother prompted me to start an early transition to help Dale to learn about grief and loss, so he got some understanding of what bereavement was like and what happened when someone died. To plant the first seed for Dale, I got myself a pet that I knew would not have a very long lifespan; this allowed me, in an emotionally tactful way, to teach Dale the early stages of grief and loss.

I got myself a goldfish and named it Goldie – Dale liked this as he knew Golden Retrievers were also known as Goldies! I took full responsibility for Goldie and would sometimes let Dale share the task of feeding Goldie or buying an ornament for Goldie's bowl. I knew Dale liked Goldie, but he loved Henry, and Dale knew the difference because of a bad incident we went through once with Dale and Henry. Inevitably, within a couple of months, one day I noticed Goldie was floating in the water and had died. I brought it to Dale's attention that I was feeling sad but also accepting of the loss in a calm and controlled way. As usual, at Dale's pace and on his terms, I used Goldie's demise to explain how Goldie's body had stopped working and how I needed to send him to Heaven to be with all the other goldfish that had died. Dale, like me, came across as being more disappointed than sad; I think because Goldie belonged to me and was just a tiny fish – therefore, it was my loss! As Dale responded so well, I involved him in the process of 'helping' me dispose of Goldie in the right socially acceptable and dignified way. I found a nicely decorated little box, into which we put a tiny flower from the garden, to be with Goldie.

I spent a while involving Dale in the decision about where in the garden we would bury Goldie. Dale helped with the entire process of giving Goldie a fitting funeral – so much so that we both stood at Goldie's graveside, quiet and reflective, and said a fond farewell.

Dale was so comfortable with the Goldie lesson that, as my mother hadn't long died, I started the next stage in Dale's grief and loss transition plan. To give Henry a different walk, I started to take Dale, with Henry in tow, on regular visits to my mother's grave. We would lay some flowers and go for walks around the vast graveyard. I would get Dale to draw a nice picture for his Granny Madge, which I would attach to the flowers, and we would lay these at her graveside. Dale was only six when my mother died and he had a very small and limited vocabulary. At my mum's graveside, I explained to Dale that this was the place where Granny Madge was sent to Heaven. I never went into detail but kept things at Dale's level and understanding (that Heaven was up in the sky and it was a very nice place – the same place Goldie went to).

On our graveyard walks, I talked to Dale about what we saw. For example, I described the array of gravestones as being like a big crowd of people who had all gone to Heaven. I would take ages to talk to Dale about the different types of gravestone (some had the deceased's picture on them) and how they were all different, just like people were all different (a rule I reinforced in Dale's mind as soon as he was able to understand it). Some graves sadly had teddy-bear-shaped headstones; Dale immediately understood these were children's or babies' graves.

I was always honest with Dale, telling him if it was a baby or young child that had died and whether it was a boy or girl, mother, father, sister, etc. that was in the grave. As Dale's understanding of loss increased with regular graveyard walks, he got so much comfort from understanding the concept that he got to know various graves on our rounds and would like to visit certain ones (particularly those that had a dog or something unusual like a footballer engraved on the headstone).

Dale got so used to the graveyard visits and walks that, while his understanding of loss grew, his sense of acceptance that death was an important part of life grew with him too. Occasionally, I would remind Dale that all pets go to Heaven too. He understood this because of Goldie, but he had also seen an animated movie called *All Dogs Go to Heaven*. I got him the DVD of the film, but he rarely watched it because he said it made him feel sad when the dog went to Heaven. In a way, Goldie, Granny Madge's demise, graveyard walks and the film had achieved their purpose.

When the fateful day of Henry's demise came, at the grand old age of 12 on 17th April 2006, I needn't have worried about Dale not coping with the enormity of Henry's loss. In the years that followed my mum's death, I had covered every detail in a transition plan for Henry's death and, when the sad day came, Dale executed the plan to the letter.

To help Amy cope, I had also buried a couple of goldfish with her in the past and had taken her on graveyard visits to her Granny Madge and Granddad George. However, her grief at Henry's loss was different and Amy wasn't coping. I realised that her sense of loss was as great as Dale's – but she was only six and wasn't coping as well. Not only had Amy lost her dog, she had also lost the favourite 'horse' she used to pretend Henry was when she played with him. I witnessed Amy's grief and saw through her play; she was quite subdued.

To help Amy cope, I found a wonderful new bereavement resource in the form of a child's story book called *Heaven*, by Nicholas Allan.[62] It was perfect for Amy's age and I adapted the book so that Amy would understand, given her lack of vocabulary and poor reading skills. The book tells the story of a little girl called Lily who one morning finds her beloved dog Dill packing a suitcase and putting all his belongings in it. The story evolves to the point where Dill explains it's his turn to go to Heaven and that two angels are coming to collect him. Dill describes to Lily how lovely Heaven is for dogs and why Lily can't go with him. (Dill tells about the place down below for naughty dogs, but I always cut that side of the story out so that all children will understand the concept.) Dill gets collected for Heaven and the book beautifully shows the impact of the loss on Lily, as I had seen with Amy, and as I myself felt with Henry's loss. There is a very fitting and hopeful ending to the story, but it was this resource alone that filled the gap of grief for Amy that Henry had left behind.

The way you use your dog as a facilitator to teach your child the concept of grief and loss is a delicate and massive subject. What I have discussed here at this stage of the programme is early transition care for this important stage of life you are at with your dog. This subject is covered in more detail in the next and final stage of the programme, 'Letting Go! Transition for the Child to Prepare for the Demise of the Dog.'

Those who have read both my previous books[63] will understand the effect our dogs have had on both my children. In Dale's case, the effects were especially powerful because, for three years, Henry had a 'voice'. One day, during a very challenging tantrum, my husband at the time developed a voice for Henry to reassure Dale. Thereafter, Dale prompted us to communicate with him via Henry's voice. We did so for three years, using Henry's voice as a facilitator until we could successfully wean Dale off Henry's voice – instead he learned to recognise Henry's canine non-verbal language.

I've heard from Neil Ashworth, dog training manager of the Irish Guide Dogs autism programme in 2008, that some parents have tried giving a voice to their facilitator dogs, some with some success. I would say as one parent to another: use your dog to facilitate meaningful progress and the best possible quality of life for your child. As long as no harm comes to either, if used wisely, your facilitator dog is a very powerful living tool and resource!

Stage 4

LETTING GO!
TRANSITION FOR THE
CHILD TO PREPARE
FOR THE DEMISE
OF THE DOG

S tage 4 is about letting go. During this stage the child learns that, just as people do, their dog is getting old. The child learns about the experiences of grief and loss.

You should start implementing this stage when you feel it's appropriate, allowing for the age or health of the dog. Parents will know best when their child's comprehension is sufficient for the concepts outlined in Nicholas Allan's book *Heaven*, described in the last chapter of Stage 3. By using the book and the loss of 'your' goldfish or similar pet, you can begin to introduce the concepts of grief and loss to give your child an insight into this complex event. Together with the recommended graveyard walks, this will give the child some insight into this difficult life experience – in an informal and subtle way.

In the months and years ahead, the task of looking after their old dog will help the child learn the concept of ageing – both the ageing of their dog and the child themselves getting older. It is hoped that the majority of dogs will live long enough to reach this last stage of the programme. However, the reality is that the dog could take ill or suddenly die; this is why it's best to plant early seeds, with this major transition in mind, during Stage 3 of the programme.

As Jim Taylor has said,[64] we cannot and should not assume that a child with autism does not have the emotional capacity to experience grief and loss simply because we think they will not understand the complex nature of death and bereavement. Due to the nature of autism, we shouldn't conclude that the child will simply accept or adapt to a dog or person suddenly disappearing from their life. We must try to give the child some strategies and resources to help them relate to this very delicate and emotionally fragile stage of life.

I feel strongly that introducing the concept of old age or death via the dog, to prepare the child for bereavement or loss, is vital for the child's well-being. Introducing the idea of loss to the child months or even a few years before the child is exposed to such an emotionally charged and life-changing event is paramount to the child's emotional health and future development.

I learned this lesson first-hand with Dale and Henry. I also learned about the impact of complacency on this subject with Amy. I assumed that, because Henry was essentially Dale's dog, somehow Amy would not be as emotionally affected by Henry's loss as Dale was. I couldn't have been more wrong. I learned a hard lesson, almost to Amy's emotional detriment. Out of us all in the family, Amy was the person most affected psychologically by Henry's passing. I am embarrassed to tell this but, because of Amy's autism and her being the youngest, we all assumed she would be less connected to Henry's demise than Dale was.

I believe it is wrong to assume that, because a child is unable to communicate, he or she doesn't have a sense of loss or bereavement. They definitely do have the same sad feelings and emotions as us; however, due to their autism, they will express their loss and grief in their own unique way.

A good film that illustrates this point well is *Snow Cake*. In this film, the main character is an adult female with autism who abruptly loses her daughter due to a car accident. The director and writer superbly depict the way grief and loss can affect a person with autism. The movie beautifully illustrates how the mother expresses her profound grief in such a different way that neurotypical people around her assume she is not grieving at all and is oblivious to the loss of her daughter.

For any child, with or without autism, it is better to begin introducing the concepts of death and Heaven early on – using the dog's passing – than for the child to experience the abrupt or traumatic loss of a close relative with no preparation. It is better for the child's emotional welfare that strategies are put in place to teach the child, at their level, about when an animal or person close to them goes away and cannot come back. How you do this is a delicate and difficult challenge, but it is possible to teach the child some understanding of the meaning of loss. The key elements to bear in mind are:

- careful planning

- ensuring the strategies you use are appropriate for the child's age, his or her individual autism and stage of development

- using the appropriate transitional resources via the dog.

It is better to be honest with your child. If you hide the dog's death or dismiss it, the child will be confused or may be frightened that he or she has done something wrong to the dog and that is why their dog is no longer with them.

The learning experience in Stage 4 can be enhanced by using the life events photo album (see 'other opportunities for using the dog as a motivator and facilitator', in the previous chapter) that shows the child and dog getting older together. Again, spending some time with the child on the computer showing them pictures of old dogs from Google Images will assist the child's understanding.

While Stage 4 is the time to plant the seed in the child's mind that the dog, like people do, is getting older and one day will go away and not come back, it is vital for the dog's welfare that you know how to adjust to meet the needs of the older dog. Teaching the child to adjust to his or her ageing dog's needs will maintain the child's feeling of autonomy with their dog and establish strong bonds of empathy.

There is no denying that taking the best care of the dog's physical and emotional welfare as it reaches old age will undoubtedly prolong and enhance its quality of life.

Now is the time for your child to adjust to the older dog's needs. Still using the elderly dog as a facilitator, your child will learn how to take care of the old dog and will begin the process of learning to let his or her dog go!

Care of the Senior Dog

Dogs age at different rates; smaller dogs may live well into their late teens, while some larger breeds may only live to around 8–10 years. The average lifespan of dogs is 10 years. Once your dog has passed middle age, it is worth considering ways to preserve its quality of life!

It is vital that you ensure your dog has a consistent daily routine.

Dogs' needs change as they get older. The stages of ageing may differ according to the type of breed; knowing how to look after your dog's changing needs as it enters old age is vital to preserving its quality of life and ensuring the longest lifespan possible for your dog.

The main things to be aware of are that:

- your dog will need more regular health checks

- you will need to keep a watchful eye for any changes to your dog's physical and emotional health.

As we age, we all become more prone to illness, and your dog is no exception. As a dog ages, several changes and processes take place within its body. Body tissues become more fragile and less flexible, muscle mass reduces and becomes wasted, and the dog's coat and colour changes, with greying of the hair around the face. The dog becomes less active and tends to sleep more.

Grooming

Daily grooming is essential in order to keep your dog's skin and coat in good condition because elderly dogs may not be able to clean themselves as well as they once did. Now your dog is getting older, it is important to groom it more often (at least twice a week), especially if it has been neutered. Older, furry coats get thicker and are more difficult to maintain!

Regular grooming will aid circulation as the brush will simulate massaging movements that can increase circulation and blood flow to the skin and hair follicles while stimulating the lymphatic nodes to boost the dog's immune system. Grooming your elderly dog will also give you the chance to check for any lumps, bumps or abnormalities. Any lumps or bumps should be regularly monitored for any change in shape and size and veterinary advice sought. Some lumps will be benign, but you want to catch potential cancerous tumours early to maximise the chances of a successful outcome.

Exercise and reduced mobility

Arthritis and other diseases of old age can affect all dogs, with some larger breeds being particularly prone to arthritic changes in their joints, particularly the hip joints. Older dogs may show signs of stiffness following vigorous exercise. The dog's mobility and happiness can be greatly improved with early treatment and measures to manage these conditions.

An older dog doesn't need as much exercise as before, but you need to ensure they still get enough exercise to maintain healthy muscle tone and joints; in this way, you'll ensure your dog stays as fit as possible. Regular gentle exercise is better than sudden bursts of exercise. Lead exercise or allowing your dog to pace itself is more beneficial than encouraging running and chasing toys. If you notice any stiffness in your dog, consult your vet immediately. An older dog may require extra help negotiating steps and stairs and jumping into cars.

Dogs that are exercised only on soft ground tend to grow longer nails which can become uncomfortable. Try to take your dog on a short pavement walk every day to help wear down nails and prevent them from becoming overgrown.

Your dog must be allowed to move at its own pace. Also bear in mind that older dogs may be able to see and hear less well. Due to this, they can become disorientated or lost when they are out for walks.

Older dogs may become confused by deviations from their routine or loud noises, particularly as their senses begin to fail. Having said that, certain types of change can enhance the dog's quality of life; since mental stimulation is as important as physical exercise, it is good to introduce a new type of toy or game to keep the dog's mind stimulated. You can teach an old dog new tricks as they can have a better attention span than younger dogs.

If your dog gets wet when out on walks, make sure you dry it thoroughly; being wet will increase the risk of infections and arthritis. The older dog is less effective at regulating its body temperature and is more sensitive to cold and heat. In addition, some dog coats get more porous and thinner with age and are therefore less able to withstand rain and cold. An older dog will therefore benefit from wearing a suitable jacket.

Feeding

Feeding older dogs smaller, less calorific but frequent meals (at least twice a day) will help reduce the work the body has to do digesting large amounts of food in one go. The older dog's digestive system may not be as efficient at breaking down food and absorbing nutrients, so dietary needs will change. However, it is essential you keep the dog's weight down and prevent obesity occurring. Your dog carrying excess weight puts an additional strain on its heart, internal organs and joints and can contribute to problems such as diseases of the internal organs, with increased incidence of cancer, pancreatitis and diabetes, as well as joint stiffness, pain and arthritis. Dogs kept at the correct weight will live longer, healthier lives.

Preventing obesity, which is common in older dogs, is essential for the dog's overall health; it is vital to get the right balance between feeding and exercise. If you cannot feel your dog's ribs, this can be a sign of obesity. Other signs include the dog being less interested in exercise and having associated breathing problems and decreased stamina.

You may need to change the dog's food to one that it is specifically suitable for a senior dog. This dog food is manufactured to meet the changing dietary needs of the older dog, providing concentrated sources of protein, reduced fat, easily digestible carbohydrates, key vitamins and minerals, and calorific value. Keep in mind that the food may need to be suitable for dogs with old teeth or a dog that has lost some teeth due to old age.

Teeth and gums

Elderly dogs need careful attention to their teeth and gums. Your dog may need a softer, more palatable food and it may need things like cooked chicken and other tastier foods added to entice it to eat.

Older dogs can lose or damage their teeth through daily wear and tear, and the build-up of tartar can encourage gum disease and infections. Dental care and regular check-ups at the vet are important to keep the dog's mouth and teeth comfortable and healthy. Providing the dog with rawhide chews or toys such as Nylabone for 10–15 minutes, two to three times a week, can help prevent the build-up of plaque and tartar.

Warning: Raw bones, soft cooked bones or poultry bones should never be given to your dog to chew.

If your dog is used to eating dried food, this helps prevent the build-up of plaque. Brushing the dog's teeth every day with dog toothpaste is also beneficial.

Bad breath, difficulty eating, excessive salivation, pawing at the mouth or rubbing the face on the floor can be indications of mouth pain or discomfort.

Deterioration in bladder control

Ensure your dog is given the opportunity to relieve itself more frequently, as bladder control often reduces with old age. For this reason, older dogs must not be left for long periods of time.

Kidney disease can be recognised by a decrease in appetite, increase in thirst or weight loss. If the kidneys are not functioning properly, the kidneys' ability to remove waste products from the dog's system is affected. Early treatment from your vet is essential in managing this problem.

Spayed bitches, especially the larger breeds, can sometimes suffer from incontinence due to depleted oestrogen levels; this is treatable if caught early enough. Look out for offensive odours, damp bedding or involuntary spotting when the bitch gets excited.

Weight loss, excessive thirst and more frequent urination may indicate the onset of diabetes. As with humans, early diagnosis is vital, and treatment may involve insulin injections and dietary management.

Heart disease

This is common in certain breeds of dog and manifests with the onset of breathing difficulties, lethargy and loss of appetite. Early diagnosis from your vet improves the success of any treatment.

Older dogs' bedding

Ensure your dog has a warm bed in a quiet place, away from draughts. Soft washable bedding can be used for the dog's comfort and will help prevent sores forming on the elbows and other bony joints. The bed needs to be in a quiet place as older dogs sleep more and do not like to be disturbed or rudely awakened by noise, children or other pets.

Veterinary care

Annual vaccinations and routine preventative treatments for worms are essential to keep your older dog healthy. Flea control on a regular basis is also important. Any signs of illness should be reported to the vet as soon as possible. Symptoms such as any sudden loss of weight, increased thirst, sudden changes in behaviour, bad breath or loss of appetite may indicate an underlying health problem. Many conditions that old dogs are prone to can be successfully controlled if caught at an early stage.

Regular veterinary examinations will increase the chances of any health problems being discovered early. Older dogs are more susceptible to conditions such as kidney disease, hyperthyroidism, high blood pressure, diabetes, cataracts and cancers; be mindful that many of these are treatable!

Osteoarthritis is very common in older dogs, although there are ways to alleviate this potentially disabling condition. Physiotherapy and hydrotherapy, combined with effective modern drugs with minimal or no side-effects, can be used to manage this condition.

Significant weight loss in old age can be the first sign of ill health. If you find your dog is refusing to eat then consult your vet immediately.

Sight, hearing and behavioural changes

Most dogs will undergo some changes in character as they reach old age. Their senses, sight and hearing may diminish as age progresses. Providing regular mental stimulation prevents boredom and lethargy and encourages elderly dogs to remain mentally alert. Elderly dogs can become confused, awkward or slow to accept change; changes to routine should be kept to a minimum. As a dog ages, it can forget some of its earlier training and behaviours; this is another reason why you must give an older dog more toilet breaks.

The older dog, like a human, can become set in its ways and, with the added reduction in some of their senses, they may appear quite wilful. Patience and understanding are essential when dealing with elderly dogs, as they become different characters as their old age progresses.

It is equally important to look out for behavioural changes in your dog; these may be related to a decrease in vision and hearing, or to cognitive dysfunction syndrome. This can cause confusion, disturbed sleep patterns, a decrease in attention span and house-training difficulties in your dog.

Older dogs can change in temperament, with some becoming friendlier and more attached to their owners, while others get grumpier. I have witnessed these two extremes of character with two very different dogs. My cousin Veronica has a great love for German Shepherds; the most loyal and strongly bonded dog she has ever owned was called Max. Max was the chubbiest boy in the litter and, from the moment Veronica took him home, Max was glued to her and would only let Veronica interact with him. Veronica alone met all his needs. Max got so protective of Veronica that she was the only one who was allowed to pat him and have contact with him. If anyone tried to approach Max to give him any attention or affection, Max made it clear no one other than Veronica was welcome. Veronica became adept at making sure anyone who came into Max's home or space knew the situation. Sadly old age wasn't kind to Max and, with it advancing, Max developed hip dysplasia. This is a canine genetic condition where there is laxity of the hip's soft tissues, ligaments and joints that affects the function of the hip joint itself. Sadly, all dogs with hip dysplasia will develop secondary osteoarthritis, and both conditions can cause limited and reduced mobility problems for the dog as well as severe pain. The condition is more common in dogs that are overweight as puppies, so, since

Max was chubby and had the affected gene, he had a bad case of the condition and it affected him severely.

Max was fortunate; because Veronica adored him, he got the best of veterinary care and treatment. However, there was another factor that Veronica couldn't have planned for. As Max's condition advanced with his old age, as he was entering the final stages of his life, his character and temperament dramatically changed. Instead of being the big protective warrior for Veronica, he literally became a gentle and loving 'pussycat', thriving on any human attention and affection (so much so, that I witnessed a stranger to Max giving him a loving and gentle massage which Max couldn't get enough of). In the final couple of weeks of Max's life, at the grand old age of 14, he had numerous people spoiling him with love and attention. I know this was pleasing for Veronica to witness, as Max's loss was so painful and devastating for her; he was such a beautiful and amazing big dog.

I also witnessed a dramatic change in personality in Dale's second dog, Henry Two, as he entered old age. Dale and Henry developed a strong bond because Dale was Henry's sole master when he came home as a pup; it was Dale who met all Henry's needs and it was Dale who trained him. Dale was so bonded to Henry because he was so friendly and sought attention and affection from anyone all the time, although Dale was 'number one' in Henry's eyes. Around the age of eight, Henry's character changed – he literally became a 'grumpy old man'. Henry became joined to Dale's hip and became a stickler for his routine; he wasn't too bothered if others interacted with him (except Dale, of course). If Henry's day wasn't going to plan, he would moan, whimper and sometimes even howl to get what he wanted. Henry even lost his tolerance towards other dogs and became somewhat indifferent to Thomas, our other Goldie, whether Thomas was in his company or not. Sadly, a year later, Dale and I were distraught to learn that Henry had suddenly died alone at home while Dale was at work. We both miss him dearly to this day, and this Henry is so memorable because he changed so much as an old man.

Remember that old dogs may become anxious because they cannot see or hear as well as they used to. A sudden personality change can be a sign of illness but, in old age, this could easily be a gradual process – so take time to monitor and observe your dog's behaviour in its advancing years. The message is clear: old age need not mean a cheerless life for your pet and there is a lot you can do to maximise its well-being. Extra vigilance and regular veterinary check-ups, with a focus on the quality of the time you have left with your dog, is sure to pay dividends for you both.

The hardest part of all when looking after a senior dog is to recognise when it is the right time to say goodbye to your dog and let go, but it is vital that you listen to the advice of your vet to help you make an informed choice in this delicate matter. As with all stressful and emotional situations, it is difficult to see things clearly when you are too close to the situation. As dog lovers, we can decide how to give our dogs the best quality of life and when it is the right time to allow them to have a pain-free and comfortable death; your vet will guide and support you through this hardest part of owning a dog.

Letting Go!

Devising a transition plan for the dog's demise

The NAS (National Autistic Society) recommend that the transition process for a major event should begin one year before the actual transition takes place. Therefore, it is prudent to make a child-centred, written plan for the dog's demise – at the child's level of understanding of the concept of loss and compiled at the child's own pace – well in advance.

The best approach is age-appropriate honesty at the child's level of understanding. When I did this with Dale, Henry was 10 years old and Dale was 15; Dale wanted to be fully involved with the entire process of Henry's demise. I explained to Dale it was better to plan ahead because, when the sad day came, we would be upset and our emotions in turmoil. Having the written plan would make sure we didn't forget anything important at that time and Dale would know he had made all the right decisions for letting go of his special dog.

With the strategies introduced in Stage 3 regarding the *Heaven* book and the graveyard walks, and of course lessons learned from Goldie the goldfish and Granny Madge's demise, Dale had a good understanding of the concept of death and bereavement.

There is a lot to think about before the demise of the dog; having an open discussion with the child and writing things down in their own words will help him or her prepare for and process what will happen in the future.

Writing down how involved the child wants to be when the dog is ill (for instance, whether he or she will go to the vet to be with the dog or not) is important. I involved Dale in giving Henry his pain-relief medicine, which gave him a sense of looking after his dog and helped Dale come to terms with the fact that Henry was ill and that his life was coming to an end.

You should discuss with your child, and write down, what you will do to involve the child so they can say goodbye under different circumstances – for instance, if your dog suddenly dies at home, has an accident or has to be euthanised. The level of involvement will depend on the child's age and stage of development and his or her understanding of loss.

A written plan really helped Dale focus when the time came to let Henry go. You can use the plan to answer questions such as whether the child wants to say goodbye to the dog in the home or go to the vet with the dog to say goodbye. I discussed with Dale what he wanted to do about keep-sakes and whether he wanted Henry's ashes. Dale came up with the idea of keeping Henry's collar afterwards – it was special to him because he had chosen Henry's blue collar as a child. He put Henry's collar under his pillow; he has kept it to this day.

Write down what will happen after the dog's demise

Discuss with your child the possible different scenarios, depending on whether the dog dies at home or at the vets. During office hours, most vets will let you take your dog's body to their premises for appropriate disposal. Alternatively, the vet can put you in touch with a private firm that can collect the dog's body and dispose of it, retaining its ashes for you; however, this can be expensive.

One of the most important lessons learned from our first Henry's demise concerned the decision about whether or not to receive Henry's ashes. Such was the amazing impact Henry One had on all our lives that Dale decided to receive Henry's ashes. We now know that, for our family's emotional well-being, this was not a wise decision. Having Henry's ashes threw up a lot of dilemmas for Dale and, with hindsight, he would rather not have obtained Henry's ashes but would have preferred to remember Henry as he was. The dilemma of where to put Henry's ashes was as emotionally draining as letting him go. Dale and the rest of the family worried about putting Henry's ashes in the garden because there was the chance that we would move house in the future. We thought about scattering the ashes in a nice place where Henry walked, but we couldn't find a place that was fitting for him; they were all too public and some had litter and old beer cans laying about that upset us. In the end, nine months after Henry's demise, it was very fitting that Val the dog breeder took Henry's ashes and had them buried in the same grave as Henry's father; that helped us a lot. We couldn't go and witness Henry's ashes being buried because it was too painful for us all – it felt like we were losing him twice.

This is a good example of why thinking of every detail of the process of letting your dog go – and writing things down in a plan – will help you avoid wrong decisions and added upset when the inevitable sad day comes.

The dog's demise and bereavement – for all children

When writing *A Friend Like Henry*, I felt it was important to share how Dale was prepared for and coped with the tragic loss of his beloved dog. I must stress that I am no expert on such a delicate and important subject; however, this section will give you some insight into strategies you can use to help children through such an emotionally important aspect of having a dog. I couldn't agree more with Mark Pinches, a vet and dad of two children, who says, 'When a pet dies, it is often the first time children encounter bereavement and, as a parent, it can be distressing to see your child so upset.'[65]

I share Mark's view that the death of your pet or dog can be one of the most valuable lessons of pet ownership – the child's emotional and psychological development can be enhanced because of the experience of losing a pet. The loss of a pet for a child can evoke powerful emotions but, if these emotions are dealt with sensitively, it can make children more robust emotionally. Mark gives some great guidance on this subject, including the following points:

- Regarding the pet's death, be honest with your child; if you try to hide it, your child will become confused or even frightened.

- Don't tell your child something like 'Rover has gone to sleep' or, worse, that the dog has run away, as the child may find it difficult to accept the finality of the dog's death. Many an adult has memories of hopefully listening for that scratch at the door because of being told such a thing as a child in explanation of a dog's demise. (I would add that a person with autism will take this type of explanation literally and may then have fears of going to sleep themselves.)

- If your child is too young or doesn't have the capacity to understand the concept of death, then explain to the child that their dog is gone and won't be coming back. You can always go into more detail later.

- If your dog has been involved in an accident and your child wants to give the pet one last stroke, this can be possible. (Mark gets his veterinary nurses to clean up the animal, so the children can say goodbye; he has found that children have coped and respond well to this gesture.)

- If your dog has to be euthanised and your child wants to be with his or her pet, ask your vet if this is possible. (Mark is happy to have children present during the procedure, if he is confident that the child understands what's going to happen and why. Mark finds that, once children have had the procedure explained to them, many want to leave; despite this, giving children this opportunity has helped them feel included at an important time.)

Preparing for euthanasia

Euthanasia is death by injection for a terminally ill dog or a dog that is suffering. This procedure is commonly described as 'putting an animal to sleep'. The finality of death is a difficult concept, especially for children under the age of five. Children could be confused and even frightened by the term 'putting to sleep', especially if they see the lifeless animal after the procedure has been performed.

When the decision is made that your dog needs to be euthanised, very small children need to know that this is final and that the dog isn't going to wake up or come back. Older children need to know the reasons why their dog needs to be euthanised and why the injection puts an end to their dog's suffering.

When children are involved, some veterinarians, like Dr Evelyn Wilson, DVM, ABVP, do not allow children under the age of five to be present for the procedure of euthanasia. Dr Wilson feels that children have a difficult enough time understanding and coping with the loss of their pet and that the young child witnessing the event won't make it easier for the child. Dr Wilson reminds us that when children and adults are upset, the pet will be too – so care needs to be taken to give adequate support to the dog in its time of need.[66]

Sudden death or finding a pet dead

If your dog is fatally injured or suddenly dies due to unknown causes, it can help reassure your child if you tell him or her that the dog is no longer suffering pain. However, the shock can have a bigger emotional impact on the child than an expected death. If veterinary care was provided, remind the child that the vet's medicines and treatments didn't work despite the best of attempts to save the dog. Remember that experiencing the death of a pet can help children develop their understanding of what happens when they lose a person in their family.

Recognising general signs of grief in children

When Henry One died, I was struck by how this loss affected Amy. Due to her autism, she didn't express her feelings of loss verbally – but I noticed signs of her grief and her lack of coping in her play and non-verbal language. Children may take longer to accept, and grieve more over, a loss than adults do. A short time of low mood, depression or gloominess can be expected but should subside with time. Warning signs of severe or prolonged grief will vary depending on:

- the child's age and stage of development

- his or her relationship with the pet

- the child's emotional maturity

- the circumstances of the dog's death.

Warning signs of severe or prolonged grief
Warning signs may include:

- the child not being interested in his or her usual activities and withdrawing from friends and family

- the child's appetite and eating habits changing (eating less than usual)

- episodes where the child reverts to pre-potty training behaviour or bed-wetting

- the child displaying signs of being afraid of being alone or going to sleep; he or she may also have nightmares

- the child becoming preoccupied with thoughts of death.

How you can help

Being available and open to talking about death with the child is helpful. You can also access professional support in the form of counselling.

Don't be afraid to show your own grief. This will help your child to learn that we all experience loss and can move on from it. I was present with Dale when both our first two dogs died and, while I remained calm and in control, I wasn't afraid to express my grief at the loss of both dogs. I know this helped Dale understand that he wasn't alone and that deep grief is a normal human emotion and reaction.

If you decide on a home burial, make sure you dig sufficiently deep to avoid the additional upset and distress of your pet being exhumed by a wild animal.

If it's appropriate for your child, encourage him or her to make a memory box or book. Include drawings, perhaps one of the dog's favourite toys or its collar, and some special photographs. For a long time, Dale slept with the two Henrys' collars under his pillows. He had personally chosen the collars and they had a real significance and connection to his dogs; he has them to this day. I made a personal photo album of Henry One for Dale and Amy to keep and look at when they wanted to. You can get remembrance plaques to put your pet's or dog's name on, which you can put into a nice spot in the garden; perhaps involve your child in planting a tree or shrub in the dog's memory. Alternatively, you can use the dog's feeding bowl to put a house plant into for the child to take care of, water, etc., in memory of the dog.

If you feel your child is deeply affected by the loss of his or her dog or pet, and is struggling to move on from the loss, talk to your health visitor; there may be support and bereavement counselling available for your child. Your vet also may be able to put you in touch with a pet bereavement counsellor who will know how the loss of a beloved pet is different but still comes with real grief and emotions.[67]

When Henry One died, I was really struck by how mature and responsible Dale was in coping with his death (Dale was 17 at the time). It was Dale who made the decision to end Henry's suffering and Dale who comforted his dying dog as he was being euthanised. As Dale said, he was so proud of what Henry did for him that he was never going to forget Henry nor let him down.

However, unlike Henry One who was in a way 'engineered' to be Dale's dog, Henry Two was definitely Dale's dog from the moment Dale chose him and took him home. Dale trained Henry Two himself and looked after all Henry's needs for nine years. Therefore, on the 23rd October 2014, it was a shock to us all, especially Dale, when he come home from his work to find his beloved Henry had suddenly died.

Yet again, Dale dealt with the practical side of his dog's demise. He spent some time just stroking his dead dog and we put a blanket over Henry so he looked secure and loved. We made sure our other dog Thomas got a good sniff at Henry's body, and allowed Thomas to witness our upset, to show him that he would be the only dog left in our family. As we had missed the time to take Henry's body to the vet, so we could spend some time with him, we got a private firm to take Henry away for us; for Dale, this was the right decision.

Dale misses Henry so much that, currently, he is still not ready for another dog. Dale misses the companionship of Henry and the relaxing walks he had with him so much that he now has shared care of my Golden Retriever, Thomas. Thomas has coped well living in two homes and Dale and I have joint custody of Thomas. I hope some day in the future Dale will find a new four-legged companion but, as he says, 'Mum, the two Henrys will always be special to me. I will never have a third dog called Henry, but I will have another dog…one day!'[68]

Death, bereavement and autism spectrum disorder

The principles of helping a child with autism relate to and deal with this life experience are similar to those you would follow with any child. However, it is important to remember that individuals with autism require clarity and planning about any event they experience in life. Death and bereavement are important issues that can't be avoided; they must be handled with the individual's specific age, stage of development and level of autism in mind.

With good planning and appropriate adjustments suited to the child's (or adult's) individual needs, death and bereavement issues can be dealt with in a sensitive and accessible manner that the individual concerned will understand.

As already discussed, a child with autism will commonly experience the death of a pet before that of a person. Taking the opportunity to cover this very delicate issue via a pet will undoubtedly help the transition when a person dies. There is an abundance of academic material available on the subject of how a person with autism experiences the death of a person, but there is very little on the impact the death of a pet has on a child or adult with autism.

I feel the best way to cover this delicate area is to combine the principles of dealing with pet bereavement with recommendations from the National Autistic Society (NAS) on what to do for those affected by autism when a person close to them dies.[69]

In the same way as you would make a plan with the child for the dog dying, the NAS advises similar principles regarding the death of a person. The NAS stresses that the ASD child will understand and adjust better if they are involved in the situation and prepared for coping with it as much as possible. Remember that unexplained changes and the unknown often scare those with autism, which can cause anxiety and even challenging behaviour. While telling the child may initially increase anxiety, doing so will reduce upset and confusion in the long run.

The NAS believes that death is better explained within a life cycle; using insects, plants or animals best demonstrates death as a process.

This biological approach is practical and clear and, for those with autism, is visual and literal. As we already know, those with autism respond to and understand concrete visual descriptions better.

As we've seen, devising a detailed plan for the dog being ill, and its demise, is vital. In one case, a school used this principle to explain death to a five-year-old child with ASD whose father had terminal cancer.[70] Here is a superb example where all the principles we have just learned about were adapted for the individual child's age, stage of development and individual level of autism. The teacher obtained a dead chicken from a local farmer and named it Charlie. Charlie was shown to the child who noticed the chicken wasn't moving. The teacher explained that Charlie would never move because he was dead. Charlie was then put in a suitable box, which was called a coffin, and they buried Charlie with a cross placed above the grave. It is thought that this approach was in line with the family's religious beliefs.

To help the child process the delicate new knowledge being portrayed, the teacher photographed the stages of the process of Charlie's 'funeral', and compiled the images in a social story book which they called 'Brett Says Goodbye to Charlie Chicken'. The process was then replicated with pictures of Brett's father, including photographs of Brett with his father, in hospital, before his death. They took pictures of the empty hospital bed after Brett's father had died. These were all placed in a book called 'Brett Says Goodbye to Daddy'.

This book was used to talk to Brett about his experience in the weeks and months that followed his father's demise. Although this may seem radical and quite morbid, the family and the teacher clearly understood Brett's need to have these visual supports to allow him to begin to understand the concept of death and loss and, more importantly, where his beloved father had gone and that his father was never coming back.

This beautiful and poignant story is a great example of how parents can use the sad death of a beloved pet to prepare a child or adult for the loss of a human counterpart. By planning for loss and bereavement, and tailoring the plan to the child's individual needs, you allow the child to move on emotionally unscathed, albeit he or she will have experienced all the normal feelings of loss. I feel strongly that doing nothing – not giving the child some knowledge or experience of what death and loss are – can have a long-term negative impact on the child's future emotional and physical development.

The NAS also recommend explaining any religious practices to the child, such as making a social story about the place where the ceremony will take place and the people involved. There is a series of books called *Books beyond Words*, which explain burial, cremation and bereavement counselling in picture format, which may be helpful.[71]

It is helpful for the child, whether your family has religious beliefs or not, to establish a familiar routine, such as putting up a picture of the deceased with some candles when someone dies, whether it is a pet, family friend or even a TV personality the child liked. This will help your child learn the concept that the deceased has gone and will hopefully lessen any inappropriate responses from the child when someone dies. As NAS founder, Helen Allison said 'by preparing people with autism for losses which can occur, they may become more able to cope with major bereavements.'[72]

Predicting someone's reaction to a death that is close to them is difficult. People with ASD are no different – how each individual reacts will be unique to them. You may not recognise how a person with ASD is responding to grief, but he or she will be expressing grief, albeit in a different way. Their overall behaviour may change and this will be an expression of their grief and loss. Howlin describes how a person with ASD 'may seem apparently unconcerned, even by the death of someone very close…'[73]

Behavioural changes may not coincide with the immediate death itself, but may occur three months, six months or even a year after the event.

The NAS has identified approximate stages of bereavement.[74] They include: shock, numbness, denial, despair, turmoil and acute grieving, including anger, guilt, anxiety, fear, panic, depression, pain, appetite disturbance, breathlessness, illness, more than usual need for sleep, sleeplessness, hyperactivity, nightmares, and regression with loss of skills.

The stages of recovery can be identified as: having acceptance, resolution of grief, the bereaved being able to think of the deceased without pain or anger, and being able to recall the times they had together in a positive way.

Be aware that many of these stages may merge together and that not everyone will experience all of them. Your child may have all of these feelings and others too. The child may experience confusion over why they do not see the person or pet any more. He or she may be anxious about why members of the family seem to be acting differently.

Children with ASD would benefit from compiling a memory book or box which is used as a reminder of the individual or pet that has died and of how the child was involved with them at different stages of life. That is why I recommend making an album of the pet growing up – including its life events with the child – in Stage 3 of this programme. This memory book or box becomes invaluable when it is time to let the pet go or when the pet dies.

In summary, the NAS advocate that, when dealing with death and bereavement, you should:

- prepare your child as much as possible

- keep changes in routine to a minimum

- use clear, simple language and use visual supports where appropriate

- show understanding for unfamiliar displays of grief, such as challenging or obsessive behaviour or an increased reliance on routines

- remember that any reactions may be delayed.[75]

Personal essay by Amy Gardner, age 17

As I was writing this delicate and difficult section of the programme, at a parents' night for Amy, her English teacher gave me a copy of a personal essay Amy had written. The content of Amy's piece sums up beautifully what our two Henrys had meant to Amy. Reading Amy's essay, it struck me that, despite the years that have gone by since the two Henrys' demises, Amy's memories are as vivid as ever and her feelings of loss continue to this day – but in an emotionally unscathed manner.

When I was five years old, we got a Golden Retriever puppy who we called Henry. Henry came from a local breeder in Gourock who lived quite close to our house. All of us were so excited especially my brother Dale who was getting the puppy to have as his own dog.

When we arrived at the breeders we heard the sounds of puppies barking before we even saw them. As we walked in the sound kept on getting louder and my heart started beating faster and faster as I got in the room where the puppies were. There were lots of puppies in the room but one of them stood out from the others and walked right up to us. We knew this would be the perfect puppy for all of us and Dale knew that this was the perfect puppy for him. Dale decided to call the puppy Henry. He was just the sweetest little thing we had ever seen.

And that was the start of a wonderful relationship.

We did so many different things with Henry like taking him to the beach to play fetch. Henry would dive into the water to try and find his ball, and then he would bring it back to get it thrown again. It made me and everyone else feel happy seeing Henry enjoying himself at the beach, running free. When Henry got out of the water he would shake all over us.

On cold nights, or nights I wasn't feeling well, Henry would lie down and comfort me and I would use him as a pillow that I called 'The Golden Pillow' since Henry was a Golden Retriever and he felt as comfy as a pillow. The Golden Pillow felt really snuggly and comfortable as I could feel Henry's soft and warm fur on my face. I also could hear his breathing and his heart beating. Henry helped lots of members in my family especially Dale who is 28 now and plays a guitar in a band from Glasgow called Century Thirteen. If Henry was not there then Dale would not be in his band or have done any of the other things that he has today.

One year later we got another dog from the same breeder who was also a Golden Retriever and we called him Thomas.

Henry when he was a puppy was actually a really well behaved puppy for his age, but Thomas on the other hand was the complete opposite. Thomas would eat anything we left out, chew lots of things in the house and make a mess all over the house. As Thomas got older he stopped doing most of these things but he still eats anything that is left out to this day. Henry as he got older was a really well behaved dog also. My mum wrote a book about Henry called *A Friend Like Henry* and a sequel called *All Because of Henry*. These books are about how Henry helped Dale and lots of other people as well.

Henry lived for nine years and sadly on 23rd October 2014, Henry passed away.

This was extremely shocking to all of us since Henry was actually a really healthy dog who was rarely ill. All of us were really sad especially Dale who was the closest to Henry in the family. This was heartbreaking for me and all my family just as much as Dale since all of us had a personal relationship with Henry; because I did the Golden Pillow with him and me and my dad took Henry to the beach and would watch Henry enjoying himself diving into the water trying to find his ball. Knowing I could not do this again was really sad for me even though it was most upsetting and heartbreaking for Dale, since Henry had helped Dale so much in his life and Dale was also Henry's owner.

Both Dale and I have autism, and before Henry there was actually a first dog we had who was also called Henry. Henry in this essay was actually named after the first Henry. My Mum and Dale have told me the story of how the first Henry helped Dale when he was a young boy who was really struggling with his autism. Henry helped Dale become more sociable with other people because he was able to understand Henry's feelings and emotions and that helped him to begin to understand other people's feelings and emotions. The dogs have also helped me cope with my autism because they have helped me build relationships with people. When I had a stressful day at school I knew one of the dogs would be waiting for me at home to give me a cuddle.

Amy Gardner

How dogs affect us

If ever I needed proof of how much our beloved dogs affect our lives, here are some facts that confirm what all dog owners have known for decades.

- One in ten animal lovers has turned to counselling or anti-depressants to cope with the loss of a pet. A survey from Animal Friends Pet Insurance revealed that half of grieving pet owners felt as sad as if they had lost a relative.[76]

- Therapists who are used to supporting those with human loss are now offering the same service to those who have lost an animal. Counsellor Shona McLean, who offers support to people who have lost an animal, said, 'Often pets are in our lives longer than a partner, so we experience grief as we would for a person.'[77]

- Pets brand tails.com found 41 per cent of dog owners spoke to their pet more than to their partner, chatting for an average of 47 minutes a day.[78]

Shona McLean says:

There's still a stigma around grieving for pets. People say, 'It's only a dog or cat, you could get another one.' But pets are loved like family. Young children confide in them. For the elderly, [their pet] may be their only companion.[79]

Writing this section of the manual has been the most challenging and most difficult of all, as it has stirred up so many memories of and emotions about the two wonderful Henrys. I hope my shared experience, together with the professional guidance I have referenced in this emotionally delicate part of the programme, meets the needs of all who will face the heartbreak of losing a beloved dog or pet.

I asked Dale what he would say if he could speak to his Henrys one more time. He told me: 'Just to say, I really miss them and thank them for the life experience they both gave me.'

As for me, I will never forget stroking Henry's head before he died, tears streaming down my face, and thanking him for what he'd done for Dale and me. That sentiment will never change. I am still very raw about how Henry Two was taken from us, but thankful for all he did for Dale in his adult life. If I could say one more thing to both of them it would be: 'I miss you both so much and I will never forget you to the day I face my own demise.'

Moving on!

Getting a new pet can be an important part of moving on. It is a personal choice that shouldn't be rushed due to the hope that the child or adult will 'get over' the deceased pet. It is commonly accepted that one pet does not replace another and that, if this is done too soon, the outcome may not be good. When the child or adult can speak openly about their deceased pet, and starts to show signs of interest in getting a new pet, only then should the subject and journey of obtaining a new pet begin!

Afterword

When I met Alberto Alvarez-Campos in October 2008 at the Assistance Dogs International conference in Frankfurt, Germany, I knew I had met a friend who shared the same values as me on how to ethically use dogs as facilitators to help children with autism. It has taken over ten years of our combined shared work and never-failing passion to create this manual.

Alberto has taught me that, with the right approach, the correctly trained dog can reach out to help so many others with varied and diverse conditions. The success of using these amazing dogs to help those affected by autism is now internationally recognised but, sadly, the supply of dogs will never meet the demand. It is my own and Alberto's desire that this manual will go a long way towards helping to bridge that gap. It is my hope that this manual enables those who seek it to gain the knowledge they need to be able to ethically source and train their own special dog, to help improve the quality of life of a child or adult with autism or any other condition.

I would never have believed that the day would come when I would desperately need the love, companionship and facilitation of my own Golden Retriever, Thomas, to help me in my time of need. After my marriage ended, I could never have survived living on my own without Thomas being by my side. As I now live with anxiety disorder, Thomas has helped me through many a difficult day and even nursed me through horrendous panic attacks.

As I leave you to start your own amazing journey with your wonderful dog, I know the joy and hope that it will bring. Life is a journey of ups and downs and many challenges. Having two children with autism has brought me much joy, but also difficult barriers to cross in order to reach the true happiness we all seek in life.

You'll have read in Amy's story how she would look forward to seeing Henry Two after school when she'd had a bad day. For two years, Amy endured lots of horrific bad days at school, facing the horror and consequences of terrible bullying. My daughter's mental and physical health got so bad that I really believed at one point that I would lose her to bullying. Thankfully, Amy's school did all they could and I fought for her, like I have never fought before, to ensure Amy got the right support and professional help. Undoubtedly, Henry and Thomas did their bit and, thankfully, with professional help and the support of Dale and Amy's father, we got Amy back to the beautiful, grounded, unscathed young woman she is today.

Dale's life hasn't been without its challenges, trying to find suitable employment and have the same opportunities in life as any other young man that doesn't have autism. He is fortunate to have employment with REACH for Autism, a social enterprise not-for-profit organisation that provides a hub of social and teaching opportunities for local children and adults who are affected by autism. As the staff there say, Dale is an integral part of REACH, where he's highly thought of by staff, parents and all the service users. To this day, he still plays in the same rock band, called Century Thirteen, who are thriving and doing the circuits as any other local bands would do. Dale has a lovely girlfriend who accepts that autism is only a small part of who Dale is; they are as happy, and looking to the future, as any other young couple are.

The deaths of Henry One and Henry Two broke our hearts, but Dale, Amy and I carry on because of the wonderful gifts – our better lives and futures – that both dogs gave us all. Both Henry One and

Henry Two gave Dale wonderful companionship and emotional support, which no human could have done, and opened up a canine and social world for Dale – worlds he would never otherwise have known. I asked Dale if there was anything he could add about his dogs. He told me:

> They were like real friends to me, and great companions, always at my side. Both of them encouraged me to go out and meet people when I learned to walk them myself. If I was worried or anxious they made me feel better and helped me cope with bad days and times.

In this manual, Alberto and I have described how much the right dog can help alleviate or reduce anxiety for their owners; Dale, Amy and I have experienced this first-hand. What a unique and wonderful talent these dogs have – but they give us so much more.

I cannot predict how successful the partnership with your own facilitator dog will be, but I can guarantee that your dog will be your child's or adult's friend! The dog will be a loyal companion and follow the child or adult everywhere. The dog's love will be unconditional, faithful and true to its very last breath. The loss of your dog will break your heart. However, your heart will be stronger, and your life will be richer, for having known your dog!

Useful Resources

www.nualagardnerautism.com
The author's website.

www.jimtaylorknowsautism.com
The website of Jim Taylor, independent autism consultant.

www.canineconcernscotland.org.uk
Information about the Therapet visiting service.

www.kennelclub.org.uk
Advice on care of the dog and sourcing the right dog from the right background – and much more!

www.learnwithdogstrust.org.uk
The Dogs Trust Education Team delivers workshops in schools and in the community, educating children about responsible dog ownership and safety.

Dog helps boy come out of autism – A Friend Like Henry
Early years video footage of Dale and Henry One on youtube.com. Search for 'Dog helps boy come out of autism A Friend Like Henry' or go to www.youtube.com/watch?v=vJSu3GoU5SY.

How an autistic child learned to say 'I love you'.
Video footage of Oliver, aged six, and his 'failed' guide dog, Lucy, now a buddy dog, on www.bbc.co.uk. Oliver is visually impaired, has cerebral palsy and epilepsy and is autistic. This is a great example of the power of the dog, with similarities to Dale and Henry's story. Search for 'How an autistic child learned to say I love you' or go to www.bbc.co.uk/news/av/magazine-30699272/how-an-autistic-child-learned-to-say-i-love-you.

Tom's Toilet Triumph

An autism-friendly cartoon on youtube.com, to help children understand all that is involved with toilet training. Search for 'Tom's Toilet Triumph' or go to www.youtube.com/watch?v=ri5RHQ58RcM.

www.pawmygosh.com

A website that has many heartwarming videos about the impact dogs have had on vulnerable people and children with disabilities. There are lots of sad stories with happy endings about how dogs themselves were rescued by people.

www.yellowdoguk.co.uk

Resources and information on dog stress and rehabilitation.

Century Thirteen – Dale's rock band, for your interest!

Official Facebook Page: www.facebook.com/centurythirteen; YouTube Channel: www.youtube.com/centurythirteen; music available at: www.centurythirteen.bandcamp.com

www.nas.org.uk

The website of the National Autistic Society.

www.scottishautism.org

An organisation dedicated to enriching the lives of people with autism.

www.friendlyaccess.org

Friendly Access brings individuals and services they wish to access together, without fear and isolation through lack of understanding and support.

Endnotes

1   Wing, L. (1996) *The Autism Spectrum: A Guide for Parents and Professionals*. London: Constable and Company Limited.

2   UNICEF (1997) *The State of the World's Children*. Oxford: Oxford University Press.

3   Source: 'Doggy Business.' *NAS Communication Magazine*. Winter 2007.

4   Grandgeorge, M., Tordjman, S., Lazartigues, A., Lemonnier, E., Deleau, M. and Hausberger, M. (2012) 'Does pet arrival trigger prosocial behaviors in individuals with autism?' *PLoS ONE 7*, 8, e41739.

5   Rederfer, L.A. and Goodman, J.F. (1989) 'Brief report: pet-facilitated therapy with autistic children.' *Journal of Autism and Developmental Disorders 19*, 3, 461–467.

6   Hall, S.S., Wright H.F., Hames A. and Mills D.S. (2016) 'The long-term benefits of dog ownership in families with children with autism.' *Journal of Veterinary Behavior 13*, 46–54.

7   Gardner, N. (2007) *A Friend Like Henry*. London: Hodder & Stoughton.

8   Gardner, N. (2013) *All Because of Henry*. Edinburgh: Black & White Publishing.

9   American Humane AssocationTM and ZoetisTM (2013) *Canines and Childhood Cancer: Pilot Study Report*. Washington: American Humane. Accessed on 31 January 2019 at www.americanhumane.org/publication/canines-and-childhood-cancer-pilot-study-report

10 Tassoni, P. (2003) *Supporting Special Needs: Understanding Inclusion in the Early Years*. Oxford: Heinemann Educational Publishers.

11 Burrows, K.E., Adams, C.L. and Millman, S.T. (2008) 'Factors affecting behavior and welfare of service dogs for children with autism spectrum disorder.' *Journal of Applied Animal Welfare Science 11*, 1, 42-62.

12 Winchester, L. (2016) 'Loyal dog refuses to leave his best friend – a young autistic boy alone in hospital.' Express, 22 February 2016. Accessed on 31 January 2019 at www.express.co.uk/news/nature/646131/Dog-refuses-leave-young-autistic-boy-master-hospital-James-Isaac

13 www.thekennelclub.org.uk

14 Burrows, K.E., Adams, C.L. and Millman, S.T. (2008) 'Factors affecting behavior and welfare of service dogs for children with autism spectrum disorder.' *Journal of Applied Animal Welfare Science 11*, 1, 45–62.

15 www.inspiredbyautism.org

16 Levinson, B. (dir.) (1988) *Rain Man*. United Artists.

17 www.hanen.org/home

18 Gillingham, G. (1995) *Autism, Handle with Care! Understanding and Managing Behavior of Children and Adults with Autism*. Arlington, TX: Future Education Inc.

19 www.autism.org.uk/sensory

20 For further information, see www.autism.org.uk

21 Grandgeorge, M., Tordjman, S., Lazartigues, A., Lemonnier, E., Deleau, M. and Hausberger, M. (2012) 'Does pet arrival trigger prosocial behaviors in individuals with autism?' *PLoS ONE 7*, 8, e41739.

22 www.thekennelclub.org.uk/breeding/assured-breeder-scheme

23 Rogers Brambell, F.W. (1965, 1970) 'Report of the Technical Committee to enquire into the welfare of animals kept under intensive livestock husbandry systems.' Presented to Parliament by the Secretary of State for Scotland and the Minister of Agriculture, Fisheries and Food by Command of Her Majesty, December 1965. London: HMSO.

24 Burrows, K.E., Adams, C.L. and Millman, S.T. (2008) 'Factors affecting behavior and welfare of service dogs for children with autism spectrum disorder.' *Journal of Applied Animal Welfare Science 11*, 1, 45–62.

25 NBCNews (2009) 'Fireman dresses as Spider-Man to rescue boy.' Accessed on 07 November 2018 at www.nbcnews.com/id/29875894/ns/world_news-wonderful_world/t/fireman-dresses-spider-man-rescue-boy

26 Smith, R. (2010) 'Dogs for autistic children help "stress and behaviour."' *The Telegraph*, 20 October. Accessed on 28 February 2019 at www.telegraph.co.uk/news/health/news/8075612/Dogs-for-autistic-children-help-stress-and-behaviour.html

27 www.rspca.org.uk

28 Rogers Brambell, F.W. (1965, 1970) 'Report of the Technical Committee to enquire into the welfare of animals kept under intensive livestock husbandry systems.' Presented to Parliament by the Secretary of State for Scotland and the Minister of Agriculture, Fisheries and Food by Command of Her Majesty, December 1965. London: HMSO.

29 A great site which covers all aspects of dog life in a fun way is www.foopets.com

30 BBC News (2016) 'Boy, 3, dies after being bitten by dog in Halstead.' Accessed on 28 February 2019 at www.bbc.co.uk/news/uk-england-essex-37129134

31 The Health and Social Care Information Centre (2015) 'Provisional monthly topic of interest: admissions caused by dogs and other mammals.' Accessed on 30 November 2018 at https://files.digital.nhs.uk/pdf/h/6/animal_bites_m12_1415.pdf

32 GfK NOP Social Research (2014) 'Stray dogs survey 2014.' Summary report prepared for the Dogs Trust. Accessed on 18 January 2019 at https://www.dogstrust.org.uk/news-events/news/stray%20dogs%202014%20report.pdf

33 See www.legislation.gov.uk/uksi/1992/901/contents

34 See www.legislation.gov.uk/ukpga/2005/16/contents

35 See www.gov.uk/government/publications/the-countryside-code

36 See www.outdooraccess-scotland.com

37 See www.legislation.gov.uk/ukpga/1987/9/section/1

38 For further information, see www.snh.gov.uk

39 Note that, of necessity, the information in this chapter regarding care of your dog is an overview. For further reading on canine health, I recommend www.kennelclub.org.uk

40 Source: Shore Veterinary Winter Newsletter 2014.

41 Proprioception is body awareness – the knowledge of where a certain part of your body is and how it is moving and relates to other objects or people.

42 A good site your child will like that covers all dog aspects and toilet games is www.foopets.com

43 For further information, see http://www.bigtickproject.co.uk/news/new-case-of-babesiosis-in-the-uk

44 Clarke-Billings, L. (2016) 'Dog owners warned of fatal tick-borne disease canine babesiosis which is likely to spread around UK.' *The Telegraph*, 16 March. Accessed on 28 February 2019 at www.telegraph.co.uk/news/uknews/12194796/Dog-owners-warned-of-fatal-tick-borne-disease-canine-babesiosis-which-is-likely-to-spread-around-UK.html

45 For further information, refer to www.bluecross.org.uk and www.petmd.com

46 Information is available from www.defra.gov.uk

47 For further information, see www.thekennelclub.org.uk

48 See www.dogstrust.org.uk/help-advice/dog-behaviour-health/sound-therapy-for-pets

49 Hall, S.S., Wright H.F., Hames A. and Mills D.S. (2016) 'The long-term benefits of dog ownership in families with children with autism.' *Journal of Veterinary Behavior 13*, 46–54.

50 See www.herts.ac.uk/kaspar

51 Grandgeorge, M., Tordjman, S., Lazartigues, A., Lemonnier, E., Deleau, M. and Hausberger, M. (2012) 'Does pet arrival trigger prosocial behaviors in individuals with autism?' *PLoS ONE 7*, 8, e41739.

52 For further information, see www.disabledliving.co.uk

53 See www.squeasewear.com/testimonials/temple-grandin

54 www.autismassistancedogsireland.ie

55 www.thekennelclub.org.uk

56 See www.thekennelclub.org.uk/barkandread

57 See www.canineconcernscotland.org.uk/therapet

58 See www.oxfordowl.co.uk/for-home/starting-school/oxford-reading-tree-explained

59 Colum Scriven is a Jan Fennell-approved Dog Listener and director of Doggy Chillin CIC. Doggy Chillin is a social enterprise that takes dogs into schools to help young people with their reading and teaches them how to understand and care for dogs (www.doggychillin.co.uk).

60 www.thekennelclub.org.uk

61 Source: *NAS Communication magazine*, Winter 2008.

62 Allan, N. (2006) *Heaven*. London: Red Fox Picture Books.

63 For further information on the story of Dale and the two Henrys, read *A Friend Like Henry* (2007) London: Hodder and *All Because of Henry* (2013) Edinburgh: Black & White Publishing, by Nuala Gardner.

64 www.jimtaylorknowsautism.com

65 Pinches, M. (2012). Quoted in 'How to help a child cope with pet bereavement.' Accessed on 11 November 2018 at www.petplan.com.au/blog/petpeople/how-to-help-a-child- cope-with-pet-bereavement

66 Tobiassen, J. (2018) 'Helping children deal with the loss of a pet: Age appropriate honesty is best.' Accessed on 11 November 2018 at www.thespruce.com/helping-children-deal-with-pet-loss-3385155

67 See also the Ally* People and Pet Loss Service: www.allyforall.co.uk

68 For further information, see Tobiassen, J. (2018) 'Helping children deal with the loss of a pet: Age appropriate honesty is best.' Accessed on 11 November 2018 at www.thespruce.com/helping-children-deal-with-pet-loss-3385155

69 Allison, H. (2001) *Support for the Bereaved and the Dying: A Guide for Managers and Staff in Services for Adults on the Autism Spectrum*. London: The National Autistic Society.

70 Ulliana, L. (1998) 'Bereavement and children with autistic spectrum disorder.' *Keynotes Newsletter*, June. Autistic Association of NSW (Australia) (ID: 10491).

71 See www.booksbeyondwords.co.uk

72 Allison, H. (2001) *Support for the Bereaved and the Dying: A Guide for Managers and Staff in Services for Adults on the Autism Spectrum*. London: The National Autistic Society.

73 Howlin, P. (2004) *Autism and Asperger Syndrome: Preparing for Adulthood*. 2nd edition. London: Routledge.

74 Allison, H. (2001) *Support for the Bereaved and the Dying: A Guide for Managers and Staff in Services for Adults on the Autism Spectrum*. London: The National Autistic Society.

75 For further reading, see www.autism.org.uk

76 Barnard, E. (n.d.) 'How do Brits cope with the loss of a pet?' Animal Friends Pet Insurance. Accessed on 11 November 2018 at www.animalfriends.co.uk/blog/how-do-brits-cope-with-the-loss-of-a-pet

77 Quoted in Spencer, R. (2017) 'Meet the therapist who helps pet owners get over the grief of losing their animals.' *The Mirror*, 22 July. Accessed on 30 November 2018 at www.mirror.co.uk/news/uk-news/meet-therapist-who-helps-pet-10851493

78 Ibid.

79 Ibid.

Index

Adams, C.I. 47, 48
adaptation of programme
19–20, 26–7
adders 197
adults with autism
communicating with 83–5
After Thomas (TV drama) 26, 31
age of child 27–8, 91–2
age of dog 94–5
All Because of Henry (Gardner)
17, 29, 34
All Dogs Go to Heaven (film)
269
Allan, Nicholas 270, 273
allergies 35–6
Allison, Henry 296
Alvarez-Campos, Alberto 28–9,
30, 46, 52, 70, 99, 117, 119,
126, 141, 257, 302, 304
American Humane Association
43
Anderson, Maureen 24, 245
Animals (Scotland) Act (1987)
153
Ashworth, Neil 110–11, 271
assistance dogs 28
for people with disabilities 25–6,
30, 39–41, 43–4, 49
in school 258–60
training 49–54
transition planning with 99–100
Assistance Dogs Australia 28,
30, 141
Assistance Dogs Europe 51
Assistance Dogs International
(ADI) 50, 51, 302
Assistance Dogs UK (ADUK)
50, 51
autism (ASD)
behaviours 38

and death 294–7
description of 19
world of 22
Autism Assistance Dogs
(AADs) programme
death of dog 61–2
development of programme
26–33
educational facilitation
60–1
purpose of programme 56
stages of 58–62
tasks of 44–5
transition planning 58–9

Babesiosis 178
Bailey 66–9
Bark and Read Foundation 259
bathing dogs 158
batteries 195
beds 121–2
behaviours of child with autism
38, 95–6, 142
behaviour of dog 128–9, 282–5
bloat 202–3
blue green algae 197–8
'bolt-hole' for dog 133, 148,
150–1
bowls for dog food 114–15
Brambell, Rogers 131, 140
breed of dog 91–4
Burrows, K.E. 47, 48

Canada Service Dogs 26
Canine Concern Scotland
Trust 259
carbon monoxide 196
chocolate 182–3
Clean Neighbourhoods and
Environment Act (2005)
152

cleaning products 186–7
collars 116–17, 149
commands
core commands 209–18
in training 221, 230–4
usefulness of 204–9 *see also*
training
communication
adults with autism 83–5
benefits of dogs 75–82
difficulties with 71–2
stages of 73–4
types of 72–3
Control of Dogs Order (1992)
37, 152
core commands 209–18
corrections in training 227–30
costs of keeping dogs 36–7
Countryside Code 153
cuddly dog 109–16
cupboard for dogs 106, 132

death of dog 61–2, 267–71,
273–6, 286–301
disabilities
adapting programme
19–20, 26–7
assistance dogs for 25–6, 30,
39–41, 43–4, 49
dog whistles 116
Doggy Chillin 260–3
dogs
family benefits 31–3
practical considerations
35–8
Dogs for Good 99
Dogs Trust 144
dried fruits 185

ear cleaning 157–8

early communication stage of communication 74
educational facilitation
  social world expansion 244–5
  feeding time 241–2
  fine motor skills 242–3
  personal hygiene 243–4
  photo albums 264
  as positive diversion 263
  reading with dogs 259–63
  road safety 257
  in school 258–60
  separation from dog 258
  sleeping arrangements 253–4
  social skills 255
  social world expansion 244–5, 264–7
  toilet training 246–52
  and transitional planning 239–41
  walking dogs 255–7
Equality Act (2010) 98
Erdwin, Maureen 27, 54
exercising dogs 37, 150, 169–71, 278

families
  benefits of dog ownership 31–3
  bonding with dog 151–2
  parental work patterns 36
  transition planning with 104–5, 108
feeding time 162–7, 241–2, 279–80
fine motor skills 242–3
fireworks 198–9
fleas 175
Friend Like Henry, A (AFLH) (Gardner) 10, 25, 26, 34, 61
Friendly Access 31

garden poisons 192–5
Gardner, Amy
  and cuddly dog 109
  death of Henry 274, 291, 298–300
  impact of Henry on 303–4
  love of horses 26, 244
  and public access dogs 46
  toilet training 247, 248–9
  transition planning with 107, 108

Gardner, Dale
  age appropriateness of 27–8
  choosing Henry for 40, 91–3, 94, 126
  commands for Henry 204–5, 207
  death of Henry 61–2, 267–70, 274, 286–8, 292–3
  educational facilitation through Henry 239–40, 241–6, 247, 251–2, 253–4, 258, 259–60, 263–5
  exercising Henry 169, 170, 171
  eye contact with Henry 53
  feeding time for Henry 166
  and Henry as older dog 284–5
  impact of Henry on 23–4, 25, 26, 33, 40, 303–4
  neutering of Henry 156
  playtime with Henry 172
  toilet routine of Henry 167
  transition planning with 48–9, 99, 102–3, 106–8, 109, 113
  world of autism 58
Gardner, Nuala
  and Andy MacGillivray 67, 68
  development of programme 26–33
  research on dogs and autism 17–18
Garrett, Heather 63–5
Goodman, J.F. 28
Grandgeorge, Marine 28, 91, 243
Grandin, Temple 253
grooming 116, 156–9, 278
Guide Dogs Queensland (GDQ) 29, 46, 117, 126
Guide Dogs UK 99, 129

Halti 122
harnesses 118–19, 149
health of dog 128–9
  Babesiosis 178
  bathing 158
  bloat 202–3
  ear cleaning 157–8
  exercise 37, 150, 169–71
  feeding time 162–7

fireworks 198–9
fleas 175
grooming 116, 156–9
heatstroke 200–1
Lyme disease 178
nail trimming 158
neutering 37, 155–6
older dogs 277–85
parasites 179–82
physical examinations 159–62
playtime 172–3
poisoning 182–98
stings 201
teeth 157, 158–9
ticks 175–7
toilet routine 167–9
vaccinations 174–5
veterinary care 38, 134, 174–5
vomiting 182
heart disease 281
heartworms 181–2
Heather 63–5
heatstroke 200–1
Heaven (Allan) 270, 273
Henry (One and Two) 34
  choosing 40, 91–3, 94, 126
  commands for 204–5, 207
  death of 61–2, 267–70, 274, 286–8, 292–3
  educational facilitation 239–40, 241–6, 247, 251–2, 253–4, 258, 259–60, 263–5
  exercising 169, 170, 17
  eye contact with Dale 53
  feeding time 166
  impact on Dale 23–4, 25, 26, 33, 40, 303–4
  neutering of 156
  as older dog 284–5
  playtime 172
  toilet routine 167
  transition planning for 48–9, 99, 102–3, 106–8, 109, 113
home
  considerations for dogs 36
  introducing dog to 69
  planning for dog's arrival 131–5
  poisons in 184–96
  settling dog into 148
hookworms 179

Human-Animal Bond Research Institute (HABRI) 32

intentional communication 73
International Guide Dog Federation 50
Irish Guide Dogs 111
Isaacs, James 53
Issacs, Wendy 53–4

Kefford, Jane 52
Keill, Valerie 26
Kennel Club 54, 92, 93, 126, 127
Kongs 119–21, 172
Kortabarria, Eneko 30–1

leads 117–18, 149
legal responsibilities 37, 152–3
lungworms 180–1
Lupien, Sonia 109
Lyme disease 178

MacGillivray, Andy 66–9
MacGillivray, Duncan 66–9
MacGillivray, Jenny 66–7, 68
Mahe 53
McLean, Shona 300
medicines as poisons 188–9
Millman, S.T. 47, 48
Mills, Daniel 32, 207
MIRA Foundation 109
Morris, Glynn 31

nail trimming 158
National Autistic Society (NAS) 22, 98, 286, 294–5, 296–7
neutering 37, 155–6
nicotine 196

older dogs 277–85
onions 185
'own agenda' stage of communication 74

PAAT 29, 46, 257
parasites 179–82
parents
    training assistance fogs 54
    working patterns of 36
Parents Autism Workshops and Support (PAWS) programme 99
partner stage of communication 74
personal hygiene 243–4
pets
    mixing with dogs 36
    and programme principles 20–1
phobia of dogs 36, 59

photo albums 264
physical examinations 159–62
plant poisons 190–2
playtime 172–3, 237
poisoning 182–98
potpourri 198
pre-intentional communication 73
public access dogs 45–6, 50, 51–3
puppy crates 133–4, 150–1

reading with dogs 259–63
Rederfer, L.A. 28
requester stage of communication 74
rewards in training 222–3, 225, 226, 233–4
road safety 257
Rodriguez, Mylos 30
roundworms 179

school
    assistance dogs in 258–60
Scottish Outdoor Access Code 153
Scriven, Colum 260–3
seasonal canine illness (SCI) 198
senior dogs 277–85
sensory issues 79–82, 112, 114–15
Service Dogs Canada 117
sleeping arrangements 133, 253–4, 281–2
Snow Cake (film) 275
social behaviour 234–6
social skills of child 255
social world of child 244–5, 264–7
socialising dogs 141–2, 143–5
songs 122–3
sourcing a dog 40–1, 56, 60, 125–30
stings 201
stress in dogs
    prevention 140–3
    signs of 137–40

tapeworms 180
Taylor, Jim 274
teeth of dogs 157, 158–9, 280–1
ticks 175–7
toads 192
toilet pen 132
toilet routine 167–9, 281
toilet training for child 246–52
towels 121

training
    assertiveness in 221
    attention of dog in 222, 230–1
    body language in 222
    clicker training 236
    commands in 221, 230–4
    confidence in 220
    consistency in 221
    corrections in 227–30
    dog psychology 219
    excitability of dog 235–6
    jumping up 234–5
    motivation in 224–7
    perseverance in 220
    personality of dog 226
    playtime 237
    positive reinforcement in 223–4
    positivity in 220
    praise in 224–7, 233–4
    puppies 134
    reasons for home training 49–54
    respect of dog 220
    responsibility for 223
    rewards in 222–3, 225, 226, 233–4
    social behaviour 234–6 see also commands
transitional kit 102–23
transitional planning
    and assistance dogs 99–100
    benefits of 48–9
    educational facilitation 239–41
    as first stage 58–9, 87–90
    importance of 98–101
    transitional kit for 102–23
treats 142–3

University of Lincoln 32

vaccinations 174–5
veterinary care 38, 134, 174–5, 282
vomiting 182

walking dogs 150, 152–3, 255–7
welfare of dogs
    importance of 40, 46–8
    rights to 96
    stress in dogs 137–43
whipworms 179
Wing, Lorna 22
working dogs 42–3

Xylitol 186